Factors Associated with Participation in Cooperative Programs of Curriculum Development

by

J. GALEN SAYLOR, Ph.D.

Teachers College, Columbia University
Contributions to Education, No. 829

Published with the Approval of
Professor Hollis L. Caswell, Sponsor

BUREAU OF PUBLICATIONS

Teachers College, Columbia University

NEW YORK · 1941

MANUFACTURED IN THE UNITED STATES OF AMERICA
BY THE HADDON CRAFTSMEN, INC., CAMDEN, N. J.

Acknowledgments

THE writer wishes to express his gratitude to the many people who have made this study possible. He is particularly indebted to Professor Hollis L. Caswell, his sponsor, for his counsel, guidance, and constructive assistance throughout the course of the investigation. His sympathetic guidance was of inestimable value in planning and carrying forward the study.

The writer also wishes to express his gratitude to Professor Helen M. Walker for guidance in the statistical treatment of the data.

The study would have been impossible without the cooperation and assistance of Dr. Sidney B. Hall, State Superintendent of Public Instruction in Virginia, and his staff in the State Department of Education. Dr. Ruth Henderson, State Supervisor of Elementary Education, and Mr. J. L. B. Buck, Director of the Division of Instruction, were particularly helpful in carrying forward the study. Dr. D. W. Peters, President of the Radford State Teachers College and formerly Director of the Division of Instruction, also rendered valuable assistance.

The author expresses his appreciation to the division superintendents, the supervisors, and the elementary teachers of the county school systems in Virginia, which were selected for study. Their cooperation aided greatly in carrying on the study.

Finally, the author is grateful to Dr. William Alexander, Mr. George Oliver, and other close friends and professional associates for their assistance in this undertaking.

G. S.

Contents

Tables

Tables

TABLE · PAGE

30. Analysis of Variance of Current Expenditures per Pupil Enrolled, All Schools (Table 29) 138

31. Effort to Support Public Education: Current School Expenditures Locally Raised per $1,000 of Locally Taxable Wealth, Selected Counties, Virginia, 1930–39 140

32. Analysis of Variance of Effort to Support Public Education (Table 31) . . 141

33. Percentage of Salaries of Instructional Staff Derived from State Funds, Selected Counties, Virginia, 1930–39 142

34. Analysis of Variance of Percentage of Salaries of Instructional Staff Derived from State Aid (Table 33) 143

35. Expenditure by Local Division for Library Books per 100 Pupils Enrolled, All Schools, Selected Counties, Virginia, 1930–39 145

36. Analysis of Variance of Library Expenditures per 100 Pupils Enrolled (Table 35) 146

37. Library Books per Pupil in Average Daily Membership, White Elementary and Secondary Schools, Selected Counties, Virginia, 1938–39 . . . 148

38. Expenditures from Board of Education Funds for Educational Supplies per 100 Pupils Enrolled, All Schools, Selected Counties, Virginia, 1930–31, 1934–35, 1938–39 149

39. Analysis of Variance of Expenditures from Board Funds for Educational Supplies per 100 Pupils Enrolled (Table 38) 150

40. Number of Pupils in Average Daily Attendance, Number of Teachers, and Average Teacher Load, White Schools, Selected Counties, Virginia, 1930–31, 1934–35, 1938–39 151

41. Analysis of Variance of Number of Pupils in Average Daily Attendance, Number of Teachers, and Average Teacher Load (Table 40) 153

42. Number of Pupils in Average Daily Attendance, Number of Teachers, and Average Teacher Load, White Elementary Schools, Selected Counties, Virginia, 1938–39 154

43. Percentage of White Elementary Schools One or Two Teachers in Size, Selected Counties, Virginia, 1930–31, 1934–35, 1937–38 156

44. Analysis of Variance of Total Percentage of White Elementary Schools One and Two Teachers in Size (Table 43) 157

Tables

TABLE

PAGE

61. Average Number of Years of Experience Outside of County of White Elementary Teachers, Selected Counties, Virginia, 1930–31, 1934–35, 1938–39 195

62. Analysis of Variance of Years of Experience Outside of County (Table 61)   196

63. Years of Previous Experience of Newly Employed White Elementary Teachers, Selected Counties, Virginia, 1930–31, 1934–35, 1938–39 . . .   197

64. Level of College Training of Newly Employed White Elementary Teachers, Selected Counties, Virginia, 1930–31, 1934–35, 1938–39 . . .   198

65. Mean Age of White Elementary Teachers, Selected Counties, Virginia, 1939   199

66. Percentage of White Elementary Teachers Teaching in Home County, Selected Counties, Virginia, 1939   201

67. Percentage of White Elementary Teachers in Each Category of Experience Who Have Attended Summer School Since Beginning Teaching or Since June, 1930, Selected Counties, Virginia, 1939   203

68. Distribution of White Elementary Teachers Who Have Attended Summer School Since Beginning Teaching or Since June, 1930, According to Number of Sessions Attended and Years of Teaching Experience, Selected Counties, Virginia, 1939   205

69. Number and Percentage of White Elementary Teachers Who Have Taken College Extension Courses Since Beginning Teaching or Since June, 1930, Selected Counties, Virginia, 1939   206

70. Percentage of White Elementary Teachers Who Subscribed to One or More Professional Magazines and Who Read One or More Professional Books from September, 1938, to December, 1939, Selected Counties, Virginia   209

71. Percentage of White Elementary Teachers Not Including Those in One-Teacher Schools, Reporting Flexible Daily Class Schedule, Class Excursions and Trips, and Class Study of Community Life, Selected Counties, Virginia, 1939   214

72. Percentage of White Elementary Teachers Not Including Those in One-Teacher Schools Reporting Development of Large Units of Work, and Introduction of Major Changes in Teaching, Selected Counties, Virginia, 1939   217

73. Percentage of Teachers, Classified by Grade Level, Following Various Teaching Practices, Selected Counties, Virginia, 1939   219

Figures

Factors Associated with
Participation in Cooperative
Programs of Curriculum
Development

CHAPTER I

Teacher Participation in Programs of Curriculum Development

THE generally accepted concept of curriculum development has changed considerably within the last two decades and more particularly in the past ten years. This modification has accompanied a broadened view of the curriculum itself. Educators formerly thought of the curriculum as the specified body of organized subject matter to be taught in the classroom, but in recent years it has come to be regarded as the sum total of educative experiences under the guidance of the school.

The planning of curriculum programs has been directly influenced by the definition and concept of the curriculum accepted by those in charge. If the curriculum is considered to be an organized body of definite subject matter which is set out to be learned, programs of curriculum development are largely concerned with the preparation of outlines of the content to be taught, or courses of study. The purpose of such programs has been well stated by a superintendent of schools:

> The major objective in organizing for curriculum improvement should be (a) to produce at the completion of the initial attack the best course of study possible for the system in view of the best scholarship and the most approved practices available at the conclusion of the work, and (b) to maintain the gradual modification, development and improvement of the course of study, so as to insure that it shall be at all succeeding times as up-to-date and serviceable to the system as it was when first issued.[1]

But under the broader concept in which the curriculum is considered to be the totality of school experiences, the purposes of a curriculum program also are broadened in scope and formulated in terms of a more basic approach to curriculum development. Under such a guiding

[1] H. B. Wilson, "Machinery and Organization for Devising, Revising, and Supervising the Curriculum—The Administrator's Viewpoint"; in *The Elementary School Curriculum*, Second Yearbook of Department of Superintendence, p. 37.

1

concept curriculum development becomes a complicated process with the philosopher, the psychologist, the sociologist, the subject-matter specialist, the research worker, the curriculum expert, the administrator, the teacher, the parent, the layman, and the child all involved. Such a program is best characterized as follows:

> The major purpose is to develop an instructional program that will contribute more significantly to the individual and social welfare of the people of Mississippi. This will require outstanding improvements in classroom instruction throughout the state . . . such improvement will take two major lines of development. First, the work of the school must be better adjusted to the social and economic conditions of the age in which we live. This may be briefly characterized as the need for social orientation of the educational program. Second, greater attention must be given to providing optimum learning conditions. That is, boys and girls must be provided a greater variety of experiences and activities than have previously been included in the school program, and more attention must be given to factors that condition learning, such as interest and purpose.[2]

Programs of curriculum development down through the years have reflected changing concepts of the curriculum. In the main, three general types of programs may be distinguished: (1) programs designed solely for the preparation of courses of study; (2) programs planned in terms of course-of-study preparation, but organized so as to promote acceptance of the completed course by teachers through participation of representative teachers in its preparation; and (3) programs planned on a broad basis for the improvement of instruction, with course-of-study preparation only one although an important aspect of the program. The first type of program is a logical outgrowth of the older traditional concept of the school and of the course of study; the last named is a necessary correlate of the new concept of the curriculum; and the second represents a transitory but nevertheless distinct stage in the fundamental shift from one point of view to a complete implementation of the other. In this phase ways were sought to bolster up a curriculum development process that had serious shortcomings in an age of rapid educational advancement. Each of these three principal types of programs will be considered in turn with attention being given particularly to the processes used and the manner in which these reflected the point of view concerning the curriculum.

[2] Mississippi State Department of Education, *Study Program*, Bulletin No. 1, 1934, p. 7.

PROGRAMS DESIGNED SOLELY FOR COURSE-OF-STUDY
PREPARATION

The program of studies for the earliest American schools was usually
stated in the law or ordinance of the town establishing the school or in
the laws of the colony. Thus the town of Dorchester, Massachusetts, in
1639 voted: "This rent of 20 lb. yearly to bee payd to such a schoole-
master as shall undertake to teach english, latine, and other tongues,
and also writing."³ And the famous "old deluder Satan" Act of 1647
in Massachusetts provided that every township of fifty householders
must appoint "one within there towne to teach all such children as shall
resort to him to write and reade." The primary objective of the early
colonial schools was religious instruction and the curriculum centered
around the religious interests of the church. Reading received primary
attention, with the Bible, church hymns, the catechism, and other de-
votional literature such as the Hornbook constituting the materials of
instruction.

Somewhat later, after other books suitable for texts began to appear,
the titles of books to be used in the school were often prescribed. These
required texts may be said to constitute the formal course of study. *The
New England Primer,* Dilworth's *A New Guide to the English Tongue,*
Noah Webster's famous *American Spelling Book,* Hodder's *Arithme-
tick; or That Necessary Art Made Most Easie,* the Psalter, the Holy
Bible, and similar widely used textbooks constituted at one time or another the framework of the curriculum during the eighteenth century
and the early part of the nineteenth. Emphasis remained as in early
days on religious materials and instruction. Noah Webster stated that
in the pre-Revolutionary period "the books used were chiefly or wholly
Dilworth's spelling book, the Psalter, Testament, and Bible. No
geography was studied before the publication of Dr. Morse's small
books on the subject, about the year 1786 or 1787. No history was read
as far as my knowledge extends for there was no abridged history of
the United States."⁴

The courses studied in the Boston Latin Grammar School in 1789,

³ Quoted in Ellwood P. Cubberley, *The History of Education,* p. 362.
⁴ Noah Webster, letter to Henry Barnard; in *American Journal of Education,* Vol. 26,
pp. 195-196.

as noted by Inglis,[5] were stated entirely in terms of textbooks, and Stout[6] likewise showed that in the early days of the public high school the program of studies was frequently stated in terms of textbook titles. Some towns adopted rules giving specifically the program of studies and the books to be used. For example, the school regulations adopted by Providence in 1820 stated that "The Instruction shall be uniform in the several schools, and shall consist of Spelling, Reading, the use of capital letters and Punctuation, Writing, English, Grammar and Arithmetic. . . . The following Books, and none others, shall be used in the several schools."[7]

Prior to the establishment of graded schools, which began, at least in the more populous towns, during the two or three decades preceding the Civil War, instruction was individual and consisted almost entirely of hearing pupils recite what had been memorized from their books or checking their answers to textbook exercises or problems. While enterprising towns like Providence might prescribe the books required to be used, often the pupil used whatever was available for him and as a result wide variation occurred. Reisner has characterized instruction and the course of study in the usual district school in the period about 1800 in these words:

The method of instruction for the most part was individual. Each pupil brought with him to school the books which were available at home, or which the teacher prompted his parents to purchase for him. . . . The main factor in the learning process was the pupil's mastery of his text. Thus he learned the lessons in his reader and his speller page by page and worked his way from the beginning of his arithmetic to the end . . .[8]

CURRICULUM MAKING BY TEXTBOOK WRITERS
AND GOVERNING BOARDS

Curriculum making, if that term can be used, under such an educational pattern rested almost entirely in the hands of the writers of textbooks and law-makers. The latter group usually fixed the subjects to be taught in all the common schools of the state, often prohibiting the local school authorities from adding to the prescribed subjects; the

[5] Alexander Inglis, *The Rise of the High School in Massachusetts*, pp. 65-66.
[6] John E. Stout, *The Development of High School Curricula in the North Central States from 1860 to 1918.*
[7] Quoted in Ellwood P. Cubberley, *Readings in the History of Education*, p. 548.
[8] Edward H. Reisner, *The Evolution of the Common School*, pp. 312-313.

local school governing body frequently went further and named the texts which had to be used. The influence of textbook authors, such as Webster, Dilworth, Cheever, and the Biblical writers, who were only inadvertently textbook authors, on the curriculum was tremendous. Books by Dilworth, Webster, and perhaps others sold millions of copies each and dominated the school curriculum for many, many years. Rugg has said that

Webster's *American Spelling Book*; his *Little Reader's Assistant* written in 1790; the *Franklin Primer* and the *Columbia Primer* (1802); graded reading books like the *American Preceptor* and compendiums of classical selections like the *Columbian Orator*; these supplied the schoolmasters with the content of their "lessons" and hence of their curriculum.[9]

If the curriculum is considered in the broader sense of total pupil experience, it is apparent that these favored textbooks also largely determined the character of the total learning experience. Teaching consisted almost exclusively of testing memorization of their contents. Procedure, method, and discipline were designed for such learning. Educational outcomes, such as attitudes, habits, understandings, and ability to deal effectively with problems and situations, which are emphasized as an important part of the total curriculum today, were decidedly influenced by this type of instruction, although often not in the manner desired. It is no wonder that the famous Boston Grammar School Examining Committee reported in 1845 that

They [the pupils] can repeat rules with great fluency and accuracy, answer printed questions in arithmetic, while the book is before them, and, in fact, recite all their lessons in the book in a manner which would seem to do them great credit. When, however, these landmarks are thrown aside, and they are called to the blackboard and requested to answer questions not found in the book, and for which they have no prescribed rules, they come to a dead stand, and lose the whole skill which before they apparently exhibited . . . the pupils learn rules rather than principles, and . . . the textbooks are made quite too much their guide.[10]

Gradation of the elementary schools gave rise to a need for the preparation of courses of study—that is, of outlines of the topics of materials to be taught in the school subjects. Gradation was initiated by the older town schools in the pre-Civil War period, was extended generally to

[9] Harold Rugg, *American Life and the School Curriculum*, p. 127.
[10] Quoted from Otis W. Caldwell and Stuart A. Courtis, *Then and Now in Education 1845:1923*, pp. 55-56.

all town systems shortly after that struggle, and was being generally adopted in rural schools by the latter part of the nineteenth century. At first, the grade system simply took the form of grouping children together so that they could be held to the same attainments in a common text. Under such a practice the text still remained the only course of study and determined the curriculum pattern. Great attention, therefore, was given to the matter of securing uniformity in textbooks, with the question of the desirability of such a practice being agitated extensively during this period. Official reports of state education departments abounded in eloquent pleas for the adoption of uniform texts, either on a local school basis or on a state-wide basis. Frequently state superintendents clamored for legislation to give them the power to prescribe the texts to be used throughout the state, and in some cases the laws were forthcoming.

USE OF COURSES OF STUDY

Thus with the advent of the graded school, curriculum making still remained largely a prerogative of the textbook writer and the governing body—the board of education or the state legislature. But as the graded system became more systematized and true school grades rather than groupings according to progress through a prescribed text became established in the larger town systems courses of study were formulated, although, as stated previously, a course of study in a very limited sense of the word existed in the earlier days in the prescription of subjects or books to be taught in the schools. Actual courses of study, or courses of instruction as they were often called, were correlates of gradation, however, and did not appear until that movement got under way after 1800. In fact, the advent of gradation was considered to make some sort of course of study necessary so that an orderly procedure could be given to the work of each grade. The early courses of study were very simple, often stating only the title of the subjects to be taught and books to be used with perhaps a statement of the part or pages to be covered, or a sentence or two on the nature of the topics to be covered.

Both the use and the content of courses of study expanded after the Civil War as the system of gradation was extended in the town schools and gradually introduced in the latter part of the century into the one-teacher rural schools. Reisner summarized the reason for this:

The factor of gradation, with each class under a single teacher, gave a great deal more time for the treatment of stated school studies and even invited the addition of new subjects in the list indicated by the state laws. . . . The graded system had made possible and had prompted a careful prescription of the work to be done in each grade. . . . Under the graded system . . . it early became the custom for the school authorities to designate much more exactly the work to be done by any given class.[11]

Barnard's American Journal of Education for 1869[12] in a published survey of the status of school administration and organization and courses of instruction in a number of the larger cities shows that most of this select group of school systems had formal "courses of study" or "courses of instruction." Accompanying statements often indicate, however, that their preparation had been a rather recent step. Thus the St. Louis, Missouri, report stated that after a visit of the superintendent to other cities in 1858 to study their schools "a gradual course of instruction was adopted."[13]

As systematization became more firmly established and often even a fetish, courses of study became more elaborate, growing from a mere list of subjects, with required texts or at the most a statement of topics to be covered, to large volumes outlining in great detail the subject matter of each subject and the procedures and methods to be used.

Philbrick, at one time superintendent of schools at Boston, complained in 1885 that,

Only a few years back the program was, in general, nothing more than a list of textbooks prescribed for each class. . . . All that is now changed. . . . The programs of the present day scarcely refer to any textbook whatever. Under the old regime the teacher found it impossible to master the whole textbook and was quite at a loss to know what to omit. Under the present regime, where subjects and topics only are named, the teacher is equally puzzled to know what to include.[14]

Courses of study for a state as a whole did not appear until after the practice had been well established in city schools, few being published until the last quarter of the nineteenth century. This was in a large measure due to the much later establishment of graded schools in rural districts (the schools for which state education departments have usually felt primarily responsible), the prevailing concept and even legal basis

[11] Reisner, *op. cit.*, p. 424.
[12] Vol. 19, pp. 401-576.
[13] *Ibid.*, p. 533.
[14] John D. Philbrick, *City School Systems in the United States*, pp. 59-60.

of the duties of the department, and the traditional lag of school practice in rural and small town districts behind that of city systems, which in turn is reflected in or from state school administration. The lateness of the appearance of state courses of study is illustrated, for example, in Massachusetts, where the Secretary of the State Board of Education maintained in his annual report as late as 1883-84 that "It [was] the duty of the school committees to make these courses."[15] But three years later a course of study for ungraded schools appeared with the statement that it should aid the school boards of the various towns in preparing courses for their own schools. And in the report for 1893-94 a more elaborate course appeared, but again with the statement that it should guide local boards.

In Ohio, the first steps toward state courses of study were not taken until 1896-97, when the state teachers' association passed a resolution asking the State Commissioner of Education to appoint committees of seven members each to prepare syllabi in the common subjects for use in the institutes of the state. A number of such outlines were prepared within the next four years, apparently for the purpose of serving as guides to teachers, first in carrying on study at institute meetings and then in planning instruction. The Superintendent of Common Schools for Pennsylvania stated in his report for 1874 that,

The branches required by law to be taught in all common schools are orthography, reading, writing, arithmetic, geography and grammar. Other branches may be introduced at the discretion of boards of directors; but practically in ungraded schools the course of study remains as fixed by law. By a careful estimate it is found that scarcely one in thirty of all children attending public schools takes a single step beyond that course; and what is worse, even within these narrow limits, the instruction given comprehends, in a general way, little more than the matter with which the authors of textbooks used have seen proper to fill their pages.[16]

The first state course of study in Indiana[17] was prepared in 1883 and adopted for use by the county superintendents in 1884. It was a bare outline of subjects, listing only texts or topics, and covering but one and a half printed pages.

[15] State of Massachusetts, *Forty-Eighth Annual Report of the Board of Education,* 1883-84, p. 80.
[16] State of Pennsylvania, *Report of the Superintendent of Common Schools,* 1874, p. xxi.
[17] State of Indiana, *Thirty-Second Report of Superintendent of Public Instruction,* 1883 and 1884, pp. 101-103.

In the state of Virginia, which is particularly the subject of this study, a formal state course of study did not appear until 1907. In his annual reports for 1873 and 1874, State Superintendent Ruffner published articles by himself and some of the city superintendents on teaching certain common school subjects. These discussed methods and content but did not pretend to constitute formal courses. In the report for 1881, Dr. Ruffner outlined a "Graded Course for Primary Schools" which merely listed the subjects to be taught, but again this was intended as a personal statement of a professional writer rather than as a required state course. In the 1888 report an article by one of the teachers in the state normal school at Farmville appeared and it too suggested a possible course of study for one-teacher graded schools. Superintendent Ruffner, in the 1889 report, noted the use of courses of study in other states and suggested "the scheme here as worthy of the thoughtful consideration of the educators of our State." It was not until the fall of 1907, however, that a formal state course of study appeared. State Superintendent Eggleston, in his introduction to the publication, discussed the need for a graded course and justified its preparation. He said: "The time seems ripe, therefore, for a graded course of study for the primary and grammar school; and numerous requests from all parts of the state indicate that such a course will be welcomed by a large body of progressive teachers."[18]

COURSE-OF-STUDY PREPARATION BY ADMINISTRATIVE OFFICIALS

During this period of curriculum development the courses of study in both the cities and the states were prepared by administrative officials. Before the school superintendency was well established in city schools, boards of education exercised major responsibility for preparation of the course, which, as was pointed out earlier, was largely a list of the school subjects and the texts to be used or the topics to be taught. With the growth of the responsibilities and duties of the superintendent, authority to determine and make the course of study passed into this officer's hands, although frequently not without a struggle with boards of education. The profession asserted its full right as educational

[18] State of Virginia, *Course of Study for the Primary and Grammar Grades of the Public Schools of Virginia*, First Edition, October, 1907, p. 1.

experts to determine the course of study, subject, of course, to formal ratification by the governing board. The Secretary of the State Board of Education in Massachusetts declared in his annual report for 1883-84 that "it is the duty of the school committee to make these courses,"[19] but in the report for 1898-99 it is stated that "no greater technical or professional work is needed anywhere than in the making of a course of studies, and the superintendent alone should do it, or be responsible for it."[20] A table in this report, which summarized a study of the authority of school superintendents in 233 Massachusetts towns, showed that seventy per cent of these officers claimed that they had full authority in "making a course of study," while eighteen per cent had advisory authority only, and nine per cent possessed joint responsibility.

Examination of city courses of study and reports of superintendents reveals that after they had once wrested the power to make courses of study from boards of education, superintendents made little or no effort to secure the cooperation or participation of teachers in this process until after 1900. In the largest cities, administrative assistants might, upon invitation, aid the superintendent in the process but by and large courses of study were administrators' brainchildren, or at least their cutting and pasting projects, and were put into effect by administrative fiat. Cubberley, drawing on a broad view of practice, wrote even as late as 1911 to the effect that,

In the smaller cities the Superintendent of Schools usually prepares the course of study, and the Board of Education formally adopts it for use in the schools, though in many cities a committee of the Board of Education on course of study attempts to do what the laws generally give it the legal right to do, but which it is no longer competent to handle. In the larger cities the Superintendent and his assistants prepare the course of study, usually after conferences with committees selected from the teaching force, and the course is promulgated by the Superintendent and altered as necessity arises.[21]

The earlier state courses of study were likewise prepared by administrative officials or under their direct auspices. In this case, however, several lines of procedure were followed by various states. In a number of states, county superintendents occupied a more strategic and

[19] State of Massachusetts, *op. cit.,* p. 80.

[20] State of Massachusetts, *Sixty-third Annual Report of Board of Education,* 1898-99, p. 318.

[21] Ellwood P. Cubberley, "Courses of Study," in *Cyclopedia of Education,* ed. by Paul Monroe, Vol. 2, p. 223.

important position than the state superintendent, particularly with respect to instruction in the schools. Demands to formulate courses of study first arose among this group of officials and they frequently took the initiative, so that course-of-study making became a cooperative effort of county superintendents. In time, with the strengthening of the position of the state superintendent and the development of more educational leadership in this office, some responsibility for preparing courses of study was frequently turned over to or assumed by this official, but he continued to work closely with county superintendents. In other states, the state superintendent assumed or was legally given responsibility for formulating the state course of study from the outset. State superintendents, once they were accepted as the proper authorities to prepare the courses, followed two methods in preparing them: the superintendent, often with the assistance of his staff, prepared the course; or small committees, usually composed of county superintendents or college professors or both, were invited to prepare the outline. In any case, actual course-of-study preparation remained an administrator's job. And this practice prevailed in many of the states until recently and even exists in a few at the present time. Examples of these procedures will illustrate the role of the administrator—county or state superintendent—in the preparation of courses of study published by the state department for use especially by rural and small village schools.

The first Indiana state course of study (1884) "was prepared by a committee appointed by the convention of County Superintendents of 1883, and was adopted by the convention of 1884."[22] From statements in the state superintendent's subsequent annual reports, it seems that this course was revised and expanded almost every year by a committee of county superintendents until "by resolution of the County Superintendents Association, June, 1894, the revision of the State Manual and Course of Study was placed in the hands of the Superintendent of Public Instruction."[23] Thereafter the courses, according to statements in the introductions, were prepared by the staff of the State Education Department, with, at least in two instances, "acknowledgments . . . due the authors and publishers of the new textbooks for their prompt

[22] State of Indiana, *op. cit.*, p. 102.
[23] State of Indiana, *Forty-second Report of Superintendent of Public Instruction,* 1895-96, p. 35.

assistance in preparing outlines in the subjects embodied in their books."[24]

After several state courses in South Dakota had appeared, prepared, according to statements in the introduction, by "a committee of county superintendents," the State Superintendent in his report for 1920 pleaded for a more adequate program, charging that "the present course of study in our state is compiled in a piece-meal and job-lot fashion at the county superintendent's meetings without any opportunity for serious and constructive investigation and research."[25] The Kansas course of study of 1896[26] was prepared by a committee composed of seven members of the State Board of Education, four city superintendents, and five county superintendents. The 1907 edition[27] was "prescribed by the Committee on Course of Study" which consisted of the State Superintendent and four county superintendents. The Colorado state course of study for 1890[28] was prepared by a committee of three county superintendents and was adopted by the State Association of County Superintendents.

Cubberley summarized the situation in regard to state courses of study during this period in these terms:

> Such courses are generally outlined by the State Board of Education or the State Superintendent of Public Instruction, though in a few cases a State Commission has been created, and in one state the State Teachers Association has been the active body in working out the course. Such courses are based on the statutory school studies and the state series of textbooks, if such exist, and try to outline the minimum quantity of work for each school year.[29]

Two factors greatly influenced the formulation of courses of study during this period. The general pattern of offerings was affected by the pronouncements of national committees, particularly the Committee of Ten, the Committee of Fifteen, and the Committees on Economy of

[24] State of Indiana, *Uniform Course of Study for Elementary Schools of Indiana,* 1916-17, p. 12.

[25] State of South Dakota, *Fifteenth Biennial Report of Superintendent of Public Instruction,* p. 8.

[26] State of Kansas, *Course of Study for the Public Schools of the State of Kansas,* 1896.

[27] State of Kansas, *Course of Study for the Common Schools of Kansas,* 1907.

[28] State of Colorado, *State Course of Study for the Public Schools of Colorado,* 1890-1893.

[29] Ellwood P. Cubberley, "Courses of Study," in *Cyclopedia of Education,* ed. by Paul Monroe, Vol. 2, p. 223.

Time. The influence of these national committees was so great following 1890 that Rugg declared that, "Curriculum making, from the day of the Committee of Ten, has been predominantly via national committees . . ."[30] Unquestionably these committees were powerful factors in curriculum making, first through their influence on the program of studies in the schools themselves and second through their dictation, in a large measure, of the seriation and nature of the content of textbooks. Significantly, the personnel of these committees was composed largely of college professors and administrators. For example, the famous Committee of Ten was made up of five college presidents, one college professor, two headmasters of private schools, a principal of a public high school, and the United States Commissioner of Education. The Committee of Fifteen consisted of a college president, a state superintendent, the United States Commissioner of Education, and twelve city superintendents.

However, during this period—that is, the last several decades of the nineteenth and the first decade of the twentieth century—the actual day-by-day curriculum in the classroom was determined in the main by adopted textbooks. Courses of study were largely outlines of the texts, a fact often proudly acknowledged in the preface, as in the case of Indiana which was cited above. Reisner stated that the course of study "was organized in topical form, but withal in fairly close dependence upon available textbooks . . . the two factors of graded textbook production and city courses of study went hand in hand and were interdependent."[31] And Rugg said that,

For nearly a century [the nineteenth] . . . professional textmakers and professors of "subjects" prepared textbooks and the textbook dominated the curriculum. The content of instruction was determined by the point of view, knowledge, and interest of the individual writer, who frequently had no direct connection with the schools. Curriculum making was an "armchair" procedure.[32]

Not only was the course of study based on textbooks, but the curriculum in the broad sense was dictated by them. Rigid, lock-step teaching pro-

[30] Harold Rugg, "Three Decades of Mental Discipline: Curriculum-Making via National Committees," in *The Foundations and Technique of Curriculum-Construction*, Twenty-Sixth Yearbook of National Society for the Study of Education, p. 38.

[31] Edward H. Reisner, *The Evolution of the Common School*, p. 426.

[32] Rugg, "Three Decades of Mental Discipline: Curriculum-Making via National Committees," *op. cit.*, pp. 36-37.

cedures predominated, with one objective foremost—mastery of the
content prescribed by the course of study and found in the text. The
organization, management, and discipline of the school, as well as
pupil activities, were predicated on the attainment of this end.

All of this evidence substantiates amply the assertion that curriculum
development in the period beginning with the gradation of schools in
the second quarter of the nineteenth century and continuing until the
second decade of the present century, and even into the present day in
numerous instances, has been largely a process of course-of-study preparation by administrative officials and the putting into effect of these
courses by administrative fiat. The courses of study were based on textbooks written largely by college-orientated subject specialists who seri-
ated the book at first according to their own judgment and later on the
basis of recommendations of national committees. Classroom experiences of pupils were dictated by the courses of study and textbooks, and
teachers adhered closely to a pattern of teaching that sought mastery
of the prescribed content. No consideration was given by those in
authority to the teacher as a curriculum maker. His function was that
of putting pupils through the ritual of textbook learning.

COURSE-OF-STUDY PREPARATION BY SMALL COMMITTEES

Curriculum making through course-of-study writing by administrative officials was gradually superseded, taking the country as a whole,
by course-of-study preparation by small committees. These committees,
whose membership might include classroom teachers, supervisors, principals, and, in the case of states, county superintendents, were under
the close jurisdiction of the superintendent, and, in fact, at first often
only advisory to him. This newer procedure, which represented a
slight modification of former practices in the transition stages, came
into vogue well after 1900, although there is no clear demarcation line
between the two methods, for even today course-of-study writing by
administrative officials occurs, particularly in state curriculum development.

At the outset, course-of-study committees seem to have been largely
advisory in function. While a cursory survey of courses and professional literature fails to reveal a stated motive for the appointment of
such committees it may have been a strategic move on the part of

superintendents in order to get teacher support for the courses, but undoubtedly a desire to get teacher help on a professional responsibility was also a motive for the appointment of advisory committees.

This early form of committee work is illustrated by Soldan's procedure in St. Louis.[33] He stated that the 1902 course was "the joint work of the teachers and principals of the public schools, of the supervisors, assistant superintendents, and of the Superintendent of Instruction." A committee for each subject was appointed, consisting of eight teachers (one from each grade), principals, and members of the supervisory force. Prior to the assembling of these committees, a circular letter had been sent to each teacher asking for suggestions on changes that should be made in the courses then in use. These suggestions were made available to the committees. But the advisory nature of the committees is shown by this statement: "A draft of a course of study made by the Superintendent formed the basis of the deliberations, and changes were freely made with the understanding that the whole course, when finished, would be subject to his revision and approval." The San Francisco, California, courses also came to be formulated by this procedure. Imprinted on the title page of the course of study issued for 1897-1898 was this statement: "Course for Primary and Grammar Grades prepared by the Superintendent; for High, Normal, and Evening Schools, by Principals."[34] But the 1900 course stated that, "The Board of Education and the Superintendent wish to thank the teachers of the city for their helpful suggestions, and particularly to thank the committees for the reports which they submitted. These have been found very helpful, and wherever possible, the suggestions of the teachers have been used."[35]

As better trained teachers began to be found in the city systems and as course-of-study preparation became more technical and elaborate in nature, committees participated more and more in the actual writing of courses. With the development of the scientific movement in education and a new emphasis on "pedagogy" the busy administrator could not hope to be an expert in all phases of the curriculum. Teachers,

[33] St. Louis, Missouri, Public Schools, *Outline of the Course of Study*, 1902.

[34] San Francisco, California, Public Schools, *Course of Study in the Public Schools of San Francisco*, 1897-1898. Title page.

[35] San Francisco, California, *Course of Study for the Public Schools*, 1900, p. 13.

principals, and supervisors assumed increasingly larger responsibilities in determining the content of the course of study, so that the period centering around 1910-1920 is marked, at least in city systems, by course-of-study writing by small professional committees whose membership was drawn from teachers, principals, and supervisors. Occasionally a college professor served as an "expert" adviser on pedagogy or content, but in the main, superintendents were seeking to utilize the professional skill and practical insight that came from actual contact with the classroom. Thus the Denver, Colorado, course of study published in 1918 makes this acknowledgment, "The Denver Course of Study for the Elementary Schools is the product of the combined efforts of teachers, principals, and directors. The course, in its first form, was the work of committees of teachers, and represents the best efforts which resourcefulness and continued study of practical teachers can offer."[36] The Philadelphia schools used a similar procedure. The preparation of three elementary English courses of study published in 1917 is described as follows: "The following Course of Study in English is the result of more than two years' work on the part of a committee of Philadelphia teachers, principals, and members of the Department of Superintendence."[37] In preparing this course an effort was also made to enlist the assistance of teachers generally, for acknowledgment is made "to the teachers of Philadelphia, many of whom were of direct assistance through detailed replies to questionnaires, through furnishing of outlines of lessons, and through their willingness to try out with their classes parts of the course while it was in the making."[38]

This small committee type of procedure in course-of-study construction was a common practice among the larger city systems in the period following 1910. A committee of the Department of Superintendence of the National Education Association[39] has reported the

[36] Denver, Colorado, Public Schools, *Course of Study in Geography and Nature Study,* 1918.

[37] Board of Public Education, School District of Philadelphia, *The Course of Study in English—Grades One to Eight,* 1917, p. 3.

[38] *Ibid.,* p. 7.

[39] Committee on Superintendents' Problems, "Report—Part I, Administrative Cooperation in the Making of Courses of Study in Elementary Schools," *Addresses and Procedures,* National Education Association, Vol. 57 (1919), pp. 675-716.

results of an extensive study into course-of-study making procedures in elementary schools in 1919. Of the 329 city systems which replied to the inquiry, 176 stated that committees were used in preparing courses while "153 superintendents out of 329 kept the work closely in their own hands." A total of 499 committees were functioning in these 176 cities. Teachers occupied about one-third of the committee positions. The committee concluded that,

> The typical procedure of a superintendent in a smaller city, who revises the course of study himself, probably includes the observation of classroom procedures and the making of mental or written notes thereon, the making of incidental inquiries from teachers as to the practical workings of various portions of the course, the observing of the results of examinations given by himself, the analyzing of courses of study in other cities, and of other literature in this field, and in some instances general discussions in grade meetings.[40]

And that this practice was common is indicated by this statement: "There are still a large number of superintendents, particularly in the smaller cities, who prepare the courses of study themselves or with only incidental and unorganized assistance of teachers and principals."[41]

However, it must be recognized that thousands of school systems had no prepared courses of study at all. The adopted textbooks were their courses of study and fixed the curriculum pattern of the school. Also, textbooks influenced greatly the printed courses of study where such existed, many being merely syllabi for particular texts. The influence of the textbook writer was still tremendous.

While, as shown above, some of the earliest state courses of study were cooperative projects of administrators—county superintendents—and hence in a sense committee projects, the procedure of utilizing committees which were representative of the entire teaching staff was seldom followed until a decade or two ago. After responsibility for preparing state courses of study had been fixed in the state departments of education, these courses, with few exceptions, were prepared until after 1920 by state department staffs or under their immediate direction by "specialists." In some cases, committees of county superintendents perfunctorily reviewed the courses or served as advisory committees. Reinoehl, writing in 1922 and well after committee activity had become firmly established in many city systems, summarized the meth-

[40] *Ibid.*, p. 697.
[41] *Ibid.*, p. 714.

ods by which forty-four state courses of study then current were formulated in these words:

There are variations in the methods used in preparing state courses. The number of writers varies all the way from 50 contributors in Arizona to State Department members in most states . . . College and normal-school professors and city superintendents have frequently helped to write courses; county superintendents and grade teachers, occasionally; successful rural teachers, seldom, if ever.[42]

Illinois offers an interesting example of state procedures followed during this period.[43] The first state course of study was drafted in 1889 by a committee of five county superintendents, who had been appointed at the instigation of the state teachers' association. This course was revised in 1894 by a committee composed of the State Superintendent of Public Instruction, three county superintendents, and a principal of a township high school. In 1895 the county superintendents' section of the state teachers' association appointed a Standing Committee on State Course of Study, and it has directed all work on state elementary course-of-study construction since that date. The Committee originally consisted of the State Superintendent, three county superintendents, and two professors from state normal schools. In 1912 it was decided that the committee should thereafter consist of the State Superintendent, a faculty member from each of the state normal schools, and from the university, and six county superintendents. Seven general revisions of the original course have appeared to date, the last being issued in 1925. In the early years, the standing committees revised the course themselves, but beginning in 1912 individuals, usually faculty members of state normals, were selected to prepare the outline for each subject. This procedure was followed until 1925 when subject committees of three persons—a faculty member of a state teachers college or of the university, who served as chairman, and two persons who were teachers or superintendents in the state—were named to write the course for their respective fields.

The Idaho state courses of study[44] beginning with 1908 and con-

[42] Charles M. Reinoehl, *Analytic Survey of State Courses of Study for Rural Elementary Schools*, pp. 2-3.

[43] County Superintendents' Section of Illinois State Teachers Association, Standing Committee on State Course of Study, *Course of Study for the Common School of Illinois*, 1925.

[44] Idaho State Superintendent of Public Instruction, *Courses of Study and Teachers Manual for the Public Schools of Idaho*, 1908 and subsequent years.

tinuing until 1923 were written by the city superintendent of schools at Pocatello. In 1925 several other people prepared outlines in certain subjects. In preparing the 1929 course a committee organization was used for the first time.

In Minnesota, after the county superintendents had instituted action in formulating a course of study in 1906, it was prepared by individuals on the state department staff of specialists selected by the state department until 1923, when committees were named for broad subject areas. These committees for both the 1923 and the 1928 editions were composed of faculty members of state educational institutions, superintendents, and occasionally a city supervisor. No teachers were listed as members of any committees. The first course of study in Michigan, published about 1890, was prepared by a committee of county superintendents, but beginning with the next edition in 1897 and continuing until as late as 1928 the courses have been prepared by members of the state education department.

The first formal state course of study for Virginia (1907) was prepared in the following manner:

On February 15-16, 1907, by invitation of the State Superintendent of Public Instruction, a committee to outline this course met at the University of Virginia. This committee was composed of Dr. Charles Kent and Dr. Bruce Payne of the University of Virginia; Dr. R. M. Fallon of Miller School; Messrs. Harris Hart, E. H. Russell, and Charles Maphis of the Board of Examiners; Mrs. M. S. Moffett of Manassas; County Superintendent E. W. Scott of Orange, and J. W. Everett of Albermarle; and the State Superintendent . . . after working for two days this committee completed the outline and requested Mrs. Moffett and Messrs. Hart and Maphis to amplify the course, as already worked out. Messrs. Hart, Russell, and J. S. Thomas had prepared, with much care, an outline which was in large measure followed by the committee.[45]

A slight revision of this course was published in 1909, without indicating who made the changes.

A new course was prepared in 1915 and the committee procedure was also used in this instance. The introduction stated that,

Fifty or 100 of the superintendents and teachers of the state were asked to collaborate in the preparation of the pamphlet. This was brought about by establishing centers for the consideration of the various subjects presented. At each center two leaders were appointed who were asked to associate other

[45] State of Virginia, *Course of Study for Primary and Grammar Grades of the Public Schools of Virginia,* First Edition, October, 1907, p. 3.

specialists with themselves in the performance of the duties assigned. The Conference of Division Superintendents also appointed a committee to act with the State School Inspectors and other representatives of the Department of Public Instruction in bringing together and harmonizing the reports of special committees.[46]

This course served until 1923 when a committee was again utilized to assist or at least advise in the preparation of a new course for the elementary schools. The work was carried out as follows:

The Department of Education invited a committee to serve with the Supervisor of Teacher Training to formulate an elementary course. This Committee was divided into appropriate divisions with specific assignments. Members of this Committee took great pains to secure courses from other states and additional related material. After careful individual study and thoughtful conference in group meetings and in the Committee as a whole the program of work herein outlined was formulated.[47]

This course with slight revision in 1926 was used until the new curriculum program was initiated in 1931.

SUMMARY

In summary, it is apparent from the foregoing discussion that curriculum development in American public schools was the prerogative of governing boards, textbook writers, national committees, and administrators until well after the opening of the twentieth century. After administrators came to exercise the dominant role in curriculum development through the formulation of courses of study, small committees, composed of subject specialists, supervisory and administrative officials, and teachers, were increasingly invited to aid the administrator in the process or even to take over the complete preparation of the courses. The characteristics of such efforts at curriculum development may be summarized as follows:

1. The purpose was to prepare courses of study.

2. Organization was planned solely in terms of the preparation of courses.

3. College professors, textbook writers, and administrative officials dominated the work.

4. Teachers made little or no contribution to formal curriculum development.

[46] State of Virginia, *State Course of Study for Elementary Schools*, 1915, p. 4.

[47] State of Virginia, *State Course of Study for Rural and Elementary Schools of Virginia*, 1923, p. 5.

5. Curriculum development was based on the concept that education is concerned primarily with mastery of a body of subject matter set-out-to-be-learned in advance by those in authority.

PROGRAMS FOR COURSE-OF-STUDY PREPARATION SO ORGANIZED AS TO FACILITATE ACCEPTANCE AND USE

While small committees, composed almost exclusively of administrative and supervisory officials, had aided in the preparation of courses of study for many city systems during the first two decades of the twentieth century, and for state systems somewhat later, several important factors prompted the expansion of this practice until highly-organized programs involving large numbers of teachers of a school system evolved in the period beginning about 1920. Many of these programs appear to be a logical development from earlier practices— the use of more and more committees as course-of-study preparation became more laborious and detailed. Nevertheless, the movement was hastened by other factors, all of which merged together to stimulate the initiation of a new procedure in curriculum making.

The first of these factors was the scientific movement in education. As one aspect of this movement, increased attention was given to the outcomes of education; first, as to what were the actual outcomes in terms of achievement as measured by standard tests and as indicated by analyses of courses of study and textbooks; and second, as to what they should be as determined by comprehensive and tedious analyses of human activities. Thus attention centered on the courses of study themselves. Courses were evaluated in terms of the findings of such research, and if found wanting plans were formulated for revision. Curriculum makers became more concerned with the nature of the content of courses of study than was true in earlier years. They were very desirous that the curriculum be made as "scientific" as possible, utilizing the latest findings of research. This brought the research worker and the curriculum specialist prominently to the fore in curriculum development. Curriculum revision became a complicated, involved procedure. Courtis,[48] for example, described a curriculum revision program in one of

[48] S. A. Courtis, "Curriculum-Construction at Detroit" in *The Foundations and Techniques of Curriculum-Construction,* Twenty-Sixth Yearbook of National Society for Study of Education, pp. 189-206.

our large cities in the period following 1920 which utilized to an extensive degree the research worker and his findings. Directly or indirectly this impact of the scientific movement on curriculum making magnified the position of the teacher in curriculum making. It was considered necessary that the teacher become familiar with research findings or at least with their implications for classroom practice. He needed to know, for example, that the new spelling course of study or spelling book was based on a scientifically determined word list so that he would be willing to discard the relics of a spelling list handed down from the days of Noah Webster; or he must be familiar with the basic generalizations which the social sciences could contribute to man's thinking so his history teaching could be directed to the acquisition of such concepts by his pupils.

Paralleling this emphasis on the scientific determination of subject matter in curriculum making was a second educational trend which greatly influenced curriculum development during the period. This was an increased emphasis on the importance of teaching procedures and methods in the educational process. This was a manifestation of the teachings of Dewey, Parker, Kilpatrick, and others of the progressive educational thinkers who so greatly influenced education after 1920. Method became equally important as subject matter, if not more so. The teaching process itself became of primary concern. Attention was centered on the classroom and what transpired there; teaching procedures, heretofore largely overlooked, were recognized as a most important factor in the educational process. Administrators came to realize that the desired outcomes of education, direct as well as the concomitant, could not be prescribed through the mere preparation of outlines of content to be taught. Even if courses of study were so organized that good teaching procedures were encouraged and facilitated, there was no assurance that teachers, who, as a body, have been notoriously lacking in adequate professional training throughout the development of the American schools, would make proper use of the suggestions and materials and realize the desired objectives. Traditional practices were hard to change with poorly prepared teachers.

Thus out of the matrix of this situation—ever-increasing demands by the educational research worker that the curriculum be "scientific" and by the educational philosopher that teaching methods be "psychological" plus notoriously untrained teachers—administrators came increasingly to realize that improvement was to be found by giving very positive assistance to teachers in applying the scientific and the psychological to classroom practice. The basis of improvement—and this is the crux of the matter—was to be more efficient and effective use of a course of study which had been formulated in terms of accepted scientific and psychological principles. There were thus two facets to curriculum development under this view: the preparation of the best possible courses of study, utilizing the best professional knowledge available; and making these courses of study effective in practice. This concept of curriculum making was well brought out by the statements of leading school administrators of that period. Newlon and Threlkeld stated:

> The task that confronts those who are responsible for the administration of large school systems is that of bringing curricula, as regards content, methods of teaching, and administrative procedures, as nearly as possible into line with the best educational knowledge and practice. The accomplishment of this objective requires an extensive and complex organization working scientifically.[49]

And Wilson emphasized the role of the course of study: "The results of the school's efforts depend mainly upon the teachers' faithful and effective use of the course of study."[50]

In line with this point of view it became necessary, as Newlon and Threlkeld stated, to set up an elaborate organization for curriculum development so that the expert and the specialist could make their contributions to the course of study. The most elaborate organization, using the latest findings of research, was a futile gesture, however, toward curriculum development, if the course of study was not used by classroom teachers. Progress was dependent on this one basis—teacher use of better courses of study. The critical problem, then, for school administrators was to insure the use of courses by teachers generally. Teachers must be "sold" on the new course of study so they would use it efficiently and effectively. Hence a new objective entered into curriculum revision programs—the organization of course-of-study con-

[49] Jesse H. Newlon and A. L. Threlkeld, "The Denver Curriculum-Revision Program," in *The Foundations and Techniques of Curriculum-Construction*, Twenty-Sixth Yearbook of National Society for the Study of Education, p. 229.

[50] H. B. Wilson, "Machinery and Organization for Devising, Revising, and Supervising the Curriculum—The Administrator's Viewpoint," in *The Elementary School Curriculum*, Second Yearbook of Department of Superintendence, p. 40.

struction programs in such a manner as to secure teacher acceptance and use of the finished product. A major task in curriculum revision programs became that of encouraging teachers to use the courses of study produced. This new aspect of the problem is well expressed in a significant statement contained in an important study of curriculum development at that time: "The biggest problem in curriculum revision, according to one superintendent of schools is not in revision at all. It is this: 'How may the teachers who are to use the new materials be brought into a sufficient familiarity with it, so that its objectives may be realized in their work?' "[51] And Alltucker, summarizing the status of curriculum development from a national viewpoint in 1925 said, "In the last analysis, the effectiveness of a course of study depends upon the intelligence with which it is used in the classroom. A course-of-study revision program must consist of more than getting proper content and technique on a printed page. Teachers must see the significance of it."[52]

The method whereby teachers were to be led to an acceptance of courses of study produced in curriculum programs was by representation on committees which formulated the courses. Rather than have committees composed exclusively of administrators and supervisors, as was formerly the case, the teachers were to be represented so that the finished course of study would be a teachers' product and hence acceptable to them. Threlkeld, who was in charge of one of the most important of these curriculum programs, epitomized this concept well: "No program of study will operate that has not evolved to some extent out of the thinking of the teachers who are to apply it. It is, therefore, necessary to have committees of teachers at work in each of the fields represented in the program."[53]

Bonser, writing in 1920, said that "The effectiveness of a curriculum depends for its detailed applications upon the teachers, and the more they put into its development the greater their sense of responsibility and power in carrying it forward in teaching."[54]

[51] National Education Association, Research Department, *Keeping Pace with the Advancing Curriculum*, Research Bulletin, Vol. III, No. 4-5, Sept.-Nov., 1925, p. 119.
[52] *Ibid.*, p. 119.
[53] A. L. Threlkeld, "The Denver Program of Curriculum Revision," in *The Elementary School Curriculum*, Second Yearbook of Department of Superintendence, pp. 118-120.
[54] Frederick Bonser, *The Elementary School Curriculum*, p. 426.

If teachers were slow to use courses of study prepared for them by administrators and supervisors and installed by administrative fiat, it was believed that they would make more of an effort to use courses in which they had had a voice. The course of study was to be "sold" to them as a product of their own labor, as something which had been formulated by co-workers who knew the practical classroom situation. Elaborate organizations for curriculum revision in which teacher representation was meticulously provided for were consequently set up by city and state school systems during this period. Much attention was given to such matters as the selection of teacher members of committees—should they be appointed by the superintendent or elected by the teachers—and the delicate definition of responsibility and authority of each committee or person included in the widespread organization.[55] Teachers apparently were not to overstep the bounds of good administrative practice but were to be given enough responsibility (and tedious work) to make them amenable to the finished product. The literature of the period abounds in lengthy discussions of these matters of proper organization of personnel.[56] Organization was so planned as to utilize to the best advantage the professional ability of the staff and yet secure widespread teacher representation. Some programs provided for a teacher representative from each building on committees, others from each grade level, and the like.

It should be pointed out that, of course, teachers performed a valiant professional service by aiding in the preparation of courses of study. The task, in view of the great advances in research and psychology, had become much too big for an administrator to perform as one of his numerous duties. But the choice among having it prepared by an employed specialist, by administrative and supervisory committees, or by committees composed largely of classroom teachers, often working hurriedly in after-school and vacation hours, was made in favor of the last method by most city school administrators because of the belief that such participation would facilitate acceptance and use of the completed course by teachers generally, as the above discussion has indicated and certainly such a procedure does represent a step forward.

[55] L. Thomas Hopkins, *Curriculum Principles and Practices*, Part II.
[56] Walter D. Cocking, *Administrative Procedures in Curriculum Making for Public Schools*.

CITY PROGRAMS

A brief description of the Denver, Colorado, program,[57] which was one of the earliest and best known of this type of enterprise, will illustrate the procedures used to secure teacher representation in course-of-study construction during this period. The program was initiated in 1922. Three sets of committees for each subject field, one each for the elementary, junior high school, and senior high school levels were appointed to revise courses of study. In addition four central committees concerned largely with administrative problems were appointed. The program was under the direction of the assistant superintendent in charge of instruction and curriculum revision. After exploration of the task, it became apparent that a far-reaching program was next to impossible to carry out through committee activity by teachers in out-of-school hours. Early in 1923, therefore, the board of education made a substantial appropriation for curriculum revision. Two curriculum specialists from the faculties of near-by teacher-training institutions were employed on a part-time basis to work with and direct the activities of the committees.

The subject-matter committees were composed almost exclusively of classroom teachers, although directors and supervisors were ex-officio members of committees in their respective areas, with responsibility for giving general advice and guidance. The chairman was always a classroom teacher. The membership of central committees, who were largely concerned with the determination of programs of study and pupil guidance, was composed, however, of principals, deans, advisers, and the like. Membership on subject committees was so arranged that each elementary school in the city was represented on some committee, and each junior and senior high school was represented on each committee for these levels. Committee members were expected to interest the teachers in their respective schools in the work, keep them informed about the program, and serve as an agent for bringing any contributions from their co-workers to the committee.

Committee members were released from teaching duties for the neces-

[57] See Denver, Colorado, Public Schools, *Course of Study Monographs.* Issued beginning in 1923. Foreword and Introductory Statement. Jesse Newlon and A. L. Threlkeld, "The Denver Curriculum-Revision Program," in *Foundations and Technique of Curriculum-Construction*, Twenty-Sixth Yearbook of National Society for Study of Education, pp. 229-240.

sary work, substitute teachers being employed in their stead from the funds made available. In the early stages of committee activity all members might spend full time for several consecutive days or more on the project, but after a certain amount of progress had been made, only the chairman, and perhaps an assistant, would spend full time on committee work. Other members would be called in at intervals for a half-day or full day largely to evaluate the work done by the chairman during the intervening period. The chairman would then "proceed to the preparation of another section of the course of study." At the proper time in the work of the committee, a specialist in the area would be brought to Denver for a series of conferences with the committee. And after completion of the course of study the manuscript was submitted to him for criticism. Certain of the central committees also reviewed the product of these committees. The work of the three sets of committees in each area was coordinated through the supervision of the two regular curriculum specialists and other administrative and supervisory officers. An extensive professional library, adequate work facilities, and clerical assistance were provided for the committees.

From the outset, curriculum revision was regarded as a continuous process and plans were made accordingly. In September, 1925, a department of curriculum revision was established and a curriculum specialist was appointed as full-time director of the work, replacing the two part-time faculty members who formerly supervised the work. Continuous activity in revision of courses of study has been in progress since the inauguration of the enterprise, with some monographs having gone through a third revision within ten years. Committee membership has been rotated whenever possible with due regard for efficiency so that as many teachers as possible could participate.

Following the lead of Denver and other forward-looking city school systems a great wave of curriculum development swept over the country after 1920.[58] Bruner[59] maintained that less than 800 courses of study had been produced in the country prior to 1923, many of which were very meager outlines in annual reports of superintendents, but, he stated,

[58] See Harold Rugg and others, *The Foundations and Technique of Curriculum-Construction,* Twenty-Sixth Yearbook of National Society for the Study of Education, for descriptions of other programs.

[59] Herbert Bruner, "Curriculum Making in American Public Schools," *South Dakota Education Association Journal,* Vol. 5, pp. 263-266, 1930.

in the six years immediately following that year the output was so great that one curriculum laboratory alone collected over 20,000 courses of study.

Courtis, on the basis of a survey study of 132 city schools made about 1926, estimated that sixty per cent of these systems had made a general revision of the curriculum during the preceding three-year period and seventy-five per cent during the previous five years. He stated that "In all types of schools a committee of teachers under the direction of administrative or supervisory officers constitutes the conventional machinery of revision."[60] Trillingham[61] reported that ninety-three out of the one hundred city school systems replying to his questionnaire had some type of curriculum program in 1931-32. Of this number thirty-three cities reported that an effort was made to use all of their teachers in certain phases of their programs, while fifty-two cities reported making no such attempt. However, committees of some type seem to have been used in practically all cities having definite programs. While the nature and extent both of the programs themselves and of teacher participation in them are open to broad interpretation in these studies, nevertheless they reveal the widespread interest in curriculum revision and the emphasis placed on teacher representation in production committees during this period.

STATE PROGRAMS

This interest in curriculum making was reflected in the states. Langvick[62] reported that courses of study were revised in whole or in part in thirty-one states during the period 1928-30, and Shearer[63] found that forty-seven conducted at least one state-wide curriculum revision program in the ten-year period of 1927-37. In state programs planned in terms of course-of-study preparation it has been more diffi-

[60] Stuart A. Courtis, "Current Practices in Curriculum-Revision in Public Elementary Schools," in *The Foundations and Techniques of Curriculum-Construction*, Twenty-Sixth Yearbook of National Society for Study of Education, pp. 119-132.

[61] Clinton C. Trillingham, *The Organization and Administration of Curriculum Programs.*

[62] Mina M. Langvick, *Current Practices in the Construction of State Courses of Study,* p. vii.

[63] Allen E. Shearer, "Procedures in Curriculum Revision Programs of Selected States," p. 1.

cult to utilize extensive teacher participation in committee work than in city systems. However, many states have given selected committees large responsibilities in the work. Shearer classified twenty-six of the forty-seven state programs carried out during the period of 1927-37 as belonging in the state-wide committee-personnel type of organization.[64] Langvick gave examples of such programs in a number of selected states.[65]

The South Dakota program best illustrates the procedure of using teacher representatives on course of study production committees in state programs. These programs, it must be remembered, differed from earlier state efforts which utilized a small committee of college teachers, principals, or superintendents in that as many teachers as possible were drawn into the program so that it would be better received in all sections and by all groups of teachers and the contributions of as wide a group as possible could be secured in preparing the course of study. The South Dakota program was initiated in 1929 by the state superintendent of public instruction.[66] A staff member of the state education department was designated state director of curriculum revision, with major responsibility for directing the program. A curriculum specialist was employed in a consultative capacity. General executive and reviewing committees for the elementary and for the secondary schools respectively were appointed. The elementary committee was composed of four city school superintendents, eight county superintendents, six college faculty members, and the state educational association executive secretary. The secondary committee consisted of six city school superintendents, two high school principals, four college faculty members, two city school supervisors, two members of the state education department, and the editor of the state professional journal. These committees were to determine aims, formulate guiding principles, advise subject committees on certain matters, review work of all subject committees, and determine form and organization of the course of study.

Subject-matter committees were appointed in each subject area. Over four hundred teachers throughout the state were actively engaged in

[64] Shearer, *op. cit.*, p. 26.

[65] Langvick, *op. cit.*, pp. 15-17; 34-49.

[66] State of South Dakota, State Superintendent of Public Instruction, *Preliminary Reports on Approaches to and Theories Regarding Curriculum Construction, General Aims and Guiding Principles of Education.*

production of courses through these committees and another four hundred acted as contributing members. All educators in the state were invited to cooperate in the work by giving suggestions to the various committees. An adaptation committee was appointed to adapt the courses to rural consolidated and small schools. A publicity committee was expected to publicize the program and a standard materials committee was to select lists of textbooks in each field, and reference and teaching materials for each subject. All of this activity eventuated in a comprehensive state elementary course of study and a number of courses for high school subjects.

The South Dakota program was, of course, outstanding from the standpoint of the number of teachers involved in committee work. Few states made any effort during this period to utilize more than a very small number of teachers in the program in any manner whatsoever, and many (and this is true even to the present day) totally disregarded teachers until the course of study was ready for use.

In the period since 1920 many cities and a large number of the state school systems have utilized the type of curriculum development program discussed in this section—programs which have centered on course-of-study preparation by committees composed in part at least of representative teachers. Without doubt it is the dominant type of curriculum program in this country at the present time. And it must be recognized that this type of curriculum program does provide a great amount of in-service education for those who are appointed as committee members. It is generally recognized by superintendents of schools and curriculum leaders that participation in a curriculum revision program is a most valuable means of promoting teacher training, and this has been an important objective of most of the programs. This objective was particularly emphasized by those in charge of the Denver program. They said, "A program of this kind, properly directed, will ultimately raise every fundamental issue pertaining to curricula and method for the consideration of teachers and administrative staffs."[67]

But the weaknesses in the teacher-committee method of curriculum development through course-of-study preparation are rather obvious.

[67] Jesse H. Newlon and A. L. Threlkeld, "The Denver Curriculum-Revision Program," in *The Foundations and Techniques of Curriculum-Construction,* Twenty-Sixth Yearbook of National Society for the Study of Education, p. 231.

In the first place, at the best only a small percentage of the total teaching corps was directly involved in the program. The rigorous training and intensive study required for such a program affected a small number of teachers. While some systems claimed that they tried to bring all teachers into the program, the great majority of teachers were drawn in only slightly or not at all until the courses of study were printed and placed in their hands. Thus a small number of teachers prepared new or revised materials for the use of other teachers who had little understanding of the plans evolved or little insight into the basis and significance of the recommended procedures or content. If a break was made with the traditional, most teachers were unprepared to use the course and, frustrated, disregarded it. If no important modification was made, the work lacked significance. In either case practice remained unaffected. Many administrators undoubtedly believed that participation in writing courses by a small number of selected teachers would encourage the rest of the staff to accept them and make honest efforts to carry them into effect. Probably this was true to some extent, but teachers found that without adequate preparation it was difficult to use materials widely different from practice, regardless of sentiment in the matter. In a recent survey, the staff made this observation relative to one of the best known of the curriculum programs of the committee type, "Ambitious to the extreme, many of these programs, while they represented sincere efforts to improve the educative experiences of children, exerted little actual influence on classroom practice."[68]

The second criticism leveled against curriculum programs of this type lies in the concept of what constitutes the curriculum. Curriculum specialists who held that the curriculum was the total flow of educative experiences in the school believed that curriculum programs concerned solely or primarily with the preparation of courses of study fell far short of the proper objective. To them, teacher growth and stimulation was a primary objective of all curriculum programs, since actual curriculum improvement in the classroom is conceived to be the direct responsibility of the teacher. This has led to a new concept of curriculum development and the formation of programs of a more comprehensive type which will be discussed in the next section.

[68] Division of Field Studies, Institute of Educational Research, Teachers College, *A Report of a Survey of the Public Schools of Saint Louis, Missouri* (Complete Report), Vol. 5, p. 1098.

But it is evident that some of the administrators and curriculum workers who had been most active in these programs of course-of-study preparation by teacher committees came to realize these weaknesses, particularly the first, and began to redirect them along lines more in conformity with the point of view which had in the meantime come into prominence in these comprehensive developmental programs. Thus the school administrators of one city emphasized that "there is no substitute possible for a maximum of teacher participation if teacher growth and effectiveness are to be provided for and if the best results are to be expected from classroom procedures."[69] And a survey staff in studying a large city school system stated that "for motivation of such professional study, no better method than participation in a continuous curriculum-revision program has ever been found, for the curriculum raises every fundamental problem of theory and practice."[70] The staff placed emphasis on both the acceptance objective and the in-service training objective of such participation. It stated, "Curriculum making solely by experts will prevent thinking on the part of the teacher. . . . Teachers must participate to understand, and they have essential contributions to make out of their own study and experience."[71] Moreover, the national organization of school administrators declared in 1930 that one of the major purposes of curriculum revision was:

To make the classroom teacher alive to changing philosophies of education and conscious of the new knowledge regarding methods and materials which is coming from educational laboratories, research agencies and classroom experience. Teacher growth is one of the chief objectives of curriculum revision. Superintendents of schools are unanimous in reporting that the intellectual life of those who participate in curriculum revision is rekindled—a keener professional attitude is developed. Curriculum revision is distinctly a supervisory procedure in the training of teachers.[72]

Thus the need for a more comprehensive, broader type of curriculum program than most of those in vogue during this period was implied.

[69] Jesse H. Newlon and A. L. Threlkeld, "The Denver Curriculum-Revision Program," in *The Foundations and Technique of Curriculum-Construction,* Twenty-Sixth Yearbook of National Society for the Study of Education, p. 231.

[70] Division of Field Studies, Institute of Educational Research, Teachers College, *Report of the Survey of the Schools of Chicago, Illinois,* Vol. 3, p. 94.

[71] *Ibid.,* pp. 96-97.

[72] National Education Association, Department of Superintendence, *The Superintendent Surveys Supervision,* p. 178.

SUMMARY

In summary, the second main method of curriculum development— that is, course-of-study preparation by teacher committees—may be characterized as follows:

1. It came into vogue about 1920 in a matrix of demands that grew out of the impact of the scientific movement and the new concepts of the teaching and learning process on education and the necessity of taking account of these demands through changed school practice.

2. Improvement was to be secured through the teachers' use of courses of study which were prepared on the basis of educational research findings and on accepted psychological principles of learning.

3. Representatives of the teaching staff were appointed to membership on course-of-study production committees so that (1) the completed course of study would be more readily accepted and effectively used by teachers generally, since they or their representatives had had a part in its formulation; (2) use could be made of the professional insight and knowledge of teachers that comes from work in the practical classroom situation; and (3) a very laborious and time-consuming task could be carried out without infringing too heavily on the duties of supervisory and administrative officials or requiring too great an expenditure of money by the school district.

4. Teachers who participated in the committee work received valuable in-service education and stimulation, but by and large this growth was limited to the very small number who actually served on committees.

5. A complex organization, consisting of an elaborate system of committees with delicately balanced responsibilities, was established to carry forward the program.

Curriculum Programs for the Improvement of Instruction

A new type of curriculum program emerged in the early 1930's out of a much broadened concept of the school curriculum and, correlative to this, of the type of program implicit in this view of the curriculum. Traditionally the curriculum had been considered to be the set body of subject matter which the teacher was expected to pass on to his pupils. Hosic expressed this concept succinctly: "Curriculum means what pupils are to learn. . . . The curriculum is the body of experience to be communicated."[73] The task of curriculum construction under such a controlling concept was to formulate the best possible course of study and to devise ways for insuring its effective use by teachers. That was the type of curriculum program organized so extensively in this country in the period beginning with 1920 and described in the previous section.

But the impact of an organismic psychology and a more fundamental view of the educational process gave rise to a new and much broader concept of the school curriculum. Under this concept, the curriculum is considered to be "composed of all the experiences children have under the guidance of teachers."[74] This view holds that the totality of the experience is of utmost importance, that learning in the school is not confined to the acquisition of prescribed facts from textbooks or the mastery of a skill through drill, but encompasses all of the activities of the pupil, and that what is learned and how it is learned are the functions of the learner, not of the teacher. According to Kilpatrick, "We learn our reactions: only our reactions, and all our reactions; and we learn them in the degree and with the conditions and limitations with which we respectively accept them."[75]

The curriculum is the sum total of these pupil reactions in the classroom. Curriculum development, then, becomes much, much broader than the mere preparation of outlines of prescribed content for pupil mastery. It involves the whole process of the guidance and direction of the learning activities of pupils. And this means that the teacher and the pupil are the real curriculum makers. Caswell, a leading exponent of this broadened view of curriculum development, has expressed this whole point of view well:

Rather than considering curriculum improvement a primary concern to committees only, this concept implies that all teachers are curriculum workers and directly associated, by the very nature of their work, with curriculum improvement. It is impossible to isolate a teacher through any administrative organization from curriculum work. Arguments may wax and wane as to whether the expert or the teacher should make the curriculum, but the fact remains that no curriculum can be made without teachers though one may be developed without experts. Teacher and pupils are the indispensable require-

[73] James F. Hosic, "What Are the Essentials of a Course of Study?" in *The Elementary School Curriculum*, Second Yearbook of Department of Superintendence, p. 127.

[74] Hollis L. Caswell and Doak S. Campbell, *Curriculum Development*, p. 69.

[75] William H. Kilpatrick, "Life, Learning, and Individuality," in *Democracy and the Curriculum*, Third Yearbook of John Dewey Society, p. 370.

ments for curriculum development. Other factors add or detract from the type of curriculum developed, but these two alone are the prerequisites."[76]

To implement this broader view of the curriculum and of the process of curriculum development a new type of curriculum program was formulated. The traditional type of program so much in vogue in the 1920's was grossly inadequate since each teacher was now conceived to be the major factor in any process of curriculum improvement. In fact, curriculum change was regarded as impossible, except as each and every teacher sought to improve the learning situation in his own classroom. Improvement could come only through the work of teachers in providing richer, more meaningful experiences for children. The teacher is the key to curriculum revision. Caswell stated this position in these words:

> Unless the teacher is expanding his interests, deepening his insights, and modifying his views, little real improvement in the curriculum of the child may be expected. A program of curriculum development, therefore, must be concerned with the rounded and continuous growth of teachers as individuals. In brief, a really adequate organization for curriculum improvement must be concerned with the education of teachers in the broad sense just as much as with the education of boys and girls.[77]

What is the function of the course of study and what part does course-of-study preparation play in curriculum development under such a concept? Certainly under this point of view the course of study cannot be considered synonymous with the curriculum. Rather, it is regarded simply as a printed manual or guide which aids teachers in guiding pupils' learning activities. It is a source book to which the teacher may turn for assistance and help in curriculum development. Several recent authors made the distinction clear:

> The *curriculum* may be defined as the totality of subject matter, activities, and experiences which constitute a pupil's school life. A *course of study* is the material, usually in pamphlet form, which sets forth for the teacher such items as the objectives and content of a given subject, and the activities and books to be used to accomplish desired results.[78]

---

[76] Hollis L. Caswell, "Administrative Considerations in Curriculum Development," in *Democracy and the Curriculum*, Third Yearbook of John Dewey Society, p. 456.

[77] *Ibid.*, p. 457.

[78] R. L. West, Charles E. Greene, and W. A. Brownell, "The Arithmetic Curriculum," in *Report of the Society's Committee on Arithmetic*, Twenty-Ninth Yearbook of National Society for the Study of Education, p. 65.

Preparation of a course of study is only one aspect of the total process of curriculum development and, hence, is but one phase of a curriculum program of the type discussed here. As long as it is seen in its proper setting, the course of study may be prepared in various ways, since curriculum revision does not begin nor end with this phase of the program. Committees of teachers, specialists, or the total teaching staff may engage in its production. However, since teacher stimulation and growth—the deepening of teachers' insight, the broadening of teachers' vision and the sensitizing of teachers to basic educational problems and issues—are the primary objectives of such programs, actual participation of teachers in some phases of course-of-study preparation offers very real opportunities for accomplishing these objectives. But withal, curriculum development programs under this concept do not stake their sole efforts for curriculum improvement on careful, tedious preparation of courses of study which are to dictate the change sought in the classroom.

Thus the framework for a more detailed consideration of a new type of curriculum program—a program for the improvement of instruction—has been given. Since Chapter II describes in detail an outstanding example of these programs, there is no need to recount the features of the procedure here. In keeping with the concept of curriculum development which has guided their formulation, the programs have numerous facets, each of which is planned to make a major contribution to the primary objective of teacher stimulation and growth, so that enriched learning of pupils will result in the classroom.

These broad programs for the improvement of instruction had their origin in state school systems. State departments of education in the states of Florida (1930), Virginia (1931), Arkansas (1932), Georgia (1933), Texas (1933), Mississippi (1934), Alabama (1935), Tennessee (1935), Louisiana (1936), and Kansas (1936) organized and carried forward significant programs of this type in the early part of the movement. The state department of education in California has proceeded along somewhat different lines, but has also made an important attack on curriculum problems. Following the lead of these states a number of other states have planned comprehensive efforts for curriculum development and are in the process of carrying them forward at the time of this writing.

Likewise a number of city school systems have organized programs of this general type, typical of which are Glencoe, Illinois, Pasadena, California, Fort Worth, Texas, and Santa Barbara, California.[79] While these programs naturally vary somewhat in procedures and organization, they represent important efforts to carry forward a comprehensive program of curriculum improvement.

Some indication of the scope of the state program is given by Shearer[80] who summarized the reported number of teachers participating in at least some phase of the program for ten of these state programs as follows:

Number of Participants	Number of States
30,000	1
13,000	1
10,000	3
8,000	2
6,000	1
5,000	1
1,500	1

Thus curriculum development within the past ten years has entered a new phase if recent state and city programs are indicative of trends, and the recommendations of outstanding curriculum specialists are followed. These new curriculum programs are designed "to improve classroom instruction . . . by encouraging teachers, through study of curriculum problems to provide children with enriched and more purposeful experiences in the classroom . . ."[81]

The distinguishing characteristics of this type of curriculum program may be listed as follows:

1. The dominating purpose of the program is the improvement of instruction in the classrooms.

2. Preparation of courses of study and curriculum materials is recognized as of great importance, but only as contributory to the larger purpose of the improvement of instruction.

[79] See Department of Supervisors and Directors of Instruction and Society for Curriculum Study, Joint Committee on Curriculum, *The Changing Curriculum,* Chapters IX and X and John Dewey Society, *Democracy and the Curriculum,* Third Yearbook, Chapters XVII and XVIII.

[80] Allen E. Shearer, "Procedures in Curriculum Revision Programs of Selected States," p. 77.

[81] Virginia State Board of Education, *Tentative Course of Study for Virginia Elementary Schools,* p. xi.

3. The programs are planned on a long-time or even continuous basis.

4. The program is designed to provide maximum stimulation and understanding for all teachers.

5. All factors directly affecting education become legitimate matters for consideration in the program.

6. The program is planned so that all agencies directly influencing the educational program are drawn into the program.

7. The procedure is made as democratic as possible.

Purposes and Procedures of This Study

The foregoing brief discussion of trends in the procedures for curriculum development shows the shift in emphasis in recent years of the controlling purpose of curriculum programs from one of course-of-study preparation to one of general improvement of instruction in the classroom through teacher stimulation and growth. This has necessitated a radical change in the planning and organization of curriculum programs. Under the former concept the most efficient program is one which utilizes the services of experts in writing courses of study; under the latter concept the best type of program is one which encourages each teacher to study carefully his own situation, and under the guidance of leaders and with the encouragement and assistance of his co-workers to seek to improve it. With this plan of organization an effort is made to secure participation of each teacher in the manifold aspects of the program, so that he will receive the stimulation and help to be derived from a joint undertaking. Such a program requires careful planning, expert direction, extensive organization, and a large expenditure of money. As a procedure for curriculum development, the comprehensive, cooperative program is widely acclaimed by curriculum workers and other educational leaders. A number of city and state school systems have organized or are planning to organize this type of program.[82]

PURPOSE OF THE STUDY

It has been ten years since the first of these programs was begun, and while at least one study[83] has surveyed the extent and nature of these programs no attempt has yet been made to determine the condi-

[82] See "News Notes" in monthly issues of the *Curriculum Journal*.

[83] Allen E. Shearer, "Procedures in Curriculum Revision Programs of Selected States."

tions under which a comprehensive, cooperative program for the improvement of instruction best functions. Curriculum workers have had to depend on subjective judgment and empirical evidence to guide them in planning these endeavors.

From the standpoint of planning, organizing, and directing state programs of this type these pertinent questions arise: Under the diverse conditions found in a typical state, in what types of situations does a comprehensive, cooperative, state program of curriculum development function best and in what types of situations is it least effective? As they have been organized and carried out in the past what factors seem to condition the success of such a program? What are some of the chief difficulties that must be overcome in carrying out a comprehensive state program? What are the chief characteristics of local school units which participate extensively in such state programs and of local units which participate little or not at all? Wherein do these local units differ? Wherein are they alike? In what respects does it seem advisable to modify or change the procedures now used in typical programs? These are crucial questions for curriculum workers, state school officials, local school administrators, and educational workers generally. The present study is planned to give at least a partial answer to these questions.

PLAN OF THE STUDY

The research procedure which seemed to offer the best possibilities for securing answers to the questions posited for this study was that of determining the characteristic likenesses and differences of local school systems which had participated extensively and of systems which had participated little or not at all in a state cooperative curriculum program of the comprehensive type. This is sometimes called the causal-comparative method of investigation.[84] The method provides a basis for determining the significance of a factor to a problem under consideration by its presence or absence in cases selected on the criterion of differentiation basic to the problem. Thus factors become significant by affiliation.

The first step in undertaking the project was to select a state which

[84] Carter Good, A. S. Barr, and Douglas Scates, *The Methodology of Educational Research*, pp. 533-548.

offered opportunities for conducting this type of study. The state selected was Virginia. Among the important factors determining this choice were these:

1. The Virginia state curriculum program is generally accepted among curriculum workers as an outstanding example of the comprehensive, cooperative type of state curriculum program.

2. It has been continuously under way since 1931, a period of eight years to the time of this study.

3. While being a continuous program it has passed through certain definite phases not yet completed in some other similar programs.

4. In its recommendation for a scope and sequence of the curriculum which are radically different from the traditional basis of curriculum organization and in the development of course-of-study materials to implement such a plan of organization, the Virginia program offers a critical test of the willingness of local school systems to participate— such a test as would not be provided in programs which made little or no departure from traditional plans of basic curriculum organization.

5. The State Superintendent of Public Instruction encouraged the study and offered the facilities of his department in promoting and carrying it forward. The expressed willingness of the members of his staff and of the superintendents of schools in local school divisions in Virginia to cooperate in every respect in the study clearly indicated the feasibility of undertaking it; and their generous assistance since its initiation has made it possible to carry it to completion in the manner planned.

6. The county system of local school districts in Virginia provided especially satisfactory units for a study of factors associated with participation.

7. Virginia was readily accessible for study, thus facilitating extensive work and travel in the state.

The next step in the study was a thorough-going analysis of the Virignia state curriculum program to ascertain what opportunities for participation by local school systems existed in the program. This analysis is given in Chapter II. The third step in the procedure involved the selection of local school systems as cases for study. Since the basic method used in this investigation was the determination of characteristic likenesses and differences of school systems varying greatly in the nature and extent of participation in a state curriculum program it was necessary first to define participation in the program and then to ascertain the extent of such participation by each local unit so proper choice of cases might be made. Participation is defined in this study to mean active engagement in one or more of the aspects of the Virginia state curriculum program—that is, engagement in any of those broad activities of a state-wide nature which were planned, developed, and organized by the State Department of Education through its division of instruction as a definite and officially sponsored aspect of the state program for the improvement of instruction.

The unit of local school control in Virginia is the county or independent city. A county school district does not include within its jurisdiction in any respect the schools of independent cities within its boundaries. A county and any independent city which happens to lie within its borders are as distinct in all governmental functions in Virginia as if they were at opposite ends of the state. Two or even three small county units may be joined together for school administrative purposes; the administrative unit, whether it be composed of one or more than one county, or of a city, is called a school division. There are twenty-four independent cities in the state, each constituting a school division. There are one hundred counties, each of which is a local school district, but administratively there are eighty-five county school divisions. In this study it was decided to select all cases from among the counties. This made for a much more comparable and homogeneous group. To have selected from both city and county systems would have made comparisons difficult. And counties were selected rather than cities because of greater homogeneity and also because it is generally recognized in Virginia that cities on the whole have not participated in the curriculum program as extensively as have counties.

One other limitation was placed on the study: only white elementary schools and teachers were to be considered in any phase of the study where segregation could be made on this basis. Thus participation by county school systems was limited in meaning to participation insofar as it affected white elementary schools and to participation by white elementary teachers, including classroom teachers, principals, supervisors, and superintendent. Where differentiation could be made in the data only white elementary schools and teachers were included.

The basis for selection of cases for study in this undertaking was thus the extent of engagement by county school systems either as a system or through white elementary teachers in the system in those phases of the Virginia state curriculum program which were planned, organized, and carried forward by the State Department of Education as a definite part of the program for the improvement of instruction in the white elementary schools of the state. The selection of counties is described in Chapter III. Through this procedure one group of eleven counties was selected as representative of the counties which had participated most extensively in the Virginia program and one group of eleven counties as representative of those counties which had participated least in the program.

The main part of the study involved a thoroughgoing analysis of likenesses and differences in these two groups of counties. Approximately forty factors were selected for investigation. Obviously these do not include all the items on which the two groups of counties could have been compared. In making the selection of factors to be studied, the investigator was guided by a number of considerations. First, a tentative list of items which seemed to the writer to be pertinent to participation or lack of it in a state, cooperative curriculum program was formulated. This list was then refined through additions, deletions, or restatement of items on these bases: (*a*) a study of factors included for investigation in recent important school surveys; (*b*) a review of the writings of curriculum directors, consultants, and other specialists for suggestions as to factors relevant to successful participation in curriculum programs; (*c*) perusal of recent researches in the area of local school adaptability; (*d*) survey of the plans and procedures of recent state cooperative curriculum programs for clues to significant items affecting participation; (*e*) use of the judgment and opinions of outstanding leaders in the field of curriculum as to factors which should be included in this particular investigation. Third, this refined list of factors was carefully appraised in terms of the practicability of securing the necessary data. Some items which seemed to be portentous for this study had to be eliminated because of lack of data or the impracticability of securing it within the limits of this project. Finally, the list of factors was modified somewhat as the study progressed. On occasion, analysis of data suggested the desirability of probing an item further than planned or of including a new item which would develop more adequately an important comparison.

Thus the factors to be included in this study were formulated. In making the final decision as to those to be included the criterion was: Is this a factor which may be congenial to participation? Is it a factor which may enter into a complex pattern of interrelationships in participation in a state curriculum program? If the investigator has gone afield in introducing any factor into the study it may be disregarded by those who discount its pertinency without affecting the rest of the study. Chapters IV, V, VI, and VII present the results of this investigation of characteristic likenesses and differences.

SOURCES AND TREATMENT OF DATA

Most of the data used in the comparisons were taken from official documents either published by or on file in the State Department of Education or, in certain cases, other state agencies. Since all the data have been summarized in tables, the source for each item is given in footnotes to the tables.

One other source of information should be considered more in detail here. In order to secure certain information not available elsewhere, a questionnaire form was distributed to all white elementary teachers in the counties selected for study. The form is reproduced in the Appendix. The form consisted of three parts: Part I requested certain information about personal and professional matters; Part II requested information about personal participation of the teacher in the state curriculum program; and Part III consisted of the opinionnaire, "What Should Our Schools Do?,"[85] plus five appended statements (Numbers 101-105 in Part III of the form) which were used in another connection in this study. This scale is a poll of opinion on the school program and has been used in several investigations of educational viewpoint.[86] It consists of 100 statements with which the respondent is asked to express agreement or disagreement. The authors report that the form has an index of reliability of .91, as determined by the Spearman-Brown formula for split halves, from the replies of 360 teachers.

[85] Paul R. Mort, F. G. Cornell, and Norman Hinton, *What Should Our Schools Do?*
[86] See George W. Ebey, "A Study of Adaptability in the City of St. Louis, Missouri," and Division of Field Studies, Institute of Educational Research, Teachers College, *A Report of the Survey of the Schools of St. Louis, Missouri,* Chapters I and II.

Table 1 shows the number and percentage of white elementary teachers in each of the selected counties who returned usable questionnaire forms. A high percentage of teachers responded in the eleven counties selected as the most-participating group of counties; in fact, the returns were exceptionally high in a number of counties. As a group, 75.7 per cent of all teachers in this set of counties returned

Table 1

NUMBER AND PERCENTAGE OF WHITE ELEMENTARY
TEACHERS RETURNING QUESTIONNAIRES, SELECTED
COUNTIES, VIRGINIA

County[a]	Number	Per Cent
Group I. Most-Participating Counties		
I-a	76	70.4%
I-b	87	78.4
I-c	14	93.3
I-d	88	64.7
I-e	85	68.5
I-f	12	85.7
I-g	45	57.0
I-h	62	69.7
I-i	31	86.1
I-j	176	97.2
I-k	17	77.3
All counties	693	75.7%
Group II. Least-Participating Counties		
II-a	24	61.5%
II-b	2	5.0
II-c	105	67.7
II-d	18	94.7
II-e	40	80.0
II-f	15	46.9
II-g	25	54.3
II-h	15	32.6
II-i	30	34.1
II-j	49	61.3
II-k	53	20.1
All counties	376	43.8%

[a] See Chapter III for explanation of coding system for the counties.

forms. The percentage of returns was very good in six of the eleven counties selected as the least-participating group. In one of the other five counties only two teachers out of a total of forty returned forms. This county is not included in any summaries of data from the questionnaire given later in the study. In the remaining four counties from twenty to forty-seven per cent of the teachers returned forms, with a minimum of fifteen returns in any case. This seemed to be a sufficiently large proportion of replies for purposes of this study. All in all, 43.8 per cent of teachers in the least-participating group of counties returned usable forms.

As will be observed in the chapters which discuss the likenesses and differences of the two groups of counties, figures for all nine years of the period from 1930 to 1939 have been presented for several factors. This was done for three reasons: first, to reveal trends in this factor during the period since the initiation of the state curriculum program in 1931 to the time of this study in 1939—a period during which the program was in continuous development; second, to determine if the same likenesses or differences existed in 1930-31, the school year prior to the inception of the program, as existed after its development; and third, to provide a more sensitive statistical test of reliable differences between the two sets of data for the two groups of counties. In the case of certain other factors, where the task of tabulating and compiling figures for each of the nine years of the period was so extensive as to be impractical, or where statistical analysis revealed the main facts without additional data, only three years were selected for comparison. These were 1930-31, the year before the program was initiated, 1938-39, the last year for which data were available for use in this study, and 1934-35, the year halfway between the other two years and also a most important year in the program, since that was the year the state tentative course of study was available for general use. For certain other factors only data for the year concurrent with the study were available and comparisons were necessarily limited to that year—1938-39.

Four statistical procedures were used in the main to determine statistically reliable differences between data for the two groups of counties. These were the analysis of variance, the Chi-square test, the *t* test for significance of the difference between two means, and the test for the significance of the difference between two percentages.

SUMMARY

A brief historical study of the process of curriculum development reveals a decided change in the objectives of curriculum development programs from one of emphasis on textbook writing in the nineteenth century to one of course-of-study preparation in the first three decades of the present century and finally to that of teacher stimulation and growth as a basis for the improvement of classroom instruction since 1930. State school officials, particularly those in the Southern states, have taken the leadership in organizing and carrying forward comprehensive, cooperative curriculum programs planned to realize the last named objective. The present study proposes to determine significant factors which are associated with extensive participation by local school systems in such cooperative programs. Virginia was selected as the state for study and two groups of counties, one of which included counties which had participated extensively in the state curriculum program and the other counties which had participated little or not at all in the program, were chosen for an intensive investigation of characteristic likenesses and differences, so that factors associated with participation might be determined.

CHAPTER II

The Virginia State Curriculum Program

THE Virginia state curriculum program was initiated in 1931 and has been in continuous progress since that date. The State Superintendent of Public Instruction, Dr. Sidney B. Hall, who took office January 1, 1931, reorganized the State Department of Education on a "functional basis," effective July 1, 1931. Under the new plan the former separate divisions of elementary schools, secondary education, physical and health education, and Negro education were coordinated into a division of instruction with a director as its head. The State Superintendent directed this new division of instruction "to carry through a state-wide curriculum revision program, believing such program to be the most effective type of supervisory service through which teachers may receive in-service training, improved teaching materials and professional stimulation."[1] State Education Department officials spent considerable time, after decision was made to inaugurate a curriculum program, in planning the nature of the program and general procedures to be used. Conferences were held with curriculum specialists and various possibilities were carefully considered. But out of all of this planning evolved a program of far-reaching significance.

The major purposes of the program were stated to be:

1. To improve classroom instruction in Virginia by encouraging teachers, through study of their own curriculum problems, to provide children with richer and more purposeful experiences in the classroom.
2. To aid teachers in developing division courses of study especially adapted to their own needs.
3. To develop state courses of study.[2]

[1] Virginia State Board of Education, *Annual Report of the Superintendent of Public Instruction*, 1932-33, p. 16.

[2] Virginia State Board of Education, *Organization for Virginia State Curriculum Program*, p. 6.

Emphasis throughout the program has, however, been primarily on the improvement of instruction in the classrooms of the state, and this objective has guided the planning of all other aspects of the project. While the preparation of a course of study loomed large in the first three years of the program, this activity was envisaged and planned in terms of its contribution to better teaching in the schools. This point was emphasized in an early publication of the program: "Although attention turns first to the assistance that courses of study may render in revising the curriculum, we would stress the fact that there are other important sources of assistance, and the State Curriculum Program will make these available also."[3] Some of these other methods by which the State Department proposed to aid teachers and local school divisions in improving instruction were: promoting cooperative study by teachers of curriculum problems; encouraging teacher-training institutions to offer suitable courses of instruction; providing specialists in various fields for consultative service; establishing curriculum centers at state institutions; providing materials for use of local divisions in curriculum construction work of their own, providing counsel and guidance for divisions in developing effective curriculum organizations.[4] The Virginia program, if correctly interpreted, must be conceived in much broader terms than that of a project designed to prepare a state course of study, such as has been the primary purpose of the committee or administrative type of state curriculum revision program in the past. The basic purpose that has been foremost throughout the program was well expressed by State Superintendent Hall when, in reviewing the program in 1939, he wrote:

The principal purpose of the program is to spread ever more widely among teachers a spirit of better understanding of children and of the kind of experiences which will best fit them to play a constructive part in our democratic society. The various courses of study are considered merely as guide books which may be helpful to teachers in acquiring this understanding.[5]

The key to improved classroom practices is conceived by those in charge of the Virginia program to be the teacher. The teacher is regarded as a curriculum worker, as the person who in the final analysis

[3] *Ibid.*, p. 5.
[4] *Ibid.*, p. 6.
[5] Virginia State Board of Education, *Brief Description of Virginia Program for Improving Instruction*, p. 5.

"makes" the actual curriculum through his guidance and direction of the learning activities of children. Any improvement in instruction and hence in the curriculum must come through the teacher, as guide of the learning process. Under such a concept the primary objective of curriculum programs of the type inaugurated in Virginia is that of teacher stimulation and growth and secondarily that of providing courses of studies and curriculum materials which will be useful to the teacher in making the improvement which he envisages as a result of study and professional growth. The full force of the undertaking revolves around teacher development, and plans are formulated in terms of this purpose. Such stimulation and growth is best fostered, according to this view, by providing extensive opportunities for teachers to participate in the program of curriculum development. In fact, the emphasis is on teacher activity rather than the production of courses of study *per se*. The latter become a means to an end, not the end product, although it is recognized that the course of study may be a valuable aid to teachers in improving instruction after they have come to understand the need for and basis of such improvement as a result of study.

The extent to which teacher activity in the form of participation in the various aspects of the project has beeen emphasized in Virginia is indicated in the following analysis of the program. This description will serve to show the nature of the widespread cooperative type of curriculum program and to illustrate the opportunities for teacher participation. Inasmuch as this study is limited in scope to the participation of white elementary teachers, only the details of the program as related to the elementary grades will be described. However, the program has been a coordinated effort involving both elementary and high school teachers. In some aspects of the program no distinction is apparent, but beginning with the production phase some differentiation was made both as to teachers involved and procedures followed. Where this has been true, this study will take no account of the high school phase. The Virginia program has progressed to date through these more or less distinct phases: a study program, production of curriculum materials, tryout of an experimental course of study, preparation of a tentative course of study, and a continuous effort, correlated with the other phases and particularly emphasized since their completion, to improve instruction in the classroom.

At its inception, the Virginia state curriculum program was announced as consisting of three phases, extending over a period of three years:

First year (1931-32). Study program: a period of education and orientation, during which teachers were to study curriculum problems.

Second year (1932-33). Production: The production of curriculum materials and formulation of an experimental course of study.

Third year (1933-34). Tryout of the experimental course of study and its subsequent revision on the basis of this experience: use of tentative materials in selected school situations as a basis for preparation of a course of study for general use.

While these three phases were all that were definitely planned and stated at the outset, the program evolved as progress was made, so that the staff of the State Department of Education continuously expanded and extended the scope of the movement. Rather than ending upon the completion of the courses of study, as has been true in most state programs of curriculum development, it became a continuous and consistent effort for the general improvement of classroom instruction in whatever channels this might lead as the situation developed. These continuous efforts, with their manifold aspects will become apparent in the description of the program.

It should be emphasized that the State Department has insisted from the beginning that participation be entirely voluntary. Local school divisions as well as individual teachers have been free either to join or not to join in any phase of the program, and if they cooperated to participate as extensively as they wished. This feature has been in marked contrast to the practice of most former state curriculum programs. Published courses of study, which usually constituted the teachers' first and only acquaintance with the program, frequently contained statements to the effect that they were the "required" courses of study. Naturally the staff of the State Department has made strenuous efforts to enlist the interest and cooperation of all school systems and all teachers in the program; they have traveled extensively throughout the state, explaining the program and encouraging participation; wide publicity has been given the program, and close contact has been maintained with division superintendents, principals, and supervisors—but nevertheless participation has remained entirely voluntary. That is the important factor in the program insofar as the present study is concerned since there would be no point in studying the characteristic likenesses and differences of counties if all were required to participate at least nominally in the program.

Attention will be given first to the study program, consideration of organization being deferred until the next section since it was not perfected until production was planned.

THE STUDY PROGRAM

The study program, the first phase of the curriculum program, was initiated in the late fall of 1931. Its purposes were to aid teachers in gaining an understanding of their role as a curriculum maker, to sensitize them to the need for improvement in classroom instruction, and to develop an underlying philosophy as a basis for progress and for effective cooperation in the program. Since the whole enterprise was designed to aid teachers in providing richer and more purposeful experiences for children, study of problems basic to curriculum making at the outset of the program was deemed to be an essential step. The study program is a distinguishing characteristic of the comprehensive type of curriculum program as exemplified by Virginia. It is one of the means by which an attempt is made to draw all teachers into the program so that general stimulation and growth of all, rather than of a limited number of teachers, will result.

To coordinate and guide study a study bulletin[6] was issued by the State Department. It was prepared by the General Curriculum Adviser for the program. Seven topics for study were outlined: (1) What Is the Curriculum?; (2) Developments Which Have Resulted in a Need for Curriculum Revision; (3) What Is the Place of Subject Matter in Education?; (4) Determining Educational Objectives; (5) Organizing Instruction; (6) Selecting Subject Matter; (7) Measuring the Outcomes of Instruction. Under each topic a brief statement of the problem, a list of questions developing it, and a limited bibliography were given.

To aid in the initiation and promotion of the study program and to get the curriculum program before the school people of the state, State Department officials held a series of meetings at various points in the

[6] Virginia State Board of Education, *Study Course for Virginia State Curriculum Program.*

state in November, 1931. The State Superintendent invited division superintendents of the surrounding areas to these meetings. They were asked to bring their supervisors, high school principals, principals of large elementary schools, two or three elementary teachers, and the same number of high school teachers to the regional meeting.

In organizing for study, the State Department recommended[7] that a division chairman for study groups be designated by the division superintendent. The chairman was to assist in forming groups in various parts of the division and to act as general counselor. It was recommended that a meeting of all teachers of the division be called at which time the plan of the state curriculum program was to be explained and organization of teachers into study groups to be effected. The State Department suggested that small study groups be organized throughout the division in order that weekly or bi-weekly meetings could be held conveniently. Each group was to select its own leader and secretary and arrange to secure necessary books and materials. It was also suggested that the division leader call joint meetings monthly of all local study groups to discuss progress and to stimulate further study. State Department officials stood ready to offer assistance and to attend division meetings if desired.

Apparently some criticism was directed at the program, at least by division superintendents, early in the development of the study program. In a circular letter of December 1, 1931,[8] addressed to all division superintendents, the State Superintendent wrote that the whole problem of curriculum revision had been discussed at some length in a state meeting of superintendents of schools held shortly prior to that date. The letter indicates that two objections to the program were voiced in this discussion—one, as to the need for a curriculum revision program at all; and the other, that the plans and procedures were not sufficiently definite. Since the program, the State Superintendent wrote, was planned primarily to assist the local divisions in the improvement of instruction, little benefit of this kind would result if the superintendent was not sympathetic to the program. To try to answer these criticisms and to discuss the need for such work and show how it would con-

---

[7] Mimeographed circular letter of December 12, 1931 and *Study Course for Virginia State Curriculum Program*, p. 6.

[8] Mimeographed letter on file in the State Department of Education.

tribute to school progress in each division, five regional meetings were called during December. Division superintendents were asked to "make it a point to attend" and urged to bring their supervisors also.

Available evidence indicates widespread participation by teachers in the study program. In a circular letter[9] of February 17, 1932, division superintendents were asked to report on an appended form the names of the division chairman and group chairmen and the "approximate" number of teachers in each study group. Figures for the number of groups and the number of teachers participating in each school division are summarized in a statement on file in the State Department. Detailed figures for white teachers only are given later in Table 4, in Chapter III. Some of these figures were "estimated," probably by State Department officials, for some divisions. Participation in the study program by white teachers for the state as a whole is shown in Table 2 below.

Table 2

PARTICIPATION OF WHITE TEACHERS IN STUDY PROGRAM, 1931–32

	Counties	Cities	Total
Number of school districts in state	100	24	124
Number reporting organized study groups ...	85	22	107
Per cent participating	85%	92%	86%
Number of white teachers employed	9,552	3,250	12,802
Number reported participating	6,384	2,066	8,450
Per cent participating	67%	64%	66%

According to these figures, which are based on informal reports to the State Department by superintendents and on some "estimates," two out of every three white teachers were enrolled in study groups. No basis exists for judging the extent or nature of participation or the vitalness of the study to individual teachers. But even these rough figures indicate the widespread nature of the study program and the extent to which teachers were at least informed of the program and aware that a state program of curriculum revision was being carried forward. However, fifteen county and two city systems apparently made no efforts to cooperate in this phase of the program. While the present study is

[9] Virginia State Board of Education, "Superintendent's Memo. No. 545."

limited to an investigation of participation as related to white elementary teachers, it is interesting to note in passing that these same reports listed only ten study groups for Negro teachers with a reported enrollment of 152. This was but four per cent of the total Negro teaching corps. The relation of Negro schools and teachers to the state curriculum program would be an interesting subject for study, but impossible to include in this endeavor.

In conjunction with the study program, teacher-training institutions of the state were encouraged to offer courses dealing with curriculum problems and development. In the fall of 1931 the State Department announced in a circular letter that the College of William and Mary at Williamsburg would offer a course on curriculum construction on Friday evenings, planned especially for teachers and administrators in service. Many teachers also enrolled in extension courses of various institutions during the year. In the summer of 1932 ten institutions offered courses labeled "Curriculum" in contrast to two offering such courses in 1931.[10] Since its inception the teacher-training institutions of the state have continued to cooperate in the program by offering wide opportunities for study and work in the area of curriculum development.

THE PRODUCTION OF CURRICULUM MATERIALS

The second phase of the Virginia state curriculum program was devoted primarily to the production of curriculum materials. This aspect was initiated in the spring of 1932 and extended in one phase or another through the summer of 1934, with major emphasis being given to it during the school year 1932-33 and the summer of 1933. Here again plans were developed for widespread teacher participation so that a maximum of teacher growth and stimulation would result.

The organization for production was explained in detail in a bulletin[11] issued in March, 1932. This bulletin carefully stated the relationship which the State Department felt should exist between it and the local school division in a program of curriculum development and proposed an administrative organization in keeping with this concept.

[10] Virginia State Board of Education, *Brief Description of Virginia Program for Improving Instruction,* p. 10.
[11] Virginia State Board of Education, *Organization for Virginia State Curriculum Program.*

The local division, according to this statement of policy, was to be primarily responsible for improving instruction. The function of the State Department was to assist in this process: first, by aiding teachers directly in providing for a cooperative study of curriculum problems, for the organization of classes in curriculum study in state teacher-training institutions, and for the counsel and guidance of specialists; second, by assisting local divisions in organizing their own curriculum programs and developing their own courses of study; and third, by providing state courses of study for those divisions which do not prepare their own. It was the hope of the State Department that ultimately this last responsibility would be unnecessary and its work would consist in aiding the local division in curriculum work by conducting research on curriculum problems, providing expert counsel and guidance, and making available outstanding examples of curriculum work done throughout the state. Admittedly, this possibility would be far in the future. The organization proposed in 1932, then, was planned so as to secure the development of state courses of study but coordinate with this development to provide the best assistance possible to local divisions who would engage in curriculum work correlative with the state program and to aid in the gradual transference of all construction work to local divisions.

The organization bulletin suggested a plan of organization for divisional curriculum production for those systems which wished to engage in this phase of the program. Briefly the plan was for the division superintendent to appoint a division chairman of curriculum or assume this duty himself. It was recommended that division production committees for elementary and secondary schools be established for as many fields as the division wished to work in. Each secondary committee might well consist of a chairman and all of the teachers in the division who wished to work in the area. Each elementary division committee might include in its membership a division chairman and the chairmen of local production committees. These local production committees were to be set up wherever small groups of teachers wished to work in that field. The division committee was to direct and plan the work and coordinate the activities of the local committees. Consultative service was to be provided division production committees by selected state teacher-training institutions, which served as regional curriculum centers for the counties and cities in their regions. It was also recommended that a division reviewing and unifying committee be established to review and unify the materials produced in the division.

The state curriculum organization was in direct charge of the Director of Instruction. He was, of course, responsible to the State Superintendent of Public Instruction, who, in turn referred matters of general policy to the State Board of Education. The State Superintendent appointed two advisory committees, one composed of laymen and one of educators, to assist in the formulation of general plans and policies. Serving on the staff of the Director was the General Curriculum Adviser, a specialist in curriculum development. As necessary, special curriculum advisers were to be called in for consultation. State committees on principles, aims, definitions, and procedures were appointed, and a state reviewing and unifying committee was also created. These committees worked directly with the Director of Instruction and the State Department staff.

State production committees both for elementary and for secondary schools were established for the various subject fields. Each state committee was composed of a chairman, appointed by the State Superintendent upon recommendation of the Director, all chairmen of division production committees organized in the region served by the curriculum center for that subject field, and in some cases other qualified persons who were appointed by the State Superintendent. An overlapping of personnel in state committees was provided since members of the principles, aims, definitions, and procedures committees were for the most part chairmen of the state production committees. This was done to assure "realization of a set of principles, aims, procedures, and definitions to which the leaders in the work of production can subscribe."[12] Also overlapping personnel occurred in that chairmen of division production committees, as stated above, became automatically members of state production committees. This was planned so as to facilitate, guide, and coordinate the work of local production. This interlocking of personnel was further carried out in the case of the state reviewing and unifying committee which was selected from among the more active chairmen of state production committees.

[12] Virginia State Board of Education, *Procedures for Virginia State Curriculum Program*, p. 6.

Each state production committee had assigned to it an expert in the subject field who served as consultant in the program. Furthermore, the four state teachers colleges for white students and the one for colored students, the University of Virginia, and the College of William and Mary served as curriculum centers, providing library and work facilities and guidance to teachers and committees in their respective regions of the state. Virginia Polytechnic Institute and Richmond City Normal served as centers for the entire state for the subjects of agriculture and industrial arts respectively. In production work each center emphasized one or two subject fields and surrounding school divisions were urged to concentrate on production in these fields. The activities of state committees revolved around the respective centers, with most if not all committee members being from the region.

Thus the plan provided that, in the main, production of materials in a particular subject field be concentrated in a designated region of the state—the state institution in the region serving as a center, membership on the state committee being limited to teachers in the area, and local divisions of that region being urged to emphasize production in that subject. However, local or division committees in other regions could be organized for work in that particular subject if local leaders so desired, and teachers throughout the state might be drawn into work on a subject during the summer at the college center.

The actual production of state curriculum materials under this widespread organization will be described briefly to show the opportunities for teacher participation. After the issuance of the bulletin describing organization, appointment of state committee members occurred. During the first week of May, 1932, the State Department called a multiple conference for the initiation of production work. Chairmen and associate chairmen, where such had been appointed, of state production committees and additional members of other state committees participated in all phases of the conference. The first phase was devoted to a consideration of the problems of elementary education. Leaders in elementary education throughout the state had been asked to submit a list of what they felt to be pressing problems that should receive consideration in the curriculum program. These formed the basis for discussion in this part of the conference. Leading elementary teachers, supervisors, principals, and superintendents all participated. In its next phase the conference considered plans and initiated the work of the principles, aims, definitions, and procedures committees. Some preliminary reports were formulated. The final two days were devoted to work of the state production committees. Tentative procedures for each committee were outlined and discussed. The General Curriculum Adviser, several special advisers, and state consultants also participated in this phase of the conference. Each state production chairman and the consultant in his field discussed and formulated plans and procedures for committee work. Out of this entire conference developed plans for the immediate work of all committees.

On May 27, 1932, a circular letter[13] by the Director of Instruction was sent to all division superintendents asking them to designate a chairman of curriculum work for their divisions or to serve in that capacity themselves and to state, at least tentatively, the subject field or fields in which the division proposed to organize for production. It was suggested that the field which would be emphasized in the curriculum center for that region might influence the choice, but there was no compulsion to work in a designated field.

Seven members of the interlocking state committees and the Director of Instruction spent the summer of 1932 working under the direction of the General Curriculum Adviser at the curriculum laboratory of George Peabody College in the development of a procedures bulletin[14] which was to guide the production work of all state committees. Two other production committee chairmen worked in the laboratory of the University of Virginia and one at the College of William and Mary. All state chairmen of production committees had been urged by the Director to work on the refinement of plans proposed at the May conference, the preparation of a bibliography of materials needed by the committee, and the development of outlines of procedure. The procedures bulletin contains tentative reports of the principles, aims, and definitions committees and a detailed section on procedures for the guidance of production committees.

With the opening of school in September, 1932, production was ready to be undertaken intensively. Steps were taken at once to com-

[13] Virginia State Board of Education, "Superintendent's Memo., No. 562."

[14] Virginia State Board of Education, *Procedures for Virginia State Curriculum Program.*

plete and perfect the organization of division production committees. Division superintendents who had not made an appointment of a division chairman in May were prompted to do so. A sheet summarizing the status of organization for production on November 28, 1932, filed in the State Department shows that sixty-nine of the 100 counties and eighteen of the twenty-four city systems had organized for production at that time. The counties reporting production organizations are listed in Table 4, in Chapter III. Regional conferences were held at the various curriculum centers during the first week in October for the purposes of familiarizing administrative officers and production officials in the divisions with the procedures of production, stimulating organization, and planning activities for the year. All division superintendents, division chairmen of curriculum, and division chairmen of production committees were invited to attend. At the meeting the respective state production committee for the region was organized for work and members were acquainted with the procedures to be followed. The General Curriculum Adviser and committee consultants met with these committees. Although some divisions organized committees in fields other than those emphasized at their centers, it was difficult for such division chairmen to work closely with the state committees, and reports indicate that but few of these were active on the state committee.

The composition and size of some of these state production committees will give an indication of the scope of participation. Table 3 shows the distribution by positions of the members of certain state elementary production committees for which this information is available in State Department records. Teachers played a prominent part in most state committees, and since much of the actual preparation of materials was done by division and local committees on which teachers undoubtedly predominated, the participation by teachers in production work was evidently extensive. Unfortunately, no records are available in the State Department showing the number or position of members of these local and division committees.

With organization developed by the fall of 1932, production was undertaken in a big way, and this was a period of intense activity in the program. Division and local committees set to work on various aspects of production. The central staff urged teachers, working with their division and local committees, to prepare various items of value in

Table 3

COMPOSITION OF STATE ELEMENTARY PRODUCTION COMMITTEES

Committee	Classroom Teachers	Principals	Supervisors	Unknown[a]	Total
Language arts	11	8	13	11	43
Elementary science	8	5	7		20
Industrial arts	4	3	3		10
Social science	4	11	7	12	34
Mathematics				20	20

[a] Records do not show positions held by some committee members.

developing courses of study, such as lists of observed interests of children and activities which grow out of these interests, records of successful teaching methods and techniques, descriptions of activities, subject matter, materials, and the like, helpful in carrying forward instruction and developing interests, and finally descriptions of good complete units of work which they had carried out. It was recommended that the procedures bulletin be used as a guide and that committees study the aims, principles, and viewpoint set forth there as bases for work. Thus the program of in-service training was carried forward through production activities of teachers. In fact, that was the primary purpose of the production program, for the Virginia staff, as well as curriculum leaders generally, recognize that a better course of study *per se* can be developed by a small group of specialists working intensively on it than by large numbers of committees of busy and often inadequately trained teachers. While no definite records are available it is evident from statements of State Department officials and others close to the program that a vast amount of curriculum materials was produced by teachers during the year 1932-33. Most of these materials went through the hands of division chairmen to state committees and were utilized by them in assembling and preparing materials for use in making the state course of study. All of this time, the state production committees were also active, although the degree of activity and interest varied from committee to committee, with some committees admittedly not very active as groups. Frequent regional conferences were held and extensive correspondence and distribution of circulars, statements, and reports occurred. Early activities of state committees centered around the

clarification of viewpoint from which the work in their respective subject fields would proceed, the selection of aims from among all the
aims proposed for the total educational program to which the field
could contribute, and the development of suggestive centers of interest, based on a study of children's interests, which could be utilized by
teachers in developing units of work and planning production activities.
For example, the chairman of the State Elementary Social Studies Committee in a circular letter to all division production chairmen in that
field asked them to "prepare a list of centers of interests out of which
worthwhile units of work may be developed in his or her division. These
centers of interests should be listed by age levels in so far as it is possible to list them and should include both general interests and interests
peculiar to the local situation."[15]

State committees were occasionally divided into subcommittees, each
with definite assignments, and individual members also often accepted
responsibility for particular aspects of the work. Meetings of state production committees were held at the regional centers in January, 1933,
for the purposes of surveying progress and planning the remainder of
the year's work so that all essential aspects of production would be
provided for. Three main types of material were desired by the state
committees from local production groups: descriptions of good activities useful in developing the subject; descriptions of teaching procedures
found most useful; and descriptions of good drill activities. Division
production chairmen were urged to indicate which of these phases
they would be responsible for.

It was during this period that the State Department staff concentrated efforts on the development of a basis for organizing the curriculum, and state production chairmen were drawn into this process
extensively, both for the contribution they could make and for guidance
in further committee work. Several methods of organizing instruction
were formulated and considered. Through conferences, criticisms, and
suggestions offered by state committee members, and the like, a progressive clarification of the basis for curriculum organization occurred.
Out of this consideration the now well-known plan of organizing instruction around the "Major Functions of Social Living" evolved.
This plan was first proposed by the leaders and advisers of the program

[15] Mimeographed letter of January 5, 1932, signed by Brancis P. Ford.

to the chairmen of state production committees at a meeting in February, 1933. It was accepted as a basis for procedure, and efforts thereafter were devoted to refining it. During all of this year production work of both state and local committees continued on a broad basis, with teachers reporting units of work and the like which would be useful in developing experimental course-of-study materials.

The second phase of production began with the summer of 1933. This again was a widespread program, revolving this time around the curriculum centers. All teachers were encouraged by the State Education Department to attend summer school and those active in the program were urged to work in laboratories of their respective centers, either as a part of a summer school program or solely in conjunction with curriculum production. It is interesting to note, however, that more positive pressure was placed on elementary supervisors throughout the state to participate in production work at the centers. A circular letter of July 13, 1933, written by the Director of Instruction states, "We are directed by (the State Superintendent) to urge you to spend a minimum of three weeks and a maximum of five weeks in the Curriculum Production work. . . . We would advise, however, that you do not delay entering this work later than the beginning of the second term. Please advise us by return mail what your plans are."[16] All of the state teacher-training institutions organized curriculum courses, both foundation courses and specialized courses for those working directly on production. Summer production activities at the centers continued the work initiated during the year, with efforts being concentrated on the analysis, selection, and organization of the materials already available and the production of additional materials.

At the same time, the Elementary Reviewing and Unifying Committee, working in the Curriculum Laboratory of George Peabody College, was engaged in preparing the experimental edition of a state course of study for elementary schools. This committee was composed of the chairmen of certain state production committees, and of the then state Assistant Supervisor of Elementary Education. The Director and the General Curriculum Adviser also worked closely with the group. They utilized material that had been prepared by state production committees and summer school groups as it was forwarded from the curriculum

[16] Mimeographed letter on file in State Education Department.

centers after collation and refinement, or from the chairman himself in the case of smaller, less active committees. The experimental edition of the course of study for the core program of secondary schools was prepared in a similar manner, except that state high school production committees worked through most of the summer at the state centers, and the Reviewing and Unifying Committee then met for two weeks late in the summer at the University of Virginia to prepare these materials for publication. Out of all this activity eventuated experimental editions of courses of study for elementary and secondary schools.[17]

Before leaving the work of the second year attention should be given to a phase of the program wherein the lay public contributed to its development. Copies of the procedures bulletin which contained the tentative statement of aims of education were sent to all the leading organizations of the state, such as civic clubs, women's groups, chambers of commerce, to college faculties, and to all newspaper editors. It was suggested that each organization study the views tentatively proposed and later send representatives to a public meeting to be called for the purpose of discussing them and making any desirable modifications. This meeting was held in January, 1933, and a thoroughgoing discussion occurred. Throughout the program newspaper editors were kept informed of the program and invited to comment.

TRYOUT AND REVISION PERIOD

The third phase of the Virginia state curriculum program consisted in: (1) experimental use of the courses of study by selected teachers; (2) subsequent revision of the courses, utilizing the results of this tryout experience, additional materials produced by committees and teachers generally, and the matured judgment of staff and committee members; (3) familiarizing teachers generally with the plan of curriculum organization adopted and the types of material to be included in the course of study. This phase of the program covered the period from the opening of school in 1933 until the following September. The tryout editions of the courses were lithoprinted and circulation re-

[17] Virginia State Board of Education, *Tentative Course of Study for Virginia Elementary Schools (Experimental Edition).*

Virginia State Board of Education, *Tentative Course of Study for the Core Curriculum of Secondary Schools (Experimental Edition).*

stricted to selected teachers. Approximately 550 teachers in fifty-two school divisions used the two tryout editions; of these about 300 were in the elementary schools. The tryout program was limited to divisions which had elementary supervision and within this group to those in which supervisors and teachers had been active in the production phases. The use of the materials by individual teachers in these divisions was wholly voluntary. The State Department staff followed this phase of the program closely. A series of conferences was held late in October at the curriculum centers, with one day of each meeting devoted to a discussion of plans for carrying forward the entire program with all teachers and the second day to a conference with teachers in the tryout program. Another series of conferences was held in January, 1934, at which teachers discussed their experiences with the tryout materials and considered plans for the remainder of the year. A final series of conferences was held in April, 1934, for the purpose of further discussing experiences in using the experimental materials and in planning the final evaluation of the materials. As one phase of this evaluation, a standard achievement test was given to all elementary and first-year high school pupils who had been in the tryout program and to a control group.[18] Teachers who were in the tryout program were also asked to give their opinions on a questionnaire regarding the effect of the use of the experimental course of study on certain aspects of pupil behavior, and, finally, all teachers using the tryout edition were urged to fill in forms contained in each section of the course, giving their criticisms and suggestions for additions and deletion and other desirable changes in the materials. Courses of study were then returned at the close of the year and these recorded observations were analyzed for guidance of committees in making revisions.

Meanwhile teachers throughout the state continued to participate in the program through two coordinated avenues. A short bulletin of illustrative materials[19] taken from the tryout edition of the elementary course of study was issued, as was a similar one for secondary teachers. Teachers were urged to study these materials carefully, particularly the plan

[18] Virginia State Board of Education, *Annual Report of the Superintendent of Public Instruction*, 1934-35, p. 18.

[19] Virginia State Board of Education, *Illustrative Materials from Tentative Course of Study for Virginia Elementary Schools.*

of organization of the curriculum, and on the basis of this study to undertake the development of units of work within this framework. Teachers were urged to keep a plan sheet for each unit, which showed its development. They were requested to submit these plan sheets for their best units to the division superintendent or supervisor for forwarding to the State Department. It was by these means that the great body of teachers were tied into the program, interest kept alive, and stimulation and growth of teachers fostered during the tryout year. Plan sheets submitted were analyzed in the State Department and useful items, such as suggested activities, procedures, and content, were summarized for use in revision of the courses. Thus, teachers not only were laying the basis for improved instruction in their classrooms and developing ability to use the state courses of study when issued generally, but were contributing worth-while materials of their own for use in preparation of the revised courses.

State production committees, or at least some of them, remained active during the year. In a circular letter of November 21, 1933, to the chairmen and consultants of state elementary production committees, the State Department listed these responsibilities of the committees for the year: suggest any revision of viewpoint or aims, prepare a statement of the scope of the work for the direct teaching program in their fields, suggest any revision or addition to the section on general teaching procedures, list activities for the direct teaching program in their fields, and suggest any revision of any section of the tryout course of study deemed advisable.

During the first three weeks of June, 1934, a large work conference was held at the College of William and Mary for the purposes of revising the experimental courses of study, familiarizing supervisors, selected teachers, and principals with the course-of-study materials through lectures, discussions, and revision work, and laying a basis for general use of the courses of study. Members of the conference consisted of the two reviewing and unifying committees (chairmen of state production committees), approximately all the elementary supervisors of the state, members of state secondary production committees, some of the consultants from curriculum centers, and State Department staff members concerned with the program—a total of about 130 persons. Practically the entire staff of general and special consultants participated in the conference in one form or another. Essentially it was an intensive training period, especially for the elementary supervisors of the state who would have the major responsibility for carrying forward the program for improved instruction in the elementary schools after the revised elementary course of study was issued. This conference was a very important aspect of the program. During the period the experimental editions of the two courses of study were critically evaluated; criticisms and suggestions of tryout teachers were studied; and new materials, utilizing activities, procedures, and references listed on the plan sheets submitted by teachers, were produced. Through these procedures, supervisors became thoroughly familiar with the proposed plan of organization of the curriculum, which differed widely from the traditional subject organization, and with teaching procedures appropriate for this organization.

Members of the reviewing and unifying committees remained after the main conference to complete refinement of the tentative materials. Following this, the then state Assistant Supervisor of Elementary Education and one of the state consultants took the elementary materials to George Peabody College, and under the direction of the General Curriculum Adviser and the Director of Instruction put them in final form for publication. They were published in September, 1934, as the tentative course of study for the elementary schools of Virginia.[20] The materials for the core program of the secondary schools were prepared for publication by several members of the Secondary Reviewing and Unifying Committee at the University of Virginia. Only core materials for the first year of high school were issued in 1934.[21]

INTRODUCTION OF THE COURSES OF STUDY

As a result of these three years of intensive efforts the tentative courses of study for the elementary grades and for the core program in the first year of high school were available for general use in the fall of 1934. In writing division superintendents in March, 1934, relative to the allotments of state aid for supervisory service, the State Superintendent made this significant statement,

[20] Virginia State Board of Education, *Tentative Course of Study for Virginia Elementary Schools, Grades I–VII.*

[21] Virginia State Board of Education, *Tentative Course of Study for the Core Curriculum of Virginia Secondary Schools, Grade VIII.*

The introduction and the installation of the curriculum program will be optional for those divisions maintaining effective supervision. It will be permissive in those divisions only which maintain supervision. It now appears that it would be quite unwise for those divisions without the services of supervision to attempt general installations of the new curriculum program.[22]

During the last week in August, 1934, a large educational conference was held at the University of Virginia to lay the basis for introducing the courses of study in the schools. Superintendents, principals, and supervisors were urged to attend and teachers were welcome to do so. About 600 people were present. Discussion, led by prominent educational leaders, centered around the philosophy of the program, the possibilities of the course of study making operative a desirable philosophy of education, the function of the courses in improving instruction, the use of subject matter in a program for the improvement of instruction, plans for installation of the courses, and future plans in the program.

In keeping with the underlying policy of the program, use of the new courses was not required of anyone, but was entirely voluntary insofar as the State Department was concerned. In fact, their use was discouraged at the outset unless supervision was available and unless teachers understood the basic philosophy and were ready to use the materials. In a letter of September 7, 1934, the State Superintendent suggested these plans as possibilities for use of the courses:

(1) Course of study used for professional study by all teachers; (2) course of study used by selected teachers in individual schools and by the remaining teachers for professional study; (3) course of study used completely in selected schools, and by the remaining for professional study; (4) course of study used in all classrooms in the divisions.[23]

The courses were sent out by the Department only upon request of the division superintendents, again emphasizing the lack of any compulsion. To aid in introduction of the courses, a series of conferences was held at sixteen cities in the state during November, 1934. All division superintendents, principals, and supervisors, and teachers selected by the superintendent were invited to attend.

[22] Mimeographed circular letter to division superintendents from State Superintendent, March 22, 1934, on file in State Department of Education.

[23] Circular letter to division superintendents from State Superintendent, September 7, 1934, on file in State Department of Education.

CONTINUOUS SUPERVISION AND IN-SERVICE STIMULATION

With the publication of the courses of study in 1934 only one of the three objectives considered contributory to the underlying purpose of improving instruction had been, even temporarily, achieved. Another announced objective, aiding teachers in developing division courses of study especially adapted to local needs, had been fostered through the organization of division production committees as a part of the formulation of state courses. While much of the material produced should have been and probably was utilized directly by teachers in the divisions, there has been little if any effort to produce formal division courses of study as such. One or two divisions have made efforts to develop local courses of study, at least for some grades, and undoubtedly most have carried on activity in curriculum development, even though a formal course of study has not been produced. The desirability of such an objective for the program may be questioned now, since the state courses provide for great flexibility in teaching, suggesting more the basis of organization of the curriculum but granting wide freedom in the nature of educative experiences to be undertaken. Perhaps this allows all the leeway desired and needed by local divisions.

But if the primary objective of the curriculum program—the improvement of classroom instruction—were to be effectively achieved throughout the state, it became evident that the program could not be terminated after three years of activity with the publication of courses of study. If the curriculum is the sum total of children's experiences under the direction of the school, improvement comes only as practice is modified, not with the mere publication of courses of study. It was logical, therefore, for the State Superintendent to report in 1935 that ". . . the school people now look upon the program of improved instruction as a continuous process which means that we will not go into it spasmodically, but rather it will be a continuous effort on the part of each and every teacher to better instruct the children under his or her guidance."[24] Rather than terminating after publication of the courses of study, the program has continued with intensified activity since 1934, but the methods followed have shifted considerably.

[24] Virginia State Board of Education, *Annual Report of the Superintendent of Public Instruction*, 1934-35, p. 15.

Efforts of the State Department since 1934 have been concentrated on the general improvement of classroom instruction so that children would have richer and more meaningful experiences. Primarily, these activities have centered around supervision and the furnishing of leadership. The program has a number of facets, most important of which is the direct supervisory program. In Virginia two-thirds of the salary of elementary supervisors in county divisions is paid from state funds. While the supervisors are hired by local authorities and are directly responsible to them, nevertheless, the State Department, largely through the State Supervisor of Elementary Education, exercises a general guidance and direction over their work. They must be selected from a list of eligible candidates compiled by the State Department and their appointment to a specific position must be approved by the officials of the Department.

It is primarily through the supervisors that the State Department carries on its continuous program to improve instruction. From the outset of the program in 1931, supervisors as well as superintendents had been invited to all regional conferences held in connection with the study program, production, and tryout of the experimental edition of the course of study. Beginning with the three weeks' conference of supervisors in the summer of 1934, when the experimental course of study was evaluated and reviewed, an annual conference of supervisors has been held. In fact, a provision has been inserted in their contracts since 1934-35 which provides that they must attend all meetings and conferences called by the State Superintendent for study of instructional problems. Since the initial one the conferences have usually lasted for a week. Also, supervisors make monthly and term reports to the State Supervisor of Elementary Education, listing their supervisory activities and plans for future activities. But most important of all, guidance and stimulation, as well as coordination of efforts toward realization of accepted goals are promoted by the division of instruction through an endless number of small group and individual conferences, visitations to the counties, correspondence, mimeographed materials, questionnaire forms, and a variety of such formal and informal methods. The importance of supervision in the efforts of the State Department to improve instruction is indicated by a statement of State Superintendent Hall: "Supervision in Virginia looks to the State Department of Education for professional leadership in the unification of efforts and for a clearing house for the exchange of experiences and materials."[25]

The annual conferences of supervisors are periods for cooperative planning. Objectives for the year's work are formulated, those being selected which promise maximum contribution to realization of the larger purposes of the curriculum program. The conference is devoted to intensive study and discussion, with committees working on group projects. The nature and function of the supervisory program has been described by the present state Supervisor of Elementary Education, formerly state Assistant Supervisor of Elementary Education, in these words:

> The supervisory program in Virginia is prepared in a cooperative manner with opportunity provided for teachers, supervisors, superintendents, and laymen to participate in its development. The program is general and broad in nature. It serves as a guide to the individual supervisor in meeting local needs, and, also, makes provision for cooperative planning in regional and state groups. Each local division decides where emphasis should be placed. The program proposes a long-time effort and, therefore, is but slightly modified from year to year. . . . The supervisory program is concerned primarily with child growth through teacher growth, and through the improvement of social and physical environment.[26]

Appropriate pre-service training of teachers is another important point of emphasis in the program.[27] State teachers colleges have been encouraged and aided in developing a training program for teachers that would better prepare them to guide instruction according to the accepted tenets of the program. Training in use of the plan of organization of the curriculum recommended in the courses of study is emphasized in most institutions.

Annual conferences of division superintendents, of high school principals, and of elementary principals are also held under the auspices of the State Department. Problems of instruction have been prominent among the subjects considered in recent years. Here again, committees work on problems of concern to the group, preparing reports, recom-

[25] Mimeographed statement concerning the supervisory program for 1937-38 on file in State Department of Education.

[26] Mimeographed statement on supervisory program for 1938-39 on file in State Department of Education.

[27] See Sidney B. Hall, "Teacher Training in Virginia in Relation to the New Curriculum," *Virginia Journal of Education,* Vol. 27, pp. 221-224, 1934.

mendations, and the like, which are published and made available to members.

The State Department encourages inter-school and inter-room visitation by teachers, so that they may profit from observing and conferring with others, particularly those who have done outstanding work in improving instruction. Bulletins containing accounts of good units of work actually developed in classrooms and similar materials have been mimeographed and distributed on occasion.

The Department has guided the study of certain school problems by teachers, two of which have been a study of retardation of first-grade children and a study of drop-outs in the upper elementary grades. The purpose of these studies is to focus the attention of teachers on certain important instructional problems and to stimulate teachers to evaluate practice.

In recent years the State Department has emphasized the purchase of library books as a means of furthering the program for improving instruction. While state aid funds have been available to assist local school divisions in purchasing library books for a number of years, the amount has been increased materially during the program. State aid funds for this purpose amounted to $11,250 in 1931-32, declined to $7,875 in 1933-34, were increased to $21,600 the next year (the year the tentative course of study was introduced), and to $33,000 in 1936-37, and were again increased to $100,000 in 1938-39. Moreover, the basis for matching local funds for library purchases has been liberalized, being changed in 1938-39 from ten dollars of state aid money for each thirty dollars of local funds to thirty dollars of state aid for each sixty-dollar order of library books.

With respect to the courses of study themselves, no important modifications have been made in the elementary course. It was reprinted in 1937, with only minor changes, chiefly in the references and bibliographies. In the secondary field, preparation of satisfactory courses of study has loomed large in the program. Admittedly, it has been much more difficult to get materials consistent with the philosophy of the program which would be workable in such a complex organization as the high school. Specialization, departmentalization, requirements for college entrance, and the like, have made it difficult to introduce an integrated program. The materials for the core program have been devised at least three times and various supplementary curriculum bulletins have been issued from time to time. An account of these efforts, which is beyond the scope of this study, may be found in a recent description of the program.[28]

The continuous nature of the program is indicated by plans formulated by the State Department for 1939-40. It was planned to call, in December, a three-day conference of selected representatives of the professional and lay groups in the state interested in education for the purpose of reviewing the program to date and recommending next steps. It seems important and significant that representatives of parents' groups, civic and professional organizations, women's organizations, business groups, and other state agencies, as well as professional organizations of teachers, supervisors, principals, and superintendents were to be invited to attend this evaluating and planning conference. Points for discussion included the possibility of inaugurating another state-wide study program in which all teachers would have an opportunity to study anew curriculum problems. Such a program, if approved, was to be launched during the school year of 1940-41. The plans for the conference also provided that present courses of study would be evaluated critically to determine the desirability of revision in the near future, and that means for aiding teachers in the improvement of instruction would be studied.

SUMMARY

By way of summarizing this chapter the following statement of the chief characteristics of the Virginia state curriculum program is given:

1. The program is evolutionary rather than revolutionary.

2. It is a continuous, widespread effort with one dominating purpose—the improvement of instruction in the classrooms of the state.

3. The program is a cooperative undertaking, with all educational forces of the state, teachers, supervisors, principals, superintendents, staffs of teacher-training institutions, members of the State Department of Education, and the lay public participating.

4. Widespread participation prevails.

5. Participation is entirely voluntary, even to use of courses of study.

[28] Virginia State Board of Education, *Brief Description of Virginia Program for Improving Instruction.*

6. The program is comprehensive, covering all levels of the school organization and being concerned with all major factors related to instruction, such as teacher pre-service and in-service training, books and supplies, materials to guide curriculum development, evaluation of the outcomes of instruction, teaching procedures, and the like.

7. An enlightened supervisory program, guided and directed by the State Department of Education, constitutes the chief method of carrying forward the program from a state standpoint.

CHAPTER III

Participation in the Virginia State Curriculum Program

IN THE preceding chapter the Virginia state curriculum program has been described in detail. It was shown that numerous opportunities existed for extensive teacher participation in the program. Since the problem of this investigation is to determine some of the important factors which were associated with participation of county school systems in such a cooperative state program, the first part of this chapter will present evidence on the extent of participation in the program by the 100 county school systems of the state as a basis for the selection of two groups of counties—those which have participated most and those which have participated least in the Virginia program—for a thoroughgoing study of the characteristic likenesses and differences of the two groups in an effort to find the factors which are associated with participation.

PARTICIPATION BY COUNTY SCHOOL SYSTEMS

Opportunities for participation have been present in all the major phases of the program; these have consisted of a study program, the production of curriculum materials, tryout and revision of tentative materials, introduction and use of the course of study, and a continuous in-service program of teacher stimulation and professional development designed to promote the improvement of instruction.

As was stated in Chapter I in the definition of the problem, participation is restricted in this study to mean the taking of an active part in one or more of the particular phases of the organized state curriculum program as it was planned, developed, and carried forward by the State Department of Education during the period from 1931 to the time of the study—that is, 1939. These organized phases of the program have been carefully described and delimited in the preceding chapter (II).

In the broad sense of the word, most administrative and supervisory activities directly or indirectly affect and are related to curriculum development—planning a school building, making a school budget, selecting textbooks, visiting and conferring with teachers: all of these influence curriculum development. But this investigation is concerned only with the participation of local school systems in the specific and organized phases of a comprehensive state program which directly attacked the problem of curriculum making in classrooms. Therefore, while they are of great importance no account was taken in the selection of counties for this study of the multitudinous efforts both formal and informal of local systems to influence curriculum development which did not constitute direct participation in the organized state program. For example, most every school system provides for some study and discussion of curriculum problems by teachers, usually through local staff meetings, over a period of years. Such a practice would be commended and encouraged to the limit by those in charge of the state curriculum program; and, considering the scope of the enterprise and its underlying philosophy, such study might be considered a part of the Virginia program. But that consideration was rejected here and participation in the study program was limited by definition to the formulation and carrying forward of a definite program of study by the county school staff during either the year 1931-32 or the fall of 1932. Similar delimitations were also made for all the other phases of the program.

No reliable, objective basis existed for selecting two groups of counties to be used as the cases for this study. This was due to three deficiencies: first, no objective method could be used to measure the extent of participation in the curriculum program since the issuance of the tentative course of study in 1934. Participation since that time has been so much a matter of the subtle application of a point of view in educational practice; it was to be found in the way teachers approach their work, their attitudes, their procedures, their methods of handling children, and of guiding and directing their learning activities; their choice of values—in short, in their operational philosophy of education. This could not be measured by objective means. Second, while some objective evidence on the nature and extent of participation in the more organized and discrete phases of the program existed, it is not complete or could not be secured for some aspects of participation. Third, objective data that were available took no account of the quality of participation, of the interest and enthusiasm of the participants, or of their accomplishments.

In view of the meager basis which existed for selection on the mere numerical type of evidence, it was felt that a sounder and hence more justifiable choice of counties could be made if the best judgments of people who were in strategic positions from which to evaluate participation were used as a primary basis of selection, with these choices being verified through use of all other available sources of information. Two kinds of ratings, therefore, were secured from certain key people: a rating on a four-point scale of all the counties of the state on the extent to which the county had been active in carrying into effect the principles and point of view of the program since 1934; and a rating on a similar scale which would be an evaluation of over-all participation throughout the entire program. The individuals who made the evaluations were persons in strategic positions in relation to the curriculum program in Virginia. They had worked closely with the program from its inception and were thoroughly familiar with the plans, organization, and development of the program, and the opportunities offered for participation in it. The ratings were made independently by each person and without any opportunity to consult other judges, and the two sets of ratings—the one on participation since 1934, the other on over-all evaluation—were made at different times with at least two weeks intervening in each case. The first set of ratings were not available to the judges at the time the second set of evaluations were made and had not been available at any time during the interval.

Table 4 presents the evidence upon which the selection of counties was made. To bring out more clearly the basis for the selection, the counties finally chosen for inclusion in the most-participating group of counties and in the least-participating group of counties are set at the head of the table. The former group will be designated throughout this study as "Group I—Most-Participating Counties" and the latter group as "Group II—Least-Participating Counties." In view of the confidential nature of some of the data presented and to prevent any embarrassment to counties included in this investigation the names of all counties are concealed. For the counties comprising the two selected groups a coding system has been used to identify individual counties; thus, Group I counties are called County I–a, I–b and so forth to I–k, and Group II counties are named County II–a, II–b and so forth to II–k. No significance attaches to the code name. Individual counties are not matched with each other in any manner whatsoever. The coding system is simply planned so as to facilitate easy identification of the group to which a county belongs.

Column 2 of Table 4 gives the average of the composite, over-all ratings of the judges on participation throughout the program in all phases relating to elementary schools or affecting elementary teachers. For these ratings the individuals making the evaluations were asked to rate all of the counties in the state on a four-point scale on the following basis:

. . . the extent of active participation of the school division in the phases of the Virginia state curriculum program for elementary schools. Active participation should be judged by the extent to which and the consistency with which the school division has cooperated in the various phases of the program for elementary schools since its inauguration by the State Department in 1931. That is, rate the counties by one composite measure on the basis of the use they have made of these opportunities and facilities: the group study program; preparation of curriculum materials; committee work in conjunction with the program; trying out and experimenting with new and illustrative course of study materials; curriculum conferences of various kinds; consultative and advisory service of the State Department staff; the tentative course of study in improving instruction; and any other definite aspect of the program.[1]

Thus persons making the ratings were asked to take account of the consistency of effort and the extent of participation of each county throughout the entire program, the implication being that not merely perfunctory appointment of committees, and the like, should be considered but the interest and enthusiasm with which the great body of teachers approached the work. The evaluators were urged to take account, among other things, of participation with respect to various aspects of the program since 1934. This meant taking recognition of the use made of the tentative course of study and the efforts of the county to carry forward the continuous program for improvement of instruction as planned and developed by the State Department of Education.

[1] Instructions accompanying rating forms sent to each person making evaluations.

Participation in Virginia Program
Table 4
PARTICIPATION OF COUNTY SCHOOL SYSTEMS IN CERTAIN ASPECTS OF THE VIRGINIA STATE CURRICULUM PROGRAM*

County	Over-all Rating[a]	Study Program[b]	Production[c]	Production Committee[d]	Tryout[e]	Revision Conference[f]	1934–39 Rating[g]
1	2	3	4	5	6	7	8
Group I. Most-Participating Counties[h]							
I–a	1	75	Yes	3	11	3	1.5
I–b	1.5	70					1
I–c	1	100	Yes	4	3	1	1
I–d	1	55	Yes	1	7	1	1
I–e	1	85	Yes	2	6		1.5
I–f	1	100	Yes	1	3	1	1
I–g	1	70	Yes	5	11	2	1.5
I–h	1	95	Yes	3	23	1	1
I–i	1	95	Yes	4	13	1	1
I–j	1		Yes	4	9	1	1.5
I–k	1	100	Yes	2	5	1	1.5
Group II. Least-Participating Counties							
II–a	4	85	Yes				4
II–b	4						4
II–c	4						4
II–d	4						3.5
II–e	4	100		1			4
II–f	4	65	Yes				4
II–g	4	65	Yes	1			3.5
II–h	4	85	Yes	1			4
II–i	4	95	Yes				4
II–j	4						4
II–k	4	45		1			4
Other Counties							
1	2.5	45	Yes		1		2
2	2.5		Yes				3
3	1.5	95	Yes	2	1	1	2
4	2		Yes	1			2
5	2.5	95	Yes	1		1	2.5
6	3	80	Yes	1			3
7	2.5	85	Yes		5	1	3
8	3.5			1		3	3.5
9	2.5	50	Yes	1	4		2.5
10	3	45	Yes				3

* See footnote on page 81.

Table 4 (*Continued*)

County	Over-all Rating[a]	Study Pro-gram[b]	Produc-tion[c]	Produc-tion Com-mittee[d]	Tryout[e]	Revision Con-ference[f]	1934–39 Rating[g]
1	2	3	4	5	6	7	8
11	2	100			2	1	2.5
12	2.5	60	Yes				3
13	2.5	95	Yes	1	8		3
14	1.5	100	Yes	2			2
15	3.5	45	Yes	2		1	3.5
16	3.5	45	Yes			1	3
17	2	75	Yes	2	3		2
18	2	80	Yes	2		1	2.5
19	3	95				1	3
20	3	70		2		1	3
21	3.5	40	Yes				3
22	2	55		1	3	1	2
23	2	100	Yes	2	3		2
24	2	100	Yes	2	1		2.5
25	2.5	100	Yes				2
26	3	75	Yes	1			3
27	3	80	Yes	1			2.5
28	2	100	Yes	1	3	1	2.5
29	3.5	95	Yes			1	3.5
30	3.5	80	Yes	1	4	2	3.5
31	2.5	90	Yes	2			2.5
32	2.5	90	Yes	3			2.5
33	3.5	85	Yes			1	3.5
34	3.5						3
35	3	50	Yes	3	1	2	3
36	2.5						3
37	1.5	35	Yes	2		1	1.5
38	2.5	95	Yes	2	1		2.5
39	2	100		1	14		2
40	2.5	100	Yes		9	1	2
41	2	90	Yes		4	1	2.5
42	2.5	30	Yes	2		2	3
43	2	100	Yes	2	5	1	2
44	2	90					3
45	2	70	Yes	2	4	1	2

Participation in Virginia Program

Table 4 (*Concluded*)*

County	Over-all Rating[a]	Study Program[b]	Production[c]	Production Committee[d]	Tryout[e]	Revision Conference[f]	1934–39 Rating[g]
1	2	3	4	5	6	7	8
46	3						3.5
47	3.5	65	Yes	1			3.5
48	2	90	Yes	4	4	3	2.5
49	2			1			2
50	2.5	100	Yes	2	1	1	2.5
51	2.5	100	Yes	3			2
52	2.5	100		3	6	3	2.5
53	1.5	75	Yes	2	4	1	1.5
54	2.5	50	Yes		9	1	2.5
55	2.5	75	Yes	1	4	1	2.5
56	3	85					3
57	2.5	85	Yes	1			2
58	3.5	100					3.5
59	2	75					3
60	1.5	70	Yes	1	4	1	2
61	3.5			2		1	4
62	3	50					3.5
63	3	65	Yes	3		1	3
64	2.5	95	Yes	2			2.5
65	3.5	55	Yes				3.5
66	2.5	90	Yes		4		2.5
67	3	100		2			3
68	1.5	100	Yes	2	4		1.5
69	3	60	Yes				2.5
70	2	100	Yes	3	6	1	2.5
71	2	100			1	1	2
72	2.5	80		1	3		2.5
73	3	65					2.5
74	2	100	Yes	3	7	1	2.5
75	2.5			2	8	1	3
76	2	100			3	1	2
77	2.5	70	Yes			2	2.5
78	3	65		1	2	1	3
Total		86	69	62	45	48	

* See footnote on page 81.

A compilation of these ratings showed that ten counties had been unanimously ranked in the top group by all the judges and eleven counties had consistent rankings by all judges in the lowest of the four groupings. These counties are those labeled as I–a to I–k in Group I, except County I–b which had an average rating of 1.5 and will be discussed later, and the counties labeled as II–a to II–k under Group II. It was believed that these twenty-one counties constituted the best possibilities for selection as the two groups of counties—the most-participating group and the least-participating group—for intensive study in this investigation. However, all other available evidence was carefully examined to verify the soundness of this tentative selection. This evidence is presented in Columns 3 to 8 in Table 4.

Column 3 shows the percentage of teachers who were reported or estimated as being members of study groups in conjunction with the organized study program in 1931-32. These figures are based on a summary of replies of division superintendents of schools to a request sent out by the State Department in February, 1932, for the names of local study chairmen and "approximate" number of teachers in each study group. The summary sheet shows that figures for some counties were estimated, but by whom is not known. All except one of the counties finally selected for inclusion in Group I, or the most-participating group of counties, had study groups which were cooperating in the state program according to these records. Four of the counties comprising the Group II, or least-participating, counties did not report the organization of study groups. Nine other counties in the state appar-

---

Source: All data except ratings secured from letters and reports on file in State Department of Education.

[a] Average of the composite, over-all ratings on extent of participation in the entire program from 1931 to 1939 as it related to elementary schools; ratings made by certain leaders in the program on a four-point scale with "1" the highest rank.

[b] Percentage of teachers reported enrolled in study groups in 1931–32.

[c] "Yes" indicates that county reported the establishment of division production organization in 1932–33.

[d] Number of members of teaching staff who served on state production committees, 1932–34.

[e] Number of teachers participating in tryout of experimental edition of elementary course of study, 1933–34.

[f] Number of members of teaching staff attending work and revision conference in June, 1934.

[g] Average rating of county on extent of participation in the program since 1934; ratings made by certain leaders in the program on a four-point scale with "1" the highest rank.

[h] Counties comprising the two groups selected for study are identified by code number as listed here throughout the study.

ently did not have organized curriculum study. These reports show, then, that ninety-one per cent of the counties tentatively selected for the most-participating counties, sixty-four per cent of those selected for the least-participating group, and eighty-six per cent of all counties in the state participated in the study program.

Column 4 shows the counties that reported to the State Department in the fall of 1932 that they had organized for production of curriculum materials, with the subject areas in which production would be carried on and the names of the division chairmen listed. Ten Group I, five Group II, and a total of sixty-nine counties reported the organization of production committees. There was no way of determining completely the nature or extent of the activities of these production committees. No records were kept in the State Department on the materials submitted by local production committees. Undoubtedly some counties which reported organizations produced few if any materials. On the other hand, some counties were very active, according to the statements of those familiar with the program. One county, County I–j in the most-participating group, is reported to have submitted plans for over 500 teaching units to the state committees. Some recognition of this extent of productive activity was taken into consideration in the ratings of counties, explained earlier.

The number of members of the teaching staff, including classroom teachers, principals, supervisors, and superintendents, who served on state production committees is shown in Column 5 of Table 4. Each of the most-participating counties except County I–b had from one to five persons on these committees; four Group II counties had one member each. Sixty-two counties in all had representation on state production committees. Again, no evidence was available on the contributions made by each member to his committee's work. The influence of active state committee members on participation in their respective counties was undoubtedly great. Such individuals did much to stimulate interest in the program and to encourage teachers to undertake production work. The presence in the system of a dynamic leader, who was keenly interested in the program, often meant the difference between desultory, half-hearted participation and a vigorous, aggressive program of local curriculum development. And active membership on these state committees often indicated the presence of such persons in the county.

Opportunity to participate in trying out the preliminary course-of-study materials for elementary grades was largely limited to counties, first, which had been active in production and, second, which had supervision. Hence participation in this phase of the program usually indicates that there had been much interest in production work. Thus, the number of teachers in the tryout program might be a crude index of the extent of production work. The number of teachers in each county who tried out the elementary materials is shown in Column 6. The counties selected as most-participating counties were a very active group in this phase of the program, while not a single teacher in any of the counties selected for the least-participating group tried out the preliminary course of study. Less than half of all the counties took part in the tryout program.

One of the important phases of the state program from the standpoint of later developments was the three weeks' conference held in June, 1934. All supervisors, chairmen of state production committees, and a few other teachers prominent in production were invited to attend. The conference provided opportunity for a careful study and review of the curriculum materials produced up to that time, the actual production of new material, revision of the experimental edition of the course of study—in short, an intensive study of the philosophy underlying the movement and training for carrying this point of view into effect, both through aid to teachers in use of the course-of-study materials and through general stimulation and development. As shown in Column 7, all except one of the most-participating counties, but none of the least-participating counties were represented at this conference.

Column 8 of the tables gives the average ratings of all the judges on the extent of participation in the program since 1934—that is, in carrying into effect the point of view of the program and in utilizing the resources made available by the program for the improvement of instruction. Five of the ten tentative Group I counties had an average rating of "1," the highest rank, and five had an average rating of "1.5." Nine of the tentative Group II counties had an average rating of "4," the lowest rank, and two an average rating of "3.5."

A careful study of all the evidence presented in Table 4 indicated the soundness of selecting the ten counties consistently ranked in the top class by all judges on the over-all evaluation as the group of counties which had participated most extensively in the state curriculum program in accordance with the criteria used in this study. Likewise the selection of the eleven counties unanimously ranked in the bottom class by all judges as the group of counties which had participated least in the curriculum program seemed reasonable.

Missing from the ten most-participating counties at this point in the selection, however, was one county which had been very active in the program in the last five years of the period. At the time of the study in 1939 it was generally recognized in educational circles in Virginia as well as by curriculum leaders elsewhere that it was one of the outstanding school systems, if not the outstanding system, in the state with respect to efforts that had been made since 1934 to carry into effect the point of view and principles of the program as it was formulated and directed by the State Department. The ratings in Column 8 show its high rank on this phase of participation. Admittedly evidence available at this stage of the investigation showed that the county had not been particularly active during the period from 1931 to 1934. But it was during this period—October, 1932—that a new superintendent of schools was employed. He became interested in the program and began to develop plans for more active participation. And evidence shows that he did much to carry forward the program in 1932-33 and 1933-34, but for some reason this participation was not reported to the State Department and does not show up in Table 4. Beginning with 1935-36 an elementary supervisor was employed who had been very active elsewhere in the program up to that time—in fact, she had served as a state consultant in one of the subject areas. There is no question about the extent or quality of participation of this county since that period. The average rank given the county by the judges on over-all participation was 1.5, and those who placed it in the second classification on the form explained that they had done so because of its record of participation in the early years. In view of all the circumstances, therefore, it was decided to include this county, which is County I–b in Table 4, in the group of most-participating counties. Thus, for the major study of characteristic likenesses and differences of local school systems which participate most extensively and those which participate least in a state curriculum program two groups of eleven counties each were chosen. They are the ones listed in the first two parts of the table.

PARTICIPATION OF THE SELECTED COUNTIES

After the tentative selection of counties it seemed essential that further investigation be made into participation in the curriculum program by the counties selected for study so that not only important differences in the nature and extent of participation between the two groups of counties could be determined but the original selection could be further validated. Just how extensively had each county participated in the program? What proportion of teachers were active in its various phases? Was the original selection of counties justified on the basis of more complete evidence? These are the questions to which answers were sought.

Three sources of information were used: replies of teachers to Part II of the questionnaire form distributed to all white elementary teachers in the twenty-two counties; interviews with division superintendents of most of the selected counties; and evidence gathered from annual reports of elementary supervisors and other materials on file in the State Department of Education. As the first evidence on the nature and extent of participation in the two groups of selected counties, a summary of replies to certain questions on the inquiry form will be given.

TEACHER OPINION

The questionnaire form used in this study gave teachers an opportunity to check one of three statements or to add their own which best described their use at the time of the reply of the state tentative course of study. Table 5 summarizes the percentage of all white elementary teachers returning forms who checked the various statements or who had stated in a previous question that they made no use of it. Very important differences between the two groups of counties are revealed. The converse percentages of those who follow the course of study closely and those who do not use it at all in the two groups are particularly interesting; about one-fifth of all teachers in the most-participating counties stated that they followed the course closely and had reorganized instruction in accordance with its plan of scope and sequence, and the same proportion of teachers in Group II counties made no use of it. Wide variation was found among the practices of teachers in the various counties in both groups.

Participation in Virginia Program

Table 5

PERCENTAGE DISTRIBUTION OF WHITE ELEMENTARY TEACHERS ACCORDING TO USE
MADE OF TENTATIVE COURSE OF STUDY, SELECTED COUNTIES, VIRGINIA, 1939

County	Use of Course of Study[a]			
	Followed Closely	Develop Some Units	Suggestions of Subjects	Not Used
Group I. Most-Participating Counties				
I–a	42.1%	42.1%	11.8%	4.0%
I–b	14.9	55.2	12.6	17.3
I–c	21.4	50.0	28.6	
I–d	21.6	48.9	26.1	3.4
I–e	21.2	38.8	32.9	7.1
I–f	25.0	50.0	25.0	
I–g	11.1	62.2	20.0	6.7
I–h	19.4	51.6	22.6	6.4
I–i	12.9	67.7	12.9	6.5
I–j	41.5	36.9	20.5	1.1
I–k	5.9	52.9	35.3	5.9
Mean	21.5	50.6	22.6	5.3
Group II. Least-Participating Counties				
II–a		45.8%	54.2%	
II–b	..b%	..b	..b	
II–c	18.1	22.9	31.4	27.6%
II–d	11.1	11.1	61.1	16.7
II–e	5.0	47.5	27.5	20.0
II–f		53.3	26.7	20.0
II–g		36.0	48.0	16.0
II–h		13.3	33.3	53.4
II–i	10.0	53.3	26.7	10.0
II–j	2.0	53.1	24.5	20.4
II–k	13.2	24.5	28.3	34.0
Mean	5.9	36.1	36.2	21.8

Source: Questionnaire form used in this study.

[a] Percentages of all teachers returning forms who checked one of the following statements as to the use made of the course of study or who stated that they did not use the course of study:

Follow it quite closely in organizing classroom instruction; class work has been reorganized in accordance with its recommendations and plans.

Use it for suggestions in developing some broad units, but do not follow it systematically and regularly.

Use it to get suggestions and ideas for activities, references, and the like in teaching the regular subjects.

[b] Insufficient returns.

Table 6 reports teacher reaction to the entire curriculum program. In one question on the inquiry form they were asked to indicate how valuable the program had been to them personally. The percentage of teachers checking various statements is shown in the table. Teachers in Group I counties by and large felt that the program had been of "much value" to them. Three-fourths of the teachers in County I–f have benefited much from the program, but on the other extreme only one-third of the teachers in County I–k made such an enthusiastic evaluation of the program. An insignificant number of teachers in Group I counties felt that the program had been of little value to them. In Group II counties, on the other hand, only one white elementary teacher in every six replying stated that the program had been of much value to him. But only a small proportion—six per cent—disclaimed any benefit from the program. Undoubtedly teachers in the Group II counties, in spite of little or no formal participation in the various phases of the program have been affected by it, even to a great extent in individual cases. In their professional training, especially of new teachers, in summer school study, in innumerable informal ways, as well as in formal study and discussion of the state course of study in local faculty meetings, teachers in most of these Group II counties have heard much about the program and have without question been influenced by it. They are not a group unfamiliar and unacquainted with the program.

In order that a clearer picture of the nature and extent of participation in the program may be secured, a brief descriptive statement of the activities of each county follows. This will provide a better basis for determining the validity of the original selection of counties and for understanding the likenesses and differences in participation.

GROUP I—MOST-PARTICIPATING COUNTIES

County I–a. This county organized study groups at twelve convenient centers. In addition some county-wide discussion meetings were held. Evidence indicates that seventy to ninety per cent of the teachers were members of study groups and that much interest was generated in this phase of the program. The study bulletin issued by the State Department was utilized. Study was continued into 1932-33 in conjunction with production activity. No formal county production committees were organized but each elementary teacher was encouraged by the

Participation in Virginia Program

Table 6

PERCENTAGE DISTRIBUTION OF WHITE ELEMENTARY TEACHERS ACCORDING TO THEIR
EVALUATION OF WORTH OF STATE CURRICULUM PROGRAM, SELECTED
COUNTIES, VIRGINIA, 1939

County	Value of Program[a]		
	Much Value	Some Value	Little or No Value[b]
Group I. Most-Participating Counties			
I–a	65.8%	31.6%	1.3%
I–b	54.0	36.8	
I–c	50.0	42.9	
I–d	45.5	51.1	
I–e	54.1	42.4	
I–f	75.0	25.0	
I–g	60.0	37.8	
I–h	46.8	45.2	3.2
I–i	45.2	48.4	
I–j	58.0	33.5	2.3
I–k	35.3	64.7	
Mean	53.6	41.8	0.6
Group II. Least-Participating Counties			
II–a	29.2%	45.8%	12.5%
II–b	..[c]	..[c]	..[c]
II–c	31.4	47.6	6.7
II–d		83.3	5.6
II–e	15.0	70.0	5.0
II–f	6.7	80.0	
II–g	8.0	72.0	16.0
II–h	20.0	73.3	
II–i	10.0	63.3	20.0
II–j	18.4	67.3	4.1
II–k	34.0	47.2	3.8
Mean	17.3	65.0	6.1

Source: Questionnaire form used in this study.

[a] Figures show percentages of all teachers returning forms who, in response to the question "Do you feel that the state curriculum program as a whole has been of value to you?" checked the statements "Of much value," "Of some value," and "Of little or no value."

[b] The remaining percentages not accounted for failed to answer the question, except that two teachers in Group II counties stated that the program was more harmful than helpful and four in Group I and eighteen in Group II counties stated that they knew nothing about the program.

[c] Insufficient returns.

supervisors to develop units of work, keeping records of children's interests, methods of evaluation, outcomes of the unit, and the like. Each teacher had copies of good published units for guides. The state bulletin on procedures was also used for study and help in production. Description of the units and other materials were submitted to the proper state committees. Teachers as a group were very active in this phase of work —the questionnaire returns show that fifty per cent of the teachers replying were actively engaged in producing materials for the state program and the division supervisors state that ninety-five per cent of the elementary teachers actually produced materials.

Eleven teachers from this county were in the tryout program. At the same time other teachers studied illustrative materials from this experimental course and continued under guidance of the supervisor to plan and develop broad units of work. Fifty per cent of the teachers state that they developed such units in their classrooms during 1933-34. Since 1934, supervisors have worked continuously in aiding teachers to implement the viewpoint underlying the state program. These efforts are described more fully in Chapter VI. Much progress has been made in recent years in carrying forward the program. The superintendent reported that some elementary teachers integrated all of the class work; others adhered to broad subject areas for organizing instruction and some, especially in the upper grades, retained the usual subjects. But all have introduced more pupil activity and a greater variety of activity and have sought to organize instruction around meaningful experiences of children. Table 5 shows that practically all teachers made use of the course of study and nearly one-half had reorganized the curriculum in keeping with its plan of organization. Two-thirds of the teachers, according to Table 6, felt that the state program had been of much value to them.

County I–b. Organized study in 1931-32 centered around local schools, although county-wide meetings were also held. The state study bulletin was followed. Practically all teachers participated and they are reported to have been much interested in this phase. After a new superintendent came to this county in 1932 arrangements were made to continue study through an extension course conducted in the county by a professor from a near-by state teachers college. This instructor continued to work in the county in 1933-34, spending one day each week in visiting schools and then meeting with all principals for a discussion and planning period. Production work was carried on by the local schools in conjunction with the extension classes. However, as Table 4 shows, no formal organization was set up to work with state committees. Many descriptions of teaching units were submitted to the state committees and an analysis was made of science textbooks for clues to centers of interest for teaching purposes. Since there was no supervision in the county at that time, none of the teachers participated in the tryout phase of the program and only a few teachers stated that they had copies of the illustrative materials taken from the experimental edition of the course of study.

In 1935 a supervisor was employed and she placed great emphasis on the reorganization of instruction in keeping with the viewpoint of the state program. The superintendent stated that every effort possible in keeping with local conditions has been put forth to further the use of the course of study. A demonstration school was established in which this plan of curriculum organization was followed exclusively. Supervision was concentrated on bringing about the general use of the course by all teachers. This county has a number of small one-teacher rural schools to which little attention, however, is given in the supervisory program. Table 5 shows that most of the teachers used the course of study for help in developing some broad units but not many followed it systematically. The superintendent reported that teachers not sympathetic to the program are replaced as rapidly as possible and new ones trained in the use of the course of study are employed.

Counties I–c and I–f. These two counties comprise one school division and have the same superintendent of schools and supervisor. These counties had started organized study prior to the state program but used the topics in the state study bulletin when it appeared. Local and county-wide meetings were held on alternate weeks during the year 1931-32. The supervisor for these counties was very active on state production committees and she encouraged teachers to develop units of work for submission to state committees. Production was largely carried on by individual teachers under the guidance of the supervisor. Three teachers in each county participated in the tryout of the elementary course of study. A very vigorous and intensive program of in-service stimulation and growth, which is described more fully in Chapter VI, has been carried on in recent years in an effort to aid teachers in improving instruction. The supervisor stated that many teachers had gone beyond the course of study and no longer depended on it extensively. Table 5 indicates that about one-fourth of the teachers followed it closely.

County I–d. In its organization for study this county followed the usual pattern—that is, local groups were organized at eight centers in the county and county-wide meetings were held to coordinate the work. The state study bulletin served as the basis for these discussions. Nearly all elementary teachers participated in this phase of the program. About fifty per cent of the elementary teachers reported that they engaged in production work. In the main this was carried out through individual schools and under the guidance of the supervisor. In her annual report for 1932-33, the supervisor stated that the county had participated in production in accordance with the state plan and that it was planned to have every elementary teacher develop at least one unit for submission to the state committees. Seven teachers tried out the experimental edition of the course of study and a majority of the others reported experimenting with broad units in their teaching during that year of the program. Since 1934 the supervisory program has centered around interpretation and use of the course of study. Each elementary teacher has been asked to submit at the opening of school a pre-plan for a broad unit of work to be developed during the year.

County I–e. An active study program was carried out in County I–e with practically all of the elementary teachers participating. The study groups were organized around the larger local schools. The county participated in the production work with both divisional and local production committees organized. The elementary supervisors guided the work. Each teacher recorded a unit of work and about seventy per cent of these were sent to the proper state committees. Six teachers were in the tryout program and about forty per cent of the others stated that they used the bulletin of illustrative materials from the experimental course. Since 1934, the work proceeded in this county much as in other Group I counties: Some of the teachers integrated all of their class work, others organized instruction around broad subject areas and, of course, some retained the usual school subjects. All teachers, according to supervisors, were, however, in accord with the viewpoint expressed in the state program.

County I–g. Four study groups were organized in this county in 1931-32 and this plan of organization for study and curriculum work has been continued during most of the period since then. At least eighty per cent of the elementary teachers engaged in study. These same four groups served as the basis of organization for production work. Units in social studies were developed for the state committees, but only a limited number actually submitted materials. The supervisor and principals have concentrated efforts on implementing the point of view of the state program in recent years.

County I–h. This county organized study groups in 1931-32 and has continued to emphasize study since then. Both local and county-wide meetings were held. All elementary teachers reported participating in this phase of the program and the supervisor stated much interest was aroused among teachers. Much was done in production work in this county. Committees were organized to compile and collate materials prepared by individual teachers. The state procedures bulletin was utilized as a guide for the work. Charts of children's interests were made and units which centered around these interests were developed. Much of the work of the committees was mimeographed and distributed to teachers in the county as well as elsewhere in the state. Over ninety per cent of the elementary teachers reported participation in production work. Twenty-three teachers in this county tried out the experimental course of study in their classrooms. Since 1934 continuous group study and discussion has been carried on and the supervisor has worked intensively with teachers in putting into practice the underlying point of view of the program.

County I–i. Every elementary teacher returning a questionnaire form in this county stated that he had participated in the study program. Topics suggested in the state study bulletin were used as a basis for discussion. Production work was also emphasized, with teachers centering their efforts on the development of materials in language arts, since the superintendent of schools was the associate chairman of the state secondary committee in this field. About seventy per cent of the elementary teachers reported that they prepared materials for the state program. Thirteen elementary teachers were included in the tryout program. Energetic superintendents (two have served during the period) and an enthusiastic supervisor have worked together to carry forward an aggressive program of curriculum improvement in this county. While a few teachers retained the traditional subject basis of organization, many have gone much beyond the state course of study and utilize pupil interests to a much greater extent than provided for in that guide. This probably explains the low percentage of teachers who, according to the data in Table 5, followed the course of study closely.

County I–j. This county carried on an intensive study program in 1931-32 and has continued to emphasize it since. Groups were organized in the local schools and occasional county-wide meetings were held. Practically all elementary teachers reported participation. Production work was carried on by local groups under the direction of the supervisor. Approximately forty per cent of the teachers reported preparation of curriculum materials for the state program. Most of these materials were descriptions of units of work in elementary science. Nine teachers participated in the tryout program. Table 5 shows that over forty per cent of the teachers reported following the course of study closely. Many teachers well versed in the plan of the course of study have gone much beyond it, according to the supervisors, and use it only for suggestions and ideas in developing their own instructional program.

County I–k. The county was divided into two districts for study and a group organized in each. All elementary teachers participated. The state study bulletin was used as a guide for these discussions. Production was largely individual in nature. Teachers worked under the guidance of the supervisor in producing units of work, inventories of children's needs and interests, and plan sheets for units. Eighty per cent of the teachers stated that they prepared materials for the state program. Five teachers used the tryout edition of the course of study. Apparently few teachers in this county followed the course of study closely; less than six per cent of the teachers themselves reported doing so and the superintendent of schools felt that no teachers followed it extensively. The subject basis of organization was adhered to by most teachers, but they did provide for a much greater variety of activities and gave more attention to individual needs and interests. The curriculum program has resulted in a richer program of pupil experiences in this county but no basic reorganization of instruction.

GROUP II—LEAST-PARTICIPATING COUNTIES

County II–a. This county participated in the study program in 1931-32, organizing study groups in each of the larger schools. The state study bulletin was followed. About ninety per cent of the teachers are reported to have participated, but the superintendent stated that there was "little interest" in this phase of the program. No production work was carried on in this county even though Table 4 shows that a nominal organization was set up in conjunction with the program. None of the teachers used the tryout course of study. After the publication of the state course of study in 1934, teachers used it as a basis for discussion in teachers' meetings. The superintendent encouraged its use but let the matter rest there. About one-half of the teachers, according to Table 5, reported that they use the course for suggestions in developing broad units but no teacher followed it closely.

County II–b. Little evidence on participation is available for this county since the superintendent was not interviewed and only two teachers out of a total of forty returned questionnaire forms. However, the information presented in Table 4, together with other bits of informal evidence, indicates that this county probably made the poorest showing of any in the state with respect to participation in the curriculum program.

County II–c. Table 4 shows the failure of this county to report the organization of study groups to the State Department. The superintendent stated, however, that group study of curriculum problems had been held in the county, although he indicated that it was in more recent years than the formal study program. In any case, he stated that little interest was aroused in organized study at any time. Production of materials for the state program was not carried on in the county and no teachers participated in the tryout program. Over one-fourth of the teachers in this county stated that they made no use of the course of study and another one-third used it only as a reference for suggestions. Six teachers even reported that they knew nothing about the program at all. The superintendent stated that while he encouraged use of the state course of study teachers made little effort to do so.

County II–d. This county engaged in organized group study one year through an extension course conducted by a near-by institution. It was not reported, however, as a part of the state study program, as indicated in Table 4, although the state study bulletin was utilized. Production work was not undertaken and no teachers participated in the tryout program. In fact, the superintendent stated that little was done to follow up the study program, and he felt that the county had done very little in carrying forward the state program. The subject basis of organization and traditional teaching procedures were followed almost to the exclusion of more vital methods. Table 6 shows that not a single teacher felt that the state program had been of "much value" to him.

County II–e. The superintendent in this county disclaimed any participation as such in the state program. However, study groups were organized and most elementary teachers reported participating. Beyond that there had been no formal cooperation in the program. Teachers had copies of the course of study and used it for suggestions for enriching the regular class work.

County II–f. Both county-wide and local groups were formulated for organized curriculum study in 1932. The state study bulletin was used and about two-thirds of the teachers participated. The superintendent reported only mild interest in the study program. Production work was carried on with the high schools serving as centers. Only a small percentage of the teachers actually produced materials. There were no teachers in the tryout program. The course of study had been used as a subject for study and discussion in teacher groups. And this resulted, according to the superintendent, in a broadening of the point of view of teachers even though few followed it to any great extent.

County II–g. Study groups were organized in the larger schools of the county and the state study bulletin used as a basis for group discussion. About two-thirds of the teachers participated. There has been no further organized study on a county basis since 1931-32. In spite of the fact that a production committee chairman was formally designated, as shown in Table 4, no materials were prepared for the state program. Also, no teachers were included in the tryout program. The superintendent frankly stated that he knew that the county had done very little in the state curriculum program and had been little affected by it. Practically all teaching continued in the traditional manner on the strict subject basis. About one-sixth of the teachers, according to Table 6, stated that the curriculum program had been of "little or no value" to them.

County II–h. Study was carried on through local schools in this county with four county-wide conferences being held during the year. Practically all elementary teachers reported participation in this phase of the program. Production work was very meager, even though a county organization was perfunctorily organized. No teachers participated in the tryout program. Efforts have been made in more recent years by a new superintendent to encourage gradual implementation of the principles of the state program. However, little had been accomplished to date. This county had the highest percentage of teachers report that they made no use of the state course of study.

County II–i. Five study groups were organized in this county with almost complete participation by teachers. Meetings were held every two weeks during the year and much interest was aroused among teachers. Participation in the state program, however, fizzled out after that effort and little if anything has been done since, in the words of the superintendent of schools. A few teachers prepared some materials for use in development of their own units but none was submitted to state committees. The superintendent said that "old-fashioned" methods of instruction and the traditional subjects were being retained in the county and would be retained for some time to come.

County II–j. The superintendent of this county said bluntly that they had done nothing with respect to participation in the curriculum program. An extension course was organized early in the period but it was unrelated to the state program. He recognized that teachers did make some use of the state course of study in securing suggestions and ideas for teaching the usual school subjects. A few teachers had tried to develop some broader units in the social studies but that, in his opinion, was the extent to which instruction had been affected by the program. Teachers themselves, according to Tables 5 and 6, indicated somewhat greater indebtedness to the program.

County II–k. Extension courses, organized through state teacher-training institutions, provided opportunity to teachers for study in conjunction with the curriculum program. These were conducted for several years in the early part of the period. The teachers enrolled in these courses developed some units for their own use but there was no participation in state production work. One-third of the teachers in this county reported that they made no use of the state course of study, although thirteen per cent did indicate extensive use of it. The superintendent stated that the main value of the program had been assistance in making the "old curriculum" work better. Teachers attending summer school had been influenced greatly by the program, he reported.

From the foregoing brief descriptions it is obvious that very important differences existed between any Group I county and any Group II county in the extent to which the counties had carried forward the state curriculum program and had tried to put its point of view and principles into practice. However, it is also apparent that none of the Group II counties had been unaffected in some way by the program. Some had made attempts, although often half-hearted, to cooperate in one or more phases of the program. Certainly the consistent, dogged efforts of all Group I counties to make a significant attack on curriculum problems through participation in the stimulative, cooperative state program was lacking in all Group II counties. But throughout this study it must be kept in mind that important likenesses and differences being discovered are not between a group of counties which participated and a group which did not participate—a control group so to speak—but between two groups that varied only in the nature and extent of participation.

Whether other of the seventy-eight counties in the state should have been included in one or the other of the two groups of counties on the basis of this further investigation is impossible to determine since no additional evidence was secured on the other counties. It seems apparent that wide differences in participation did exist between the counties comprising the two groups, and that serves the purpose of this study.

SUMMARY

The basis for selection of the county school systems to be used in this study was considered in this chapter. Available evidence on participation of each of the 100 counties of the state in various organized phases of the program and the ratings of certain key people, each of whom classified all counties into four groups on the basis of extent of active participation throughout the entire program, determined the selection of counties.

By this procedure eleven counties were selected to comprise the group of counties which had participated most extensively in the state curriculum program. These are designated as Group I—Most-Participating Counties throughout the study. Likewise eleven counties were chosen as the group of counties which had participated least in the state curriculum program. These counties are called Group II—Least-Participating Counties. These two sets of counties typified extreme conditions with respect to participation in the Virginia program. In no sense is the least-participating group a control group, for these counties had participated in and had been affected by the program.

Following the initial selection of counties a more extensive investigation of participation of the twenty-two counties was made through use of interviews, questionnaires, and records. Major differences were found in the extent and nature of participation between any county in Group I and any Group II county. Very important differences between teachers in the two groups were revealed in use made of the state course of study and in appraisal of the program.

CHAPTER IV

Likenesses and Differences in Geographic, Sociologic, and Economic Factors

As THE first aspect of this investigation, it seems logical to ascertain the likenesses and differences which existed between the group of most-participating counties and the group of least-participating counties in certain important geographic, sociologic, and economic factors which might be relevant to participation or lack of participation by local school systems in a cooperative state curriculum program. A number of significant associations may be found which would be of importance to state school officials and curriculum directors generally in planning a state program of curriculum development.

GEOGRAPHIC FACTORS

DISTANCE FROM CURRICULUM CENTER

As was stated in Chapter II, six curriculum centers for white teachers were established throughout the state as a part of the Virginia program. A definite group of near-by counties was assigned each institution. Production work during the years 1932-34 converged in these centers, and they also served as focal points throughout the program, with numerous regional conferences being held there, and other types of activities being carried forward from time to time. Distance of a county from its center conceivably might be an important factor associated with participation or lack of it, since difficulty and inconvenience in reaching a center might deter the teaching staff from taking an active part, particularly in production work, while nearness might facilitate participation. Table 7 shows the distance of the county seat of each county in the two groups from its respective curriculum center.

While the most-participating counties were, on the average, approximately twenty miles nearer their centers than were the least-participating

Table 7

DISTANCE OF COUNTY SEAT FROM ITS CURRICULUM CENTER, SELECTED COUNTIES,
VIRGINIA

GROUP I Most-Participating Counties		GROUP II Least-Participating Counties	
County	Miles to Center	County	Miles to Center
I–a	0	II–a	72
I–b	75	II–b	64
I–c	49	II–c	165
I–d	45	II–d	60
I–e	51	II–e	40
I–f	65	II–f	61
I–g	76	II–g	30
I–h	50	II–h	35
I–i	46	II–i	57
I–j	37	II–j	32
I–k	46	II–k	157
M	49.09		70.27
σ	19.64		44.88
d_m		21.18	
σ_d		15.50	
t value			
Obtained		1.37	
1% level		2.85	
5% level		2.09	

Source: Mileage figures furnished by the Virginia Department of Highways.

counties, this difference is not statistically reliable, the t value[1] being
1.37 whereas the t value should be 2.85 if the difference is to occur in
only one per cent of the random samples. The five per cent level of
probability has a value of 2.09. Group II, or least-participating, counties
varied much more than Group I counties in distance from centers, the
distance ranging from 30 to 165 miles in the former group, while in
Group I counties the distance ranged from 0 to 76 miles. Probably

[1] For a discussion of the t test of significance see:
E. F. Lindquist, *Statistical Analysis in Educational Research*, pp. 48-58.
George W. Snedecor, *Statistical Methods* (Revised Edition, 1938), pp. 46-65.
Helen M. Walker, "Reliability of a Difference Between Means" and "Formulas for
the Standard Error of a Mean."

extreme distance tends to discourage participation, but apparently nearness does not facilitate it.

GEOGRAPHIC LOCATION

Though distance from a curriculum center may not be significantly
associated with participation or the lack of it, such a factor as location
in the state, involving accessibility or isolation, may be. Geographically,
Virginia is usually divided into three physical divisions:[2] Tidewater or
Coastal Plain, including the Eastern Shore; The Piedmont Plateau, often
subdivided into Middle Virginia and Piedmont Virginia; and the Appalachian Mountain Province, in turn subdivided into the Blue Ridge, the
Great Valley, and the Allegheny sections.

Location of the twenty-two counties within these physical divisions is
shown in Table 8. The two groups had the same number of counties
located in the Piedmont Plateau division, but the contrast was marked in
the other two divisions. None of the least-participating counties were
situated in the Tidewater region, but six were located in the Appalachian
Mountain region. On the other hand, five Group I counties were in the

Table 8

LOCATION OF THE SELECTED COUNTIES WITHIN PHYSICAL DIVISIONS OF VIRGINIA

Physical Division	Group I Most-Participating Counties	Group II Least-Participating Counties	All Counties in State
Tidewater	5		28
Piedmont Plateau			
Middle Virginia	2	4	27
Piedmont Virginia	3	1	14
Appalachian Mountain Province			
Blue Ridge			3
Great Valley	1		15
Allegheny		6	13
Total	11	11	100

Source: Virginia State Department of Agriculture and Immigration, *Virginia*, p. 115.

[2] Virginia State Department of Agriculture and Immigration, *Virginia*, pp. 13
and 115.

Tidewater region and one in the Appalachian Mountain region, this one being in the Shenandoah Valley.

Travel is easy and convenient and counties are accessible in the Tidewater and Piedmont Plateau regions. The only obstacle is the necessity for a long ferry trip or a devious journey by land to reach the mainland from the Eastern Shore. But travel within the Allegheny section and from counties in this section to other parts of the state is much more difficult and circuitous because of the mountainous topography. All of the Allegheny counties are quite rugged; roads are not as well developed as in most regions and travel usually follows natural courses along the valleys and through gaps. By and large it would be much more difficult for teachers in these counties to hold joint meetings or to attend an after-school or Saturday conference at some central point. To illustrate this situation, a division superintendent in one of the least-participating counties stated that it was necessary for him to travel about one hundred miles to reach one of his schools and that the distance by automobile route from his office in the county seat to each school in the county added together totaled approximately 3,400 miles. It is apparent that a cooperative curriculum program of the Virginia type would be somewhat more difficult to carry forward under such circumstances, particularly if many of the schools were small, isolated units, than would be the case in other sections of Virginia.

Not only is travel within these Allegheny counties tedious, but it is quite inconvenient to travel to near-by counties. Thus superintendents, principals, and teachers were under a handicap in attending regional conferences, meetings of curriculum committees and other activities held at curriculum centers, in attending state meetings, and in visiting schools in other counties for observational purposes. In none of the eleven most-participating counties was it necessary for school people to transverse a mountain ridge or travel a circuitous mountain road to reach their curriculum center, and for only one county was this necessary to reach the state capital, and travel was easy and direct in this case. In short, then, six of the least-participating counties were faced with the impact of isolation so common to mountainous districts in America, particularly in the southern Appalachian region. Evidence is presented in Chapter VII to show that a smaller percentage of the teachers in these counties attend state educational meetings. Perhaps this is due to other factors, such as low salaries or a lack of professional spirit, but it should be considered in connection with sheer geographic isolation.

SOCIOLOGIC FACTORS

SIZE, POPULATION, AND DENSITY OF POPULATION

Population factors, particularly density of population, may be factors associated with participation, since small or less densely settled counties may find it difficult to carry forward a cooperative program. None of the counties in Virginia have an extremely dense population since all large cities in the state have an independent status, and data concerning them are not included in any of the figures used in this study for counties, even though the independent city falls within the bounds of the county. Table 9 gives the land area of each county in square miles, the population, and average population per square mile for 1930.

Group II counties averaged slightly larger in size, 42.36 square miles, but this difference is not significant, since there is a possibility that such a difference will occur in from fifty to sixty per cent of random samplings of such comparisons. Group I counties were much more variable than Group II counties, ranging from 239 to 791 square miles, and had a standard deviation of 184.99 square miles; Group II counties ranged from 333 to 669 square miles and had a standard deviation of 89.58 square miles.

The mean population of Group I counties in 1930 exceeded the mean for Group II by 5,238 persons, but again the difference is not significant, the t value falling far under the five per cent level. Group II counties had greater variability in this instance although both groups showed a wide variance in population. One Group II county, County II–d, had the smallest total population of any county in the state, and the largest county in this group, County II–k, was second in size in the entire state. Thus within the same group practically the two extremes in population were found.

Group I counties were denser in population in 1930, having at that time a mean of 58.45 persons per square mile compared to a mean of 34.95 persons in Group II counties. This difference, while large, is again not significant, the probability of occurrence being between ten and twenty per cent. The error variance is so large in all these sets of data that significance of the difference of the means is hard to establish.

Table 9

LAND AREA, POPULATION, AND DENSITY OF POPULATION, SELECTED COUNTIES, VIRGINIA, 1930

County	Area in Sq. Miles	Population	Population per Sq. Mile
Group I. Most-Participating Counties			
I–a	747	26,981[a]	36.1
I–b	791	29,091	36.8
I–c	258	6,976	27.0
I–d	416	25,264	60.7
I–e	255	30,310[a]	118.9
I–f	320	7,618	23.8
I–g	519	19,852	38.3
I–h	373	30,082[b]	80.6
I–i	239	18,565	77.7
I–j	295	35,289[a]	119.6
I–k	515	12,100	23.5
M	429.82	22,011.64	58.45
σ	184.99	9,262.35	34.44
Group II. Least-Participating Counties			
II–a	545	8,137	14.9
II–b	360	6,031	16.8
II–c	514	16,740	32.6
II–d	333	3,562	10.7
II–e	512	17,009	33.2
II–f	422	4,525	10.7
II–g	516	14,309	27.7
II–h	430	14,058	32.7
II–i	669	32,622	48.8
II–j	473	16,345	34.6
II–k	420	51,167	121.8
M	472.18	16,773.18	34.95
σ	89.58	13,356.43	29.71
d_m	42.36	5,238.46	23.50
σ_d	65.00	5,139.90	14.38
t value			
Obtained	0.65	1.02	1.63
1% level	2.85	2.85	2.85
5% level	2.09	2.09	2.09

Source: U. S. Bureau of the Census, *Fifteenth Census of the United States: 1930. Population*, Vol. I.

[a] Independent city lies within boundaries of county, but is not included in population figures.

[b] Three independent cities lie within boundaries of county, but are not included in population figures.

In spite of this lack of statistical reliability, sparsity of population may be given some consideration as a factor associated with lack of participation. Eight Group I counties exceeded the mean density of Group II counties, while but two Group II counties exceeded their own group mean. Moreover, the mean for Group I was 167 per cent larger than the mean for Group II.

COMPOSITION OF POPULATION

The composition of the population of a county may color the general attitudes of the people toward education and educational change, and their willingness to support innovations and a reorganization of the curriculum. Mort and Cornell,[3] for example, suggest a number of population factors, such as density, age distribution, racial composition, and rate of population growth, that may influence local school adaptability. To explore the possible influence of the characteristics of the population upon participation in a progressive curriculum program, race, nativity, age, illiteracy, place of residence, and occupational status were compared in the two groups of counties.

Table 10 shows the percentage of population in 1930 of white race, the percentage of white persons native born and foreign born, and the percentage of population under forty-five years of age. Negroes constituted over one-half of the population in four of the most-participating counties, but in only one of the least-participating group; five of the latter group but only one Group I county had less than ten per cent Negro population. However, the difference between the group mean percentage—compared on the basis of white persons—is not significant, having a probability of occurrence in from five to ten per cent of such random samples.

On the average, less than one per cent of all the population of these two groups of counties was born in foreign countries. All of the Negro population was native born and of the 64.33 per cent of the population which was white in Group I counties, 63.56 per cent was native born and 0.77 per cent foreign born. The 79.16 per cent of the population which was white in Group II counties was composed of 78.81 per cent native born and 0.35 foreign born. The differences between these mean percentages of native-born and foreign-born white population

[3] Paul R. Mort and Francis G. Cornell, *Adaptability of Public School Systems.*

Table 10

PERCENTAGE OF POPULATION OF WHITE RACE, OF WHITE POPULATION NATIVE AND
FOREIGN BORN, AND OF WHITE POPULATION UNDER FORTY-FIVE YEARS
OF AGE, SELECTED COUNTIES, VIRGINIA, 1930

County	Per Cent White Race[a]	Per Cent of White Persons[b]		Per Cent of White Persons Under 45 Years of Age
		Native Born	Foreign Born	
Group I. Most-Participating Counties				
I–a	76.9%	76.3%	0.6%	78.37%
I–b	76.0	75.7	0.3	74.93
I–c	45.1	45.1		73.91
I–d	81.0	79.3	1.7	74.84
I–e	78.5	76.1	2.4	78.07
I–f	45.2	45.1	0.1	73.92
I–g	78.1	77.4	0.7	72.02
I–h	55.8	54.5	1.3	81.19
I–i	46.5	46.1	0.4	74.29
I–j	90.7	90.3	0.4	82.07
I–k	33.8	33.2	0.6	74.84
M	64.33	63.56	0.77	76.22
σ	18.38	18.12	0.70	3.08
Group II. Least-Participating Counties				
II–a	85.9%	84.5%	1.4%	78.93%
II–b	97.9	97.9		81.80
II–c	99.2	99.1	0.1	87.50
II–d	99.6	99.5	0.1	75.53
II–e	63.4	62.9	0.5	73.60
II–f	96.6	96.6		74.75
II–g	59.2	58.9	0.3	75.53
II–h	55.8	55.3	0.5	78.53
II–i	47.3	47.2	0.1	79.99
II–j	72.1	71.9	0.2	79.23
II–k	93.8	93.1	0.7	86.55
M	79.16	78.81	0.35	79.27
σ	19.05	19.09	0.39	4.36
d_m	14.83	15.25	0.42	3.05
σ_d	8.37	8.32	0.24	1.69
t value				
Obtained	1.77	1.83	1.75	1.80
1% level	2.85	2.85	2.85	2.85
5% level	2.09	2.09	2.09	2.09

Source: U. S. Bureau of the Census, *Fifteenth Census of the United States: 1930. Population*, Vol. III, Part 2.

[a] Remaining percentage is Negro, except that in a few counties other races comprise 0.1 per cent or less of the population.

[b] All Negroes are native born.

for the two groups of counties are not significant. Race and nationality, then, do not constitute factors of difference between extensive participation and little participation in this program. In any case the most-participating counties suffered from whatever handicap may be assumed to exist in a larger proportion of Negro and foreign-born people. In four Group II counties over ninety-five per cent of the population was white native-born stock.

The last column of Table 10 shows the percentage of the white population which was under forty-five years of age in 1930. The least-participating counties have a slight advantage, if this is a favorable factor, with a mean of 79.27 per cent in this age group compared to 76.22 per cent in Group I counties. Again the difference is not significant, having a probability of from five to ten per cent of occurrence in random samples.

ILLITERACY

Rather surprisingly, Table 11 shows that Group I counties, in spite of a larger percentage of Negro population, which is commonly supposed to increase the incidence of illiteracy, had a smaller average percentage of illiterates over ten years of age than had Group II counties, the means being 9.77 and 10.29 respectively. This difference, however, is so small as to be insignificant. If only white persons over ten years of age are considered, the proportional difference increases greatly, but still lacks a high degree of significance, the difference having a probability of occurrence in from two to five per cent of all such samples. Nevertheless, the mean percentage of white illiteracy was twice as large for Group II counties as for Group I counties, although relatively small in both cases.

RURALISM AND URBANISM

As a further study of the characteristics of the population of the two groups of counties, Table 12 presents data on the place of residence of the people in 1930, classified according to basis used in the federal Census, which is urban, rural-farm, and rural-nonfarm. Urban residence is defined as residence in any incorporated town of 2,500 population and over, rural-farm residence as living on a farm, and rural-nonfarm residence as living in nonfarm homes in open country or in towns under

Table 11

PERCENTAGE OF PERSONS TEN YEARS OF AGE AND OVER
ILLITERATE, SELECTED COUNTIES, VIRGINIA, 1930

County	All Persons	White Persons
Group I. Most-Participating Counties		
I–a	11.4%	8.4%
I–b	10.2	6.4
I–c	13.5	3.0
I–d	3.7	1.9
I–e	5.1	1.5
I–f	11.3	2.7
I–g	6.3	3.1
I–h	10.9	2.1
I–i	8.6	2.1
I–j	4.9	3.8
I–k	21.6	2.0
M	9.77	3.36
σ	4.82	2.05
Group II. Least-Participating Counties		
II–a	5.8%	5.1%
II–b	6.7	6.2
II–c	17.4	17.4
II–d	7.6	7.6
II–e	9.2	3.4
II–f	7.3	7.0
II–g	10.8	4.5
II–h	11.0	2.0
II–i	13.2	3.8
II–j	13.3	9.0
II–k	10.9	9.3
M	10.29	6.85
σ	3.30	4.00
d_m	0.52	3.49
σ_d	1.85	1.42
t value		
Obtained	0.28	2.46
1% level	2.85	2.85
5% level	2.09	2.09

Source: U. S. Bureau of the Census, *Fifteenth Census of the United States: 1930. Population*, Vol. III, Part 2.

Table 12

PERCENTAGE OF POPULATION WHICH IS URBAN, RURAL-FARM AND RURAL-NONFARM,
SELECTED COUNTIES, VIRGINIA, 1930

County	Per Cent		
	Urban	Rural-Farm	Rural-Nonfarm
Group I. Most-Participating Counties			
I-a	..[a]%	57.6%	42.4%
I-b	12.8	70.3	16.9
I-c		86.2	13.8
I-d	..[a]	27.6	72.4
I-e		22.5	77.5
I-f		92.4	7.6
I-g		51.5	48.5
I-h	..[b]	26.1	73.9
I-i	13.6	41.9	44.5
I-j	23.9[a]	26.5	49.6
I-k		67.0	33.0
M	4.57	51.78	43.65
σ	7.92	23.90	23.29
Group II. Least-Participating Counties			
II-a	%	45.2%	54.8%
II-b		65.8	34.2
II-c		81.5	18.5
II-d		70.0	30.0
II-e		65.7	34.3
II-f		78.7	21.3
II-g		66.2	33.8
II-h		74.5	25.5
II-i		78.1	21.9
II-j		70.4	29.6
II-k	20.7	21.5	57.8
M	1.88	65.24	32.88
σ	5.95	16.69	12.21
d_m	2.69	13.46	10.77
σ_d	3.13	9.22	8.32
t value			
Obtained	0.86	1.46	1.29
1% level	2.85	2.85	2.85
5% level	2.09	2.09	2.09

Source: U. S. Bureau of the Census, *Fifteenth Census of the United States: 1930. Population*, Vol. III, Part 2.

[a] Independent city lies within boundaries of county, but is not included in population figures.

[b] Three independent cities lie within boundaries of county, but are not included in population figures.

2,500 population. Only three Group I and one Group II counties had any towns of 2,500 population or over within their legal jurisdiction. However, four Group I counties, one of the three included above as having urban towns, and three others, had independent cities within their boundaries but their population was not included in these data. Another Group I county is located near a very large city in an adjoining commonwealth and is largely a suburban residential district. In actuality, then, five of the most-participating counties had a much more urban character than is shown by the table, with a large percentage of the population in at least four of these five Group I counties being suburban in character. One Group II county lies near a large city, but is not suburban in type and all the others are highly rural in character. Over fifty per cent of the population in each group of counties lived on farms. Although Group II counties had a larger mean percentage of farm population the difference is not reliable, the probability being greater than five per cent.

Table 13

NUMBER AND POPULATION OF INCORPORATED TOWNS AND INDEPENDENT CITIES IN
THE SELECTED COUNTIES, VIRGINIA, 1930

County	Group I Most-Participating Counties				County	Group II Least-Participating Counties			
	Incorporated Towns		Independent Cities			Incorporated Towns		Independent Cities[a]	
	No.	Pop.	No.	Pop.		No.	Pop.	No.	Pop.
I–a	1	341	1	15,245	II–a				
I–b	1	3,713			II–b				
I–c	1	427			II–c	1	815		
I–d	6	4,702			II–d	1	259		
I–e			1	182,929	II–e	1	1,297		
I–f					II–f	2	375		
I–g	8	3,953			II–g	2	717		
I–h			3	183,271	II–h	2	2,321		
I–i	2	2,878			II–i	5	4,695		
I–j	2	8,443	1	69,206	II–j				
I–k	3	2,701			II–k	9	14,184		

Source: U. S. Bureau of the Census, *Fifteenth Census of the United States: 1930. Population*, Vol. I.

[a] There are no independent cities included within boundaries of Group II counties.

The predominantly rural character of the Group II counties is further shown in Table 13, which gives the number and combined population of the incorporated towns in each county and the same information for independent cities within the bounds of the county. Only four Group II counties had any towns over 1,000 population within their limits, while nine Group I counties had one or more towns of this size.

In conclusion, no statistically significant difference can be found in the urban or rural character of the two groups of counties due to the wide variation that exists, but the evidence indicates that on the whole the Group II, or least-participating, counties were much more rural in character than the Group I counties. If the independent cities encompassed by these counties were included in the data, which from a practical standpoint would be sound since these cities have as much influence culturally and in other ways as if no legal distinctions existed, significant differences would be found, with Group I counties having a much more urban character. Nevertheless, some Group I counties were strictly rural and were no more influenced by large cities than several of the Group II counties, so the mere fact of ruralism does not in itself predicate lack of progress.

OCCUPATIONAL STATUS

According to Table 14 a slightly larger percentage of all persons ten years of age and over was gainfully employed, on the average, in the Group I counties than in the Group II counties, the percentages being 44.93 and 43.14 respectively. The difference is not significant. Approximately fifty-five per cent of all persons ten years of age and over who were gainfully employed in Group II counties were engaged in agriculture as an occupation; in Group I counties the percentage was about forty-five. This again shows the more rural character of the least-participating counties and confirms the facts presented in Table 12, which showed that a larger proportion of people in the Group II counties lived on farms. Nevertheless the difference of 10.80 points is not significant, having a t value of 1.43 and a probability of occurrence in ten to twenty per cent of all samples. In nine Group II and six Group I counties over fifty per cent of the gainfully employed were engaged in agricultural pursuits.

Table 14

PERCENTAGE OF POPULATION TEN YEARS OF AGE AND OVER GAINFULLY
EMPLOYED AND PERCENTAGE OF THOSE IN GAINFUL OCCUPATIONS
ENGAGED IN AGRICULTURE, SELECTED COUNTIES,
VIRGINIA, 1930

County	Gainfully Employed	Engaged in Agriculture
Group I. Most-Participating Counties		
I–a	43.2%	51.1%
I–b	43.3	57.9
I–c	45.1	66.0
I–d	48.2	26.9
I–e	47.9	17.0
I–f	38.5	70.9
I–g	45.5	52.8
I–h	49.4	34.2
I–i	44.1	44.2
I–j	43.2	19.7
I–k	45.8	50.8
M	44.93	44.68
σ	2.88	17.26
Group II. Least-Participating Counties		
II–a	50.4%	29.1%
II–b	44.8	59.0
II–c	43.6	70.5
II–d	41.1	62.4
II–e	42.9	53.1
II–f	43.5	70.2
II–g	42.5	55.7
II–h	42.5	65.6
II–i	42.6	69.2
II–j	41.4	58.8
II–k	39.2	16.7
M	43.14	55.48
σ	2.69	16.54
d_m	1.79	10.80
σ_d	1.24	7.56
t value		
Obtained	1.45	1.43
1% level	2.85	2.85
5% level	2.09	2.09

Source: U. S. Bureau of the Census, *Fifteenth Census of the United States: 1930.
Population*, Vol. III, Part 2.

HOME OWNERSHIP AND STABILITY OF POPULATION

Such factors as home ownership and stability of the population may influence the extent to which a school system takes on newer practices. It is usually assumed that these factors are desirable characteristics of good communities and that they have a favorable influence on community progress. Thorndike[4] includes the former item, which is also an index of stability, as one of the measures of the "goodness" of a city. It is worth investigating possible likenesses and differences of the two groups of counties in these respects.

Table 15 shows the tenure of home, giving the percentage of all families and of all white families in 1930 who were owner families, that is, families in which one member of the immediate family owned in whole or part the dwelling in which the family lived. Also, since the counties are chiefly rural, the percentage of all farm operators who were full owners or part owners—the latter being those who owned part and rented part of the land they farmed—is shown as calculated from the agricultural census for 1935. Group I counties on the average had a slightly better record on home ownership than did the Group II counties, even when Negro families were included, but the differences in both cases are so small as to lack significance. The two groups were practically alike with respect to the percentage of farmers who were owners in full or part, with a difference in means of only 0.22 per cent and in standard deviation of 0.28 per cent. Obviously, then, the percentage of families of a community—county in this case—who own their home or farm is a factor not associated with participation of the schools in a curriculum revision program of the Virginia type.

Another indication of the stability of population of these counties, since they are largely rural, is provided by a tabulation in the agricultural census which shows in frequency groups the number of years each farmer had lived on his farm as an operator at the time of the census in 1935. Table 16 gives the percentage of owners and tenants belonging in the frequency groups listed. For farm owners, differences between the mean percentages in all three groupings are of no significance. It will be noted that approximately one-half of the owners had lived fifteen or more years on their respective farms in 1935. With respect to tenants, Group I counties oddly enough had a larger percentage of

4 Edward L. Thorndike, *Your City*, pp. 189-190.

Table 15

PERCENTAGE OF FAMILIES WHO OWNED THEIR HOMES, AND OF FARMERS WHO OWNED
THEIR FARMS, SELECTED COUNTIES, VIRGINIA, 1930 AND 1935

County	Per Cent of Owner Families, 1930		Per Cent of Farmers Owning Farms, 1935
	All Families	White Families	
Group I. Most-Participating Counties			
I–a	56.8%	53.1%	80.4%
I–b	59.6	61.1	65.6
I–c	72.0	67.6	75.8
I–d	69.3	69.5	83.8
I–e	70.3	70.5	81.1
I–f	79.8	78.9	82.2
I–g	56.3	57.6	76.3
I–h	53.9	61.7	71.8
I–i	34.5	47.7	44.7
I–j	64.2	64.0	82.4
I–k	44.7	61.9	54.0
M	60.13	63.05	72.46
σ	12.40	8.21	12.17
Group II. Least-Participating Counties			
II–a	51.8%	50.7%	82.3%
II–b	61.6	61.2	84.8
II–c	55.6	55.9	61.7
II–d	66.7	66.7	79.6
II–e	67.2	68.2	77.3
II–f	71.9	71.9	87.5
II–g	77.6	74.3	83.9
II–h	55.9	62.9	60.5
II–i	43.9	51.8	46.9
II–j	55.8	53.0	66.0
II–k	36.9	39.0	64.1
M	58.63	59.60	72.24
σ	11.46	10.12	12.45
d_m	1.50	3.45	0.22
σ_d	5.34	4.12	5.50
t value			
Obtained	0.28	0.84	0.04
1% level	2.85	2.85	2.85
5% level	2.09	2.09	2.09

Source: U. S. Bureau of the Census, *Fifteenth Census of the United States: 1930. Population,*
Vol. VI and *United States Census of Agriculture: 1935*, Vol. I.

Table 16

PERCENTAGE DISTRIBUTION OF FARM OWNERS AND TENANTS ACCORDING TO NUMBER
OF YEARS OPERATION OF PRESENT FARM, SELECTED COUNTIES,
VIRGINIA, 1935

County	OWNERS			TENANTS		
	Up to 5 Years	5–14 Years	15 Years and Over	Under 1 Year	1–4 Years	5 Years and Over
Group I. Most-Participating Counties						
I–a	20.0%	29.6%	50.4%	35.0%	36.2%	28.8%
I–b	20.7	31.2	48.1	36.3	34.6	29.1
I–c	20.4	24.5	55.1	25.3	43.5	31.2
I–d	19.3	35.3	45.3	29.4	38.1	32.5
I–e	21.6	30.7	47.6	32.6	35.2	32.2
I–f	13.3	24.7	62.1	28.8	37.6	33.6
I–g	21.2	28.6	50.2	26.0	36.0	38.1
I–h	22.6	37.5	40.0	26.6	39.4	34.0
I–i	17.5	21.1	61.4	20.6	25.7	53.6
I–j	27.2	34.7	38.1	37.2	43.0	19.8
I–k	18.7	29.0	52.3	22.9	38.3	38.8
M	20.23	29.72	50.05	29.15	37.05	33.79
σ	3.25	4.75	7.27	5.27	4.53	7.92
Group II. Least-Participating Counties						
II–a	23.6%	22.7%	53.8%	21.7%	56.5%	21.7%
II–b	20.9	33.1	46.0	29.9	48.0	22.0
II–c	34.3	29.8	35.9	26.5	49.9	23.7
II–d	18.3	32.3	49.3	27.6	42.5	29.9
II–e	20.5	25.8	53.7	18.5	36.4	45.1
II–f	16.7	34.2	49.1	5.5	53.4	41.1
II–g	15.4	29.3	55.3	27.6	39.1	33.2
II–h	18.7	29.2	52.2	34.5	38.6	26.9
II–i	17.1	28.5	54.4	29.9	41.1	29.0
II–j	18.7	28.9	52.4	30.9	38.4	30.7
II–k	24.6	33.3	42.1	19.8	46.2	34.0
M	20.80	29.74	49.47	24.76	44.55	30.66
σ	5.04	3.28	5.73	7.68	6.39	7.11
d_m	0.57	0.02	0.58	4.39	7.50	3.13
σ_d	1.90	1.83	2.93	2.95	2.48	3.37
t value						
Obtained	0.30	0.01	0.20	1.49	3.02	0.93
1% level	2.85	2.85	2.85	2.85	2.85	2.85
5% level	2.09	2.09	2.09	2.09	2.09	2.09

Source: U. S. Bureau of the Census, *United States Census of Agriculture: 1935*, Vol. 2.

farmers who had been on their farms a very short period—less than one year—and of those who had farmed the same farm five years or more. This means that the Group II counties had a larger percentage who had been on the farm from one to four years. This difference, through this combination of circumstance where two degrees of freedom and three factors exist, is significant, having a probability of less than one per cent. However, because of the small percentage of farmers who are tenants and the fact that this particular significant difference results from a grouping in a frequency distribution, the factor is of little if any importance.

Stability of population, as revealed by home ownership and length of residence of farmers on their farms, is not a characteristic difference between participating and non-participating counties in the Virginia curriculum progam.

ECONOMIC FACTORS

It is possible that many of the likenesses and differences which are found to exist between the most-participating and least-participating counties are due either directly or indirectly to economic factors. Certainly it is important to investigate at the outset of the study likenesses and differences with respect to wealth and income. Valid and reliable measures or indexes of these factors are difficult to secure, but available evidence has been utilized to make certain important comparisons.

LOCALLY TAXABLE WEALTH PER PUPIL ENROLLED

In Virginia, property subject to local taxation includes land and its buildings and improvements, timber and minerals, tangible personal property, machinery and tools, merchants' capital, and the property of public service corporations and railroads. It is from taxes on these sources that the county's funds for local support of the schools are derived. In other words, this is the wealth available for the local maintenance of an educational program.

The annual reports of the Department of Taxation[5] show the assessed valuation of these various items of wealth for each county. However,

[5] Virginia State Department of Taxation, *Report of the Department of Taxation,* Table 17.

since assessment is made by county officials for all items except the property of public service corporations and railroads, which is assessed by the State Corporation Commission, the proportion that assessed valuation is of true valuation is likely to fluctuate greatly from county to county. The reported assessed totals would not give an accurate measure of the true wealth of the counties. The Department of Taxation has made several thoroughgoing studies of the ratio of assessed value of real estate to its true value in each county of the state, the most important ones covering the years 1931 and 1936.[6] By dividing the assessed valuation by the average assessment ratio for the county the true value of all real estate, except that held by public service corporations and railroads, can be obtained for these years.

To secure wealth data for each of the nine years of 1930-1938 included in the present investigation, it was decided to use an assessment ratio for each of the other seven years obtained by using the figures for 1931 and 1936 as two points to determine a straight line graph and reading the ratio for other years directly from this graph. Russell states that

While, of course, there are conditions of local and temporary character which produce considerable change in the assessment ratio of a county or city from year to year, the ratios in general remain fairly constant, barring institutional change by governing authorities. Confirmation of this fact is found in the results of an extension of the study of assessment ratios into years subsequent to 1936 for a random selection of fourteen counties. In eight of these the variation from 1936 to 1938 was one point or less, while the average change in all fourteen was less than two points.[7]

The Department of Taxation's studies covered only real estate valuations and no ratios are available for tangible personal property, machinery and tools, and merchants' capital. It was decided, therefore, for the purposes of the present investigation to apply these same ratios —the obtained ones for real estate for 1931 and 1936 and the derived ones for the other seven years from 1930 to 1938—to these items of wealth to secure an estimate of their true value. Use of these ratios

[6] The results of the study for 1931 are unpublished, but are on file in the office of Dr. John H. Russell, Director of Research, Virginia State Department of Taxation. The 1936 study is reported in John H. Russell, "Diversity of Real Estate Assessments Levels Among Political Subdivisions," *The Commonwealth,* Vol. 6, pp. 7-11, 1939.

[7] John H. Russell, "Diversity of Real Estate Assessments Levels Among Political Subdivisions," *The Commonwealth,* Vol. 6, p. 8, 1939.

Table 17

LOCALLY TAXABLE WEALTH PER PUPIL ENROLLED IN PUBLIC SCHOOLS, SELECTED COUNTIES, VIRGINIA, 1930–1939

County	1930–31	1931–32	1932–33	1933–34	1934–35	1935–36	1936–37	1937–38	1938–39
Group I. Most-Participating Counties									
I-a	$ 8,277.57	$ 7,409.66	$ 6,682.16	$ 6,041.69	$ 5,693.67	$ 5,728.90	$ 5,553.63	$ 5,366.02	$ 5,289.01
I-b	4,447.55	4,467.75	4,403.51	4,320.72	4,302.16	4,429.69	4,519.75	4,617.70	4,803.06
I-c	4,375.71	3,809.57	3,691.78	3,391.93	3,123.41	3,051.31	3,014.38	3,139.23	3,084.08
I-d	10,589.63	11,118.01	10,783.26	10,159.34	10,025.28	10,065.48	10,278.27	10,705.20	11,666.09
I-e	10,574.80	10,440.62	10,770.68	10,747.41	11,035.19	11,246.77	11,964.18	12,733.73	14,058.92
I-f	2,070.56	2,160.28	2,203.63	2,247.70	2,356.78	2,605.71	2,896.80	3,267.03	3,502.17
I-g	8,467.38	7,789.23	7,476.81	7,405.33	7,043.48	7,086.03	7,043.16	7,036.30	7,510.09
I-h	5,625.03	5,459.31	5,218.28	5,075.22	5,134.88	5,087.77	5,199.89	5,136.42	5,541.27
I-i	7,622.50	7,016.73	6,463.50	5,888.54	5,513.63	5,039.25	4,731.04	4,670.07	4,978.87
I-j	8,048.67	7,401.58	6,813.17	6,185.44	5,801.22	5,559.00	5,359.56	5,156.10	5,397.85
I-k	3,928.02	3,650.65	3,599.52	3,391.30	3,451.36	3,415.07	3,334.80	3,557.33	3,985.85
Mean	6,729.77	6,429.40	6,190.66	5,895.87	5,771.01	5,755.91	5,808.68	5,944.10	6,346.93
Group II. Least-Participating Counties									
II-a	9,989.76	9,256.10	8,628.52	7,915.24	7,455.58	7,167.66	6,947.99	6,478.88	6,437.30
II-b	4,769.67	4,568.04	3,784.10	3,530.87	3,467.74	3,212.44	3,306.20	3,267.53	2,909.99
II-c	3,405.51	3,441.15	3,168.25	2,986.69	2,694.73	2,500.47	2,521.09	1,930.73	2,119.07
II-d	4,047.39	4,044.05	3,712.79	3,702.33	4,022.68	4,161.20	4,613.00	4,735.27	5,439.67
II-e	4,906.80	4,518.28	4,215.53	4,108.42	3,613.40	3,582.96	3,497.16	3,541.91	3,878.25
II-f	7,503.86	6,799.31	6,570.94	6,209.19	5,862.21	5,508.03	5,521.92	4,995.89	5,181.51
II-g	3,308.59	3,114.25	2,980.06	2,917.12	2,916.02	2,996.19	3,142.35	3,263.32	3,459.51
II-h	3,124.29	2,891.45	2,481.91	2,351.70	2,323.88	2,367.11	2,417.01	2,397.39	2,484.36
II-i	2,912.31	2,620.28	2,337.23	2,192.83	2,195.53	2,257.72	2,265.52	2,296.40	2,480.80
II-j	4,125.14	4,075.57	3,842.65	3,642.06	3,404.32	3,253.65	3,364.51	3,280.55	3,558.73
II-k	2,892.85	2,755.77	2,670.07	2,491.88	2,286.33	2,150.49	2,103.57	1,975.58	2,169.54
Mean	4,635.11	4,371.30	4,035.64	3,822.58	3,658.40	3,559.81	3,609.12	3,469.40	3,647.16

Sources: Locally Taxable Wealth calculated from Virginia State Department of Taxation, *Report of the Department of Taxation.* Public School Enrollment from Virginia State Board of Education, *Annual Report of the Superintendent of Public Instruction.*

in the manner described should give the best estimates of the true value
of all locally assessed wealth available.

Russell[8] states that the State Corporation Commission generally uses
an assessment ratio of 0.40 in appraising the properties of public service
corporations and railroads, so true value of these items for each county
can be obtained by dividing the reported assessed value for each of the
nine years by this ratio.

The sum of the true value of all real and personal property assessed
locally and the true value of public service and railroad property has
been taken as the amount of locally taxable wealth of each county.
Table 17 shows the amount of such wealth per pupil enrolled in the
public schools for each of the twenty-two counties for the years 1930-
1938. The analysis of variance[9] of these data given in Table 18 shows

Table 18

ANALYSIS OF VARIANCE OF LOCALLY TAXABLE WEALTH PER PUPIL ENROLLED

(Table 17)

Source of Variation	Sum of Squares	df	Mean Square	F Values		
				Obtained	5% Level	1% Level
Between two groups of counties	246,066,889	1	246,066,889	42.87	3.89	6.76
Among years	22,549,660	8	2,818,708	2.04	2.96	4.91
Among counties in one group for one year ..	1,032,922,963	180	5,738,461			
Interaction	2,059,543	8	257,443	22.29	2.96	4.91
Total	1,303,539,055	197				

a highly significant difference between the two groups of counties on
locally taxable wealth per pupil. The average amount of wealth available for the support of each school child in the most-participating counties varied from a high of $6,729.77 in 1930-31 to a low of $5,755.91

[8] *Ibid.,* p. 10.

[9] For a discussion of the analysis of variance see:

E. F. Lindquist, *Statistical Analysis in Educational Research,* Chapter V.

George W. Snedecor, *Statistical Methods* (Revised Edition, 1938), Chapters 10
and 11.

Helen M. Walker, "Analysis of Variance."

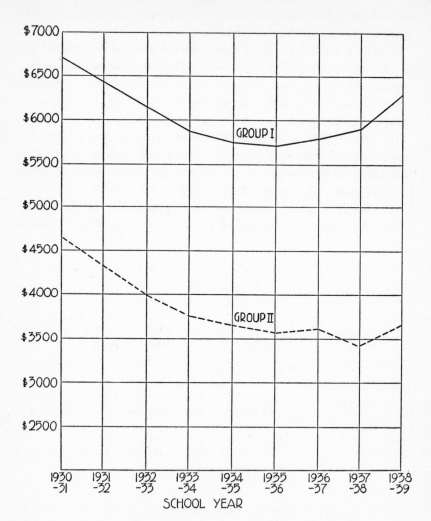

FIGURE I. Locally Taxable Wealth per Pupil Enrolled, Selected Counties,
Virginia, 1930-1939

——— Group I ------- Group II

in 1935-36, while each child in school in the least-participating counties had on the average but from $4,635.11 to $3,469.40 each year during the period to support his schooling. Moreover, the amount of wealth per pupil in 1938-39 showed a much greater decline from the 1930-31 level in the least-participating counties than in the most-participating counties, the former group showing a loss of 21.3 per cent and the latter of 5.7 per cent. This fact is strikingly revealed in Figure I, which gives in graphic form the group means for the amount of locally taxable wealth per pupil enrolled in each county, as taken from Table 17. The wide difference between the two groups of counties in this characteristic is also shown.

Not only was there a significant difference between the groups in the amount of wealth per pupil but it will be noted from Table 17 that not more than two Group II counties exceeded the mean for the Group I counties in any one year for the first five years of the period, and thereafter but one county exceeded the Group I mean. However, not all of the Group I counties individually were favored counties. County I–f in particular had a low per-pupil wealth in the early years of the period during which the curriculum program was being initiated. Within this group of eleven most-participating counties other wide differences existed during these years.

The fact remains, however, that with respect to the amount of locally taxable wealth per pupil enrolled there was a very significant difference between the most-participating and the least-participating groups of counties.

TOTAL WEALTH PER CAPITA

Locally taxable wealth does not include all of the wealth of the people in Virginia, although it is the only wealth available to support schools. In addition to the items of real wealth included in this category, there are evidences of wealth, or token wealth, taxed only by the state. This intangible wealth includes all evidences of debt—such as mortgages, bonds and notes, money, stocks, the excess of bills and accounts due over those owed—and other forms of capital. The total wealth of each county was determined by adding the reported assessed valuation of all these intangible items of wealth to the true value of all real property used in calculating Table 17. It is true that the inclusion of the value of notes, bonds, mortgages and such evidences of debt which are liabilities against real property in the same county inflates by that much the true wealth of the county, but it is believed that error due to such inclusion is negligible. In any case such amounts could not be segregated.

Figures for total wealth per capita, using population figures from the 1930 census, are presented in Table 19 for the years 1931 and 1936,

Table 19

WEALTH PER CAPITA OF POPULATION, SELECTED COUNTIES, VIRGINIA, 1931 AND 1936

Group I Most-Participating Counties			Group II Least-Participating Counties		
County	1931	1936	County	1931	1936
I–a	$1,938.75	$1,449.63	II–a	$2,037.50	$1,585.80
I–b	1,170.40	1,140.11	II–b	1,152.62	959.76
I–c	1,057.84	790.87	II–c	1,049.24	965.63
I–d	2,562.04	2,893.75	II–d	1,116.34	1,294.57
I–e	2,538.76	2,986.30	II–e	1,312.96	1,145.13
I–f	634.48	721.62	II–f	1,865.01	1,438.32
I–g	2,148.41	1,901.37	II–g	888.97	754.90
I–h	1,407.32	1,363.41	II–h	876.82	675.15
I–i	1,699.75	1,134.60	II–i	837.55	682.45
I–j	2,084.20	1,754.84	II–j	1,223.29	1,038.08
I–k	1,163.84	983.66	II–k	864.62	660.45
Mean	$1,673.25	$1,556.38	Mean	$1,202.27	$1,018.20

Sources: Wealth calculated from Virginia State Department of Taxation, *Report of Department of Taxation.*

Population from U. S. Bureau of the Census, *Fifteenth Census of the United States: 1930. Population,* Vol. I.

the years for which the assessment ratios for real estate were determined, as explained above, by field studies of the Department of Taxation. Some error may be introduced in the 1936 figures if a disproportionate change in population had occurred in any of the twenty-two counties since 1930, but if so, such error is believed to be minor. Since the same population figures would be used throughout, it seemed unnecessary to calculate per-capita wealth for all nine years.

The analysis of variance of these data, reported in Table 20, again shows a highly significant difference existed between the two groups of

Table 20

ANALYSIS OF VARIANCE OF WEALTH PER CAPITA OF POPULATION (Table 19)

Source of Variation	Sum of Squares	df	Mean Square	F Values		
				Obtained	5% Level	1% Level
Between two groups of counties	2,800,626	1	2,800,626	8.82	4.03	7.31
Between years	249,049	1	249,049	1.28	251	6,286
Among counties in one group for one year	12,707,394	40	317,685			
Interaction	12,413	1	12,413	25.59	251	6,286
Total	15,769,482	43				

counties in wealth per capita. The per-capita wealth for the eleven most-participating counties was on the average from about forty to fifty per cent greater than the per-capita wealth for the eleven least-participating counties. And this is true in spite of the fact that the Group I counties had an appreciably larger percentage of Negro population.

VALUE OF FARMS AND OF NONFARM HOMES

Certain other data, largely from census sources, provide means of comparing the two groups of counties on economic status. These data are presented in Tables 21 and 22. Since Table 12 shows that one-half or more of the population in the two groups of counties lived on farms, the comparisons of farm economic conditions in Table 21 provide a good insight into the economic status of the counties. The first set of figures shows the average value of farms, and the second the average value of farm land per acre in these counties. In both values the most-participating counties, on the average, far exceeded the least-participating counties, with the differences in the first instance being questionable in significance and in the second of high significance.

However, the percentage of farms operated by their owners which were mortgaged was much greater in the Group I counties, with the difference being of doubtful significance. The ratio of the amount of

Table 21

VALUE OF FARMS, PERCENTAGE OF FARMS OPERATED BY OWNERS WHICH ARE MORTGAGED
AND PERCENTAGE MORTGAGE IS OF VALUE OF FARM, AND PERCENTAGE OF
RURAL POPULATION LIVING ON MARGINAL OR SUB-MARGINAL LAND,
SELECTED COUNTIES, VIRGINIA

County	Value of Farms, 1935		Farm Mortgages, 1930		Per Cent of Rural Population on Marginal Land, 1930
	Per Farm	Per Acre	Per Cent Mortgaged	Per Cent Mortgage Is of Farm Value	
Group I. Most-Participating Counties					
I–a	$5,079	$ 44.52	24.7	26.79	11.79
I–b	2,316	25.28	21.1	30.80	10.81
I–c	2,368	22.46	16.8	28.05	5.85
I–d	7,589	107.29	35.8	26.43	6.25
I–e	4,762	85.67	27.2	29.40	
I–f	1,729	18.27	15.7	29.20	
I–g	7,620	53.95	30.4	31.29	3.87
I–h	4,597	63.22	40.6	46.84	5.88
I–i	7,541	88.53	38.6	41.28	
I–j	5,842	94.45	27.3	26.13	9.36
I–k	2,456	16.28	31.3	42.10	3.52
M	$4,718.09	$ 56.36	28.14	32.58	5.21
σ	2,161.37	32.06	7.89	6.94	4.04
Group II. Least-Participating Counties					
II–a	$3,898	$ 18.84	18.8	26.42	72.04
II–b	3,602	23.68	17.0	23.92	53.91
II–c	1,138	16.67	4.1	31.90	57.53
II–d	3,492	21.62	12.9	28.19	56.89
II–e	2,847	31.07	15.6	33.90	52.03
II–f	5,427	23.53	25.2	29.71	0.82
II–g	1,819	20.65	18.9	31.11	
II–h	1,851	17.44	32.5	43.13	14.01
II–i	1,904	22.23	30.9	39.73	7.46
II–j	2,380	25.76	20.1	29.93	5.14
II–k	1,087	32.44	6.4	23.87	25.81
M	$2,676.82	$ 23.08	18.40	31.07	31.42
σ	1,265.02	4.86	8.49	5.74	25.78
d_m	2,041.27	33.28	9.74	1.51	26.21
σd	791.95	10.25	3.67	2.85	8.25
t value					
Obtained	2.58	3.25	2.65	0.53	3.18
1% level	2.85	2.85	2.85	2.85	2.85
5% level	2.09	2.09	2.09	2.09	2.09

Sources: Value of Farms from U. S. Bureau of the Census, *United States Census of Agriculture: 1935*, Vol. I.

Farm Mortgages from U. S. Bureau of the Census, *Fifteenth Census of the United States: 1930 Agriculture*, Vol. II, Part 2.

Population on Marginal Land. Virginia State Planning Board, *Land Use and Agriculture*, Vol. IV-A, Sections 1 and 2.

the mortgage to the value of the farm was about the same in both groups. The last column of Table 21 shows that six times as high a percentage of rural population lived on marginal or sub-marginal land in the Group II counties as in the Group I counties—a difference which is highly significant.

Table 22 shows the percentage of nonfarm population who rent homes that paid less than $15 per month rent and the percentage of owners living in nonfarm homes who valued their homes at less than $3,000. In both cases, the Group I counties make the best showing, although the difference in means is of doubtful significance for the former item, and of no significance for the latter.

ANNUAL INCOME

Figures on the annual income of the people living in any county are impossible to secure. A number of indexes might be used, but some of these have serious shortcomings for this study. Retail sales and payrolls, for example, are available from the Census of Business,[10] but these data would have little significance in the case of these twenty-two counties. In the present day, trade has little relation to county boundaries. Also, many workers earn their livelihood in a political subdivision other than the one in which they live, particularly in communities near large cities. Four of the counties have large independent cities within their boundaries which draw trade and workers from a large area. Either inclusion or exclusion of figures for these cities in adding the county totals would be apt to distort the true facts. One county is largely suburban to a city in another political unit, and several depend largely on stores and industries in near-by cities for goods and work. Sales and payroll figures were discarded as unsound for purposes of comparing the two groups of counties in this study.

One good index of income is provided, however, by the number of state income tax returns made in each county. Virginia requires all single persons who have a net income of $1,000 or more and all married couples with a net income of $2,000 or more to pay a state income tax. The number of residents of each county who pay a tax is published annually. The number of such returns per 1,000 population as enu-

[10] United States Department of Commerce, Bureau of Foreign and Domestic Commerce, *Census of Business,* 1935.

Table 22

PERCENTAGE OF RENTED NONFARM HOMES RENTING FOR LESS THAN
$15.00 PER MONTH AND OF OWNED HOMES VALUED AT
LESS THAN $3,000.00, SELECTED COUNTIES,
VIRGINIA, 1930

County	Per Cent Renting for Less than $15.00	Per Cent Valued at Less than $3,000.00
Group I. Most-Participating Counties		
I–a	71.1	58.3
I–b	72.1	46.3
I–c	76.7	64.7
I–d	43.6	35.2
I–e	39.1	35.7
I–f	85.1	88.2
I–g	47.5	47.4
I–h	59.8	55.0
I–i	66.7	56.0
I–j	38.0	31.4
I–k	81.7	67.5
M	61.95	53.25
σ	16.51	15.91
Group II. Least-Participating Counties		
II–a	55.1	50.3
II–b	89.7	76.0
II–c	78.1	53.1
II–d	79.1	47.4
II–e	70.0	56.9
II–f	90.0	52.5
II–g	88.3	69.6
II–h	58.1	52.0
II–i	73.7	47.4
II–j	78.4	69.4
II–k	84.4	61.6
M	76.81	57.84
σ	11.35	9.42
d_m	14.86	4.59
σ_d	6.34	5.85
t value		
Obtained	2.34	0.79
1% level	2.85	2.85
5% level	2.09	2.09

Source: U. S. Bureau of the Census, *Fifteenth Census of the United States: 1930. Population*, Vol. VI.

merated in the 1930 census is shown in Table 23 for the years 1930, 1934, and 1938.

It will be observed from this table that proportionately from two to three times as many persons had taxable net income in the most-participating group of counties as in the least-participating group. Table 24, giving the analysis of variance for these data, shows a highly

Table 23

NUMBER OF PERSONS PER 1,000 POPULATION PAYING STATE INCOME TAX, SELECTED COUNTIES, VIRGINIA, 1930, 1934, 1938

County	1930	1934	1938
Group I. Most-Participating Counties			
I–a	13.009	8.710	16.678
I–b	7.012	3.781	8.628
I–c	2.724	2.294	5.447
I–d	13.022	10.885	25.491
I–e	37.215	30.320	64.995
I–f	2.232	0.394	2.232
I–g	11.888	8.110	12.996
I–h	7.912	5.086	12.067
I–i	14.059	4.902	7.272
I–j	21.225	11.222	23.237
I–k	4.132	5.207	5.868
Mean	12.220	8.264	16.810
Group II. Least-Participating Counties			
II–a	17.697	8.603	11.429
II–b	1.492	0.166	0.995
II–c	2.091	0.239	4.719
II–d	3.369	4.492	4.492
II–e	12.346	7.467	13.463
II–f	0.884	0.663	1.768
II–g	3.285	1.468	3.884
II–h	8.109	4.126	6.971
II–i	5.640	2.452	5.273
II–j	4.466	3.181	4.711
II–k	6.508	3.322	6.293
Mean	5.989	3.289	5.814

Sources: Tax Returns from Virginia State Department of Taxation, *Report of the Department of Taxation.* Population from U. S. Bureau of the Census, *Fifteenth Census of the United States: 1930. Population,* Vol. I.

Table 24

ANALYSIS OF VARIANCE OF TOTAL NUMBER OF PERSONS PER 1,000 POPULATION PAYING
A STATE INCOME TAX (TABLE 23)

Source of Variation	Sum of Squares	df	Mean Square	F Values		
				Obtained	5% Level	1% Level
Between two groups of counties	903.75	1	903.75	10.36	4.00	7.08
Among years	341.66	2	170.83	1.96	3.15	4.98
Among counties in one group or for one year (Error)	5,234.87	60	87.25			
Interaction	110.95	2	55.48	1.57	19.47	99.48
Total	6,591.23	65				

significant difference between the two groups of counties with respect to the number of persons per thousand of population who paid state income tax.

GENERAL PROGRESSIVENESS

Extensive participation in a curriculum program may be an indication of a spirit of progressiveness which exists among the people of a county. Perhaps counties which engage extensively in curriculum revision work also participate in other activities and programs of a forward-looking nature.

It is, of course, impossible to get any measure of progressiveness; authorities disagree as to what constitutes progress and what persons best exemplify enterprise. Even if a list of factors were selected as indexes, valid measures of them would be difficult to secure in most cases. While it seems futile to try to measure progressiveness, some comparison of the two groups of counties with respect to adoption of new services, participation in other programs of a voluntary nature, and cooperation in stimulative programs may be helpful for this study.

Table 25 shows the number of counties in each of the two groups and in the state as a whole which have participated in specified programs of service. Except for the farm bureau and the grange, all of these

Table 25

NUMBER OF THE SELECTED COUNTIES WHICH ARE COOPERATING IN VOLUNTARY
PROGRAMS OF SERVICE

Service	Group I Counties	Group II Counties	State Total
Total number of counties	11	11	100
Participated in state-aid program of special education, 1938–39	6	0	17
Will participate in state-aid program of special education, 1939–40	8	0	32
Employed rural elementary school supervisors, 1938–39	11	0	75
Will employ rural elementary school supervisors, 1939–40	11	2	72
Maintained a local health unit, 1939	6	4	45
Employed county farm demonstration agent, 1939	11	11	99
Employed county home demonstration agent, 1939	9	5	60
Maintained child welfare service, 1939	2	1	9
Had county farm bureau, 1939	3	2	26
Had farm grange organization, 1939	5	1	25

Sources:
Virginia State Department of Education, Division of Rehabilitation, Special and Adult Education, *Special Education*, cover page.
Virginia State Board of Education, "Supervisors of Elementary Education," Mimeograph Lists, 1938–39, 1939–40.
Virginia State Department of Health, "County and District Health Departments in State of Virginia." Typed statement on file in office.
Virginia Cooperative Extension Work in Agriculture and Home Economics. Mimeographed list of County Demonstration Agents.
Virginia State Department of Public Welfare. List of counties maintaining Child Welfare Service. Typed statement.
Virginia Farm Bureau Federation, "County Farm Bureaus." Typed statement.
Virginia State Grange, *Official Roster*, 1939.

activities are subsidized by state aid, and the county may voluntarily take on these services if it so desires. The program of special education was inaugurated in 1938-39. Under this plan state aid is granted to cooperating school divisions for the purchase of materials and supplies for a program of education for mentally and physically handicapped children. Six Group I counties participated in the first year and eight plan to participate in 1939-40, while none of the Group II counties

Table 26

NUMBER OF PASSENGER AUTOMOBILES, RADIOS, RESIDENTIAL TELEPHONES, AND
DOMESTIC ELECTRIC METERS, AND THE CIRCULATION OF 12 NATIONAL
MAGAZINES, PER 100 FAMILIES, SELECTED COUNTIES, VIRGINIA

County	Passenger Cars Registered 1936	Radios 1938	Residential Telephones 1935	Domestic Electric Meters 1930	Circulation 12 National Magazines 1937
Group I. Most-Participating Counties					
I–a	71[a]	76[a]	30[a]	10	29
I–b	49	64	10	16	31
I–c	57	60	8	6	30
I–d	87	70	30	30	43
I–e	70[a]	97[a]	50[a]	26	117
I–f	59	58	1	3	14
I–g	74	66	27	17	54
I–h	50[b]	93[b]	36[b]	21	65
I–i	55	70	10	28	51
I–j	68[a]	95[a]	46[a]	72	80
I–k	56	64	9	20	29
M	63.27	73.91	23.36	22.64	49.36
σ	11.14	13.76	15.90	17.68	27.98
Group II. Least-Participating Counties					
II–a	61	67	37	23	43
II–b	38	63	1	3	26
II–c	29	61		6	28
II–d	50	63	21	9	31
II–e	80	64	12	9	41
II–f	55	61	52	6	46
II–g	51	63	5	6	26
II–h	41	62	6	18	28
II–i	44	62	7	12	33
II–j	49	62	5	3	30
II–k	33	72	8	30	42
M	48.27	63.64	14.00	11.36	34.00
σ	13.51	3.08	15.67	8.34	7.16
d_m	15.00	10.27	9.36	11.28	15.36
σ_d	5.54	4.47	7.04	6.16	9.14
t values					
Obtained	2.71	2.30	1.33	1.83	1.68
1% level	2.85	2.85	2.85	2.85	2.85
5% level	2.09	2.09	2.09	2.09	2.09

Source: U. S. Department of Commerce, Bureau of Foreign and Domestic Commerce,
Consumer Market Data Handbook, 1939 Edition.

[a] Includes independent city located within county.

[b] Includes three independent cities located within county.

are cooperating. Rural supervision is discussed more fully in Chapter VI. The State Department of Health aids counties in maintaining local health units if they wish to establish a full-time service meeting certain minimum requirements. Six Group I counties and four Group II counties cooperated in the maintenance of such units. County demonstration agents are supported from state, federal, and county funds. Every county in the state except one urban center had a farm demonstration agent. Nine Group I counties and five Group II counties had home demonstration agents. Child welfare service is subsidized by the Department of Public Welfare from federal and state funds. Two Group I counties and one Group II county had such service. County farm bureaus were found in three Group I counties and two Group II counties and granges in five and one county respectively.

Nothing conclusive can be proved from the data, but insofar as these items indicate a spirit of progressiveness or at least the willingness of a county to cooperate in providing services considered to be desirable, the most-participating or Group I counties made the best showing. Undoubtedly the greater average per-capita wealth and income of these counties influenced and may account entirely for the differences that existed.

Another type of comparison which may prove interesting in this connection is that of the extent of material comforts found in the homes of people living in these two groups of counties. Information on the number of passenger cars registered, the number of families having a radio or radios, the number of residential telephones and domestic electric meters, and the circulation of twelve popular magazines per 100 families is available.[11] Table 26 gives these figures for the two groups of counties. Figures for automobiles, radios, and telephones include independent cities where such exist within any of the counties. While Group I counties show a much larger average number of these five comforts per 100 families, none of the differences are statistically significant, because of high variation among counties within a group.

SUMMARY

In this chapter, several important differences and a number of important likenesses in geographic, sociologic, and economic condi-

[11] United States Department of Commerce, Bureau of Foreign and Domestic Commerce, *Consumer Market Data Handbook, 1939 Edition,* pp. 428-437.

tions were shown to have existed between the group of counties which have participated most extensively and the group which have participated least in the Virginia curriculum program.

DIFFERENCES

The chief differences were as follows:

1. The most-participating group of counties far exceeded the least-participating group in the amount of wealth subject to local taxation per pupil enrolled in public schools.

2. The most-participating group of counties had a much higher per-capital wealth than did the least-participating counties.

3. Although both groups of counties were highly rural, farms and farm land per acre were worth much more in the most-participating counties than in the least-participating counties. There is also evidence, although not conclusive, that renters living in the towns paid more rent per family in the most-participating counties than did families in the least-participating counties.

4. A much larger proportion of the population paid state income tax in the most-participating counties than in the least-participating counties, which means that a much larger percentage had if single net incomes of $1,000 or more and if married net incomes of $2,000 or more per year.

5. While it is difficult to measure the rural or urban character of a county, partly because of the fact that in Virginia large cities are politically coordinate in rank with counties and are treated independently in all governmental and census data, and the fact that present-day ease of travel erases division lines between political units with respect to cultural and social influence, there is substantial evidence of both a subjective and a statistical nature that the least-participating counties, in the main, were much more rural and provincial, and in fact, geographically isolated than the most-participating counties.

6. Coupled with the rural character and isolation of the least-participating group of counties is evidence to indicate that a somewhat general lack of progressiveness and of ability or desire to participate in state enterprises usually considered to be for the betterment and advancement of the people existed.

7. While the difference is not conclusively established, the most

participating group of counties had less illiteracy among white persons.

LIKENESSES

The important likenesses of the two groups of counties may be summarized as follows:

1. Although great variations occurred among individual counties, the counties as groups showed no reliable difference in distance from a curriculum center. It is possible that great distance was associated with lack of participation, but on the other hand, proximity was not a facilitating factor.

2. Size of a county either in land area or in population and hence density of population was not associated with the extent of participation.

3. Composition of the population as to race, nativity, or age was not a distinguishing characteristic of participation.

4. The two groups of counties were not unlike in the extent of employment and both groups of counties were alike in that most persons were engaged in agricultural pursuits.

5. In both groups of counties approximately the same proportion of families owned their homes and about the same proportion of farmers owned their own farms.

6. No important differences existed with respect to stability of the population as measured by length of tenure of both owners and renters of farms.

7. About an equally large percentage of home owners valued their homes at less than $3,000.

8. Possession of automobiles, radios, telephones and electric lights, and subscription to national magazines of wide circulation by families, while showing wide variation from county to county, was not a distinguishing characteristic of the two groups of counties.

CHAPTER V

Likenesses and Differences in the Educational Program

INVESTIGATION of the likenesses and differences between the group of most-participating and the group of least-participating counties in pertinent aspects of the educational program is important for this study. This chapter presents evidence on these characteristic likenesses and differences.

EXPENDITURES FOR INSTRUCTION

PER-PUPIL EXPENDITURES FOR INSTRUCTION

The two groups of counties were compared on the cost per pupil enrolled of instruction in white elementary schools. Instructional cost is used as an accounting item in Virginia to include salaries paid teachers, principals, and supervisors, expenditures for free textbooks, instructional supplies, and materials, and traveling expenses of supervisors and vocational teachers. Number of pupils enrolled was used as the factor to reduce these expenditures to a comparable basis. These figures on per-pupil expenditures for instructional costs in white elementary schools for Group I, the most-participating counties, and Group II, the least-participating counties, for the eight year period of 1930-1938[1] are given in Table 27.

These data were compared by means of the analysis of variance, which is shown in Table 28.

It is apparent from this analysis that these two groups of counties are not random samples from the same population. In other words, the most-participating counties differed significantly from the least-partici-

[1] The year 1938-39 is not included in these data, since a different method of reporting per-pupil costs was used in the annual report for that year.

Table 27

COST OF INSTRUCTION PER PUPIL ENROLLED, WHITE ELEMENTARY SCHOOLS, SELECTED COUNTIES, VIRGINIA, 1930–38

County	1930-31	1931-32	1932-33	1933-34	1934-35	1935-36	1936-37	1937-38
Group I. Most-Participating Counties								
I-a	$22.83	$20.55	$18.26	$17.11	$16.60	$18.06	$20.04	$21.11
I-b	22.24	18.49	16.25	15.90	18.15	17.52	16.09	21.82
I-c	21.00	19.58	18.17	16.56	17.75	16.91	18.45	22.72
I-d	24.36	23.46	23.65	24.20	23.62	24.43	24.32	25.63
I-e	29.10	27.54	25.23	23.77	24.14	24.59	26.66	31.93
I-f	25.33	23.50	20.73	19.23	21.58	20.03	21.34	22.40
I-g	27.41	26.74	26.24	22.86	23.68	22.81	29.94	24.92
I-h	33.09	30.61	26.44	24.70	22.50	26.21	26.51	26.98
I-i	36.43	38.92	28.85	30.95	33.47	23.47	29.12	32.01
I-j	18.97	19.25	15.47	17.79	17.03	18.45	19.98	20.86
I-k	41.00	25.35	29.40	30.97	34.72	37.92	37.25	39.58
Mean	$27.43	$24.91	$22.61	$22.19	$23.02	$22.76	$24.52	$26.36
Group II. Least-Participating Counties								
II-a	$25.26	$24.11	$22.72	$20.40	$20.96	$21.75	$23.11	$23.57
II-b	21.47	15.73	13.35	11.89	12.37	14.62	12.76	14.00
II-c	15.59	14.74	13.27	15.30	13.24	13.98	14.25	10.35
II-d	15.82	14.17	11.85	10.27	11.91	13.26	14.00	15.28
II-e	16.42	17.00	16.50	16.00	20.00	18.77	21.00	21.00
II-f	25.35	24.30	21.77	19.83	21.54	20.89	21.47	21.34
II-g	22.02	20.59	17.42	15.36	17.37	16.15	19.97	20.95
II-h	22.95	20.75	18.45	18.07	20.32	22.18	22.12	21.89
II-i	20.34	18.82	18.81	16.90	18.59	19.34	18.91	23.39
II-j	18.04	15.90	15.94	15.45	15.01	17.95	18.56	18.28
II-k	17.70	16.47	14.88	15.28	15.18	14.84	19.23	17.06
Mean	20.09	$18.42	$16.81	$15.89	$16.95	$17.61	$18.67	$18.83

Source: Virginia State Board of Education, *Annual Report of the Superintendent of Public Instruction.*

Table 28

ANALYSIS OF VARIANCE OF COST OF INSTRUCTION PER PUPIL ENROLLED, WHITE
ELEMENTARY SCHOOLS (TABLE 27)

Source of Variation	Sum of Squares	df	Mean Square	F Values		
				Obtained	5% Level	1% Level
Between two groups of counties	1,755.32	1	1,755.32	72.87	3.91	6.81
Among years	399.21	7	57.03	2.37	2.07	2.76
Among counties in one group for one year ..	3,854.27	160	24.09			
Interaction	24.01	7	3.43	7.02	3.25	5.70
Total	6,032.81	175				

pating in the per-pupil expenditures for instruction in white elementary schools. The mean of the per-pupil cost for the counties of Group I for the eight-year period was $24.22 and for the least-participating group it was $17.91. An examination of Table 27 shows that not a single county in Group II expended as much per pupil as the average expenditure for Group I counties in any one of the eight years, except that County II–a slightly exceeded the Group I mean in 1932-33. It is interesting to note that these large differences existed prior to the initiation of the curriculum program in 1931-32 and that the difference does not seem to be accentuated in the years since its inception.

The above data are for the cost of instruction in white elementary schools only, in accordance with the limitations of this study, but it seemed advisable nevertheless to compare total current expenditures per pupil in all schools, white and Negro, elementary and secondary. This would be a comparison of over-all current costs for all children and would show the adequacy, as measured by expenditure per pupil, of the educational program in the counties. These figures are given in Table 29. A comparison of these data by an analysis of variance gives the results shown in Table 30.

Again in this comparison a highly significant difference between the two groups of counties is found. The variance between the two groups of counties remains practically the same as in the case of instructional

Table 29

CURRENT EXPENDITURES PER PUPIL ENROLLED, ALL SCHOOLS, SELECTED COUNTIES, VIRGINIA, 1930–38

County	1930–31	1931–32	1932–33	1933–34	1934–35	1935–36	1936–37	1937–38
Group I. Most-Participating Counties								
I–a	$37.09	$26.48	$30.33	$29.60	$28.27	$27.54	$30.07	$36.57
I–b	32.79	29.42	26.40	25.62	28.05	31.38	34.21	30.47
I–c	30.86	29.54	26.96	25.26	26.21	28.59	31.87	36.89
I–d	37.79	38.28	35.35	35.37	35.70	36.80	38.14	41.63
I–e	43.71	46.93	36.73	43.85	45.06	45.49	50.59	53.89
I–f	26.51	24.84	21.82	21.88	24.57	24.69	28.54	27.99
I–g	40.92	38.74	34.67	33.62	32.31	33.39	37.66	43.53
I–h	39.27	36.23	38.50	34.81	36.86	30.70	33.62	36.19
I–i	51.89	39.69	33.99	34.21	38.61	44.07	38.23	41.41
I–j	30.98	30.15	23.96	28.48	28.94	31.13	31.76	38.42
I–k	31.07	29.00	25.41	28.64	30.07	31.14	34.15	35.93
Mean	$36.63	$33.57	$30.37	$31.03	$32.24	$33.17	$35.35	$38.45
Group II. Least-Participating Counties								
II–a	$44.30	$44.98	$41.73	$39.83	$42.34	$42.27	$44.45	$43.70
II–b	28.83	24.91	29.35	18.51	28.66	26.21	40.74	30.00
II–c	19.13	18.48	16.17	19.81	17.25	18.14	18.17	13.82
II–d	32.59	34.81	24.02	25.62	36.68	36.12	33.33	41.25
II–e	35.46	27.97	19.00	27.00	28.00	25.00	27.00	25.00
II–f	40.09	37.05	35.05	30.87	34.19	32.53	34.67	38.48
II–g	28.68	24.87	23.91	21.99	24.55	25.49	29.49	30.95
II–h	25.79	24.11	21.50	20.56	24.12	25.80	28.70	28.55
II–i	23.62	20.23	19.00	19.03	20.93	15.91	24.29	24.41
II–j	24.68	21.63	20.45	21.29	21.18	22.84	25.02	27.13
II–k	26.77	27.15	22.31	22.73	21.04	21.46	23.70	26.55
Mean	$29.99	$27.84	$24.78	$24.29	$27.18	$26.52	$29.96	$29.99

Source: Virginia State Board of Education, *Annual Report of the Superintendent of Public Instruction.*

Table 30

ANALYSIS OF VARIANCE OF CURRENT EXPENDITURES PER PUPIL ENROLLED, ALL SCHOOLS
(TABLE 29)

Source of Variation	Sum of Squares	df	Mean Square	F Values		
				Obtained	5% Level	1% Level
Between two groups of counties	1,736.29	1	1,736.29	34.44	3.91	6.81
Among years	961.57	7	137.37	2.73	2.07	2.76
Among counties in one group for one year ..	8,066.34	160	50.41			
Interaction	45.25	7	6.46	7.80	3.25	5.70
Total	10,809.45	175				

costs in white elementary schools, but the variance within a group for each year has increased. From these two comparisons it is evident that the most-participating counties on the whole spent significantly more per pupil for both instruction and all current costs than did the least-participating counties.

CURRENT EXPENSES LOCALLY RAISED PER $1,000
OF LOCALLY TAXABLE WEALTH

The two groups of counties were compared with respect to the effort they made in supporting education. The accepted effort formula is:[2]

$$\text{Effort to Support Education} = \frac{\text{Amount Spent for Education}}{\text{Financial Resources}}$$

The "amount spent for education" should be the amount of current expenditures raised by the school unit under consideration. For the county school systems in Virginia this was found by subtracting the amount of state aid for schools from the current expenditures for school purposes. Since all state aid in Virginia must be used in paying instructional costs the total amount should be deducted from total current expenditures to determine the amount raised locally. County school districts do have a very small income on occasion from other

[2] National Education Association, Research Division, *The Efforts of the States to Support Education*, Research Bulletin, Vol. 14, No. 3, p. 111.

non-local sources which may be used for current expenses. These are accounted for under "Receipts from Other Funds," but since this accounting item also covers some current receipts from local sources and some non-local receipts for capital outlay, it was impractical to try to segregate the non-local receipts usable for current expenses for deduction from total current expenditures. The amount of such non-local revenues usable for current expenses is so small in any case that its inclusion can have little effect on the data. Gifts from foundations and grants from the Jeanes and Slater funds for Negro education are examples of this type of income. The numerator of the effort fraction, then, was secured for each county by deducting from its total current disbursements for school purposes for the year the total amount of state school aid granted during the year.

For a measure of financial resources, the figures for wealth locally taxable, which were used to determine the amount of wealth per pupil in Chapter IV, were utilized. These figures give the total estimated true value of all property subject to local taxation, and hence constitute the best measure of ability to support public education. In calculating effort by means of the above formula each $1,000 of wealth was used as the denominator of the fraction. These data on the efforts of the two groups of counties to support public education—that is, current expenditures raised locally per $1,000 of locally taxable wealth—are given in Table 31. As a group the least-participating counties have made more effort as measured by this formula to support education than have the most-participating counties. In all nine years except 1931-32, they spent more money locally raised for current expenses per $1,000 of wealth than did the Group I counties. The means of the county figures for the entire period were $3.727 for the Group II counties and $3.472 for the Group I counties. The difference is $0.255 or 7.3 per cent of the smaller figure.

When these measures of effort, however, were tested for the significance of difference between the two groups of counties by means of the analysis of variance no significant difference was found. The F ratio of the variance between groups to the error variance is 3.27, hence such a difference in effort between the groups could occur in more than five per cent of such random samples of two groups of counties selected on the criterion of extent of participation in a state curriculum program.

Table 31

EFFORT TO SUPPORT PUBLIC EDUCATION: CURRENT SCHOOL EXPENDITURES LOCALLY RAISED PER $1,000 OF LOCALLY TAXABLE WEALTH, SELECTED COUNTIES, VIRGINIA, 1930–39

County	1930–31	1931–32	1932–33	1933–34	1934–35	1935–36	1936–37	1937–38	1938–39
Group I. Most-Participating Counties									
I-a	$2.259	$2.275	$2.268	$2.506	$2.819	$2.668	$3.098	$3.207	$3.354
I-b	4.581	3.762	3.304	3.803	4.128	4.622	4.433	4.777	4.593
I-c	2.753	3.254	2.871	3.230	3.994	4.125	4.255	5.026	5.329
I-d	2.318	2.179	2.245	2.563	2.392	2.518	2.465	2.573	2.440
I-e	2.939	3.367	2.390	2.409	2.108	2.445	2.446	2.679	2.754
I-f	5.264	3.931	3.296	3.862	4.292	3.504	2.939	3.128	2.965
I-g	3.177	3.198	2.984	3.108	2.654	2.843	3.309	3.399	3.602
I-h	4.930	4.583	4.039	3.896	3.833	3.969	4.182	4.752	5.168
I-i	3.079	2.903	2.430	2.943	3.309	4.025	4.627	5.066	3.779
I-j	2.399	2.601	2.175	2.763	3.085	3.752	3.980	4.518	4.066
I-k	4.258	4.224	3.467	4.200	4.210	4.714	4.932	4.485	4.500
Mean	$3.451	$3.298	$2.861	$3.208	$3.348	$3.562	$3.697	$3.962	$3.868
Group II. Least-Participating Counties									
II-a	$3.131	$3.444	$3.525	$3.695	$3.653	$3.350	$4.515	$4.241	$4.655
II-b	2.978	2.397	2.267	2.638	2.353	2.379	2.903	3.047	4.694
II-c	2.066	1.827	1.626	3.306	2.686	3.128	2.861	3.080	1.759
II-d	3.879	3.490	2.837	3.146	2.683	3.435	2.915	4.117	3.359
II-e	3.308	2.868	2.809	3.040	3.570	3.677	3.508	3.170	4.017
II-f	3.149	3.100	3.202	2.993	2.898	3.157	3.262	3.737	3.969
II-g	3.379	3.557	3.021	3.251	3.670	3.907	3.977	4.030	5.498
II-h	4.290	4.060	4.255	4.656	5.063	5.293	5.139	5.335	6.594
II-i	3.675	3.025	3.317	3.391	4.092	4.030	4.029	5.153	5.440
II-j	3.107	2.425	2.620	2.984	2.539	3.434	3.347	3.836	4.088
II-k	5.292	5.353	4.169	5.852	5.282	5.347	6.141	7.975	8.582
Mean	$3.478	$3.231	$3.059	$3.541	$3.499	$3.740	$3.872	$4.338	$4.787

Source: Virginia State Board of Education, *Annual Report of the Superintendent of Public Instruction.*

The conclusion is that there was not a significant difference between the groups of counties on effort. This analysis is shown in Table 32.

Table 32

ANALYSIS OF VARIANCE OF EFFORT TO SUPPORT PUBLIC EDUCATION (TABLE 31)

Source of Variation	Sum of Squares	df	Mean Square	F Values		
				Obtained	5% Level	1% Level
Between two groups of counties	3.208	1	3.208	3.27	3.89	6.76
Among years	32.813	8	4.102	4.19	1.98	2.60
Among counties in one group for one year ..	176.367	180	.980			
Interaction	3.536	8	.442	2.22	2.96	4.91
Total	215.924	197				

DEPENDENCE ON STATE AID

In Virginia, state funds allocated to the local school divisions must be used for payment of salaries of teachers, supervisors, and principals, except for very minor grants for vocational education equipment and, in recent years, for music equipment.[3] Most of this state aid is apportioned on the basis of teaching units, which are defined as each group of twenty-five to forty pupils, the exact figure being determined by a scheme set up by the State Board of Education which takes into account the density of population. No discrimination is made against Negro children in calculating teaching units. A small percentage of state-aid funds for salaries is distributed on other bases, such as payment of part of the contracted salaries of supervisors and vocational education teachers.

In Virginia it is often charged that under the present state aid plan counties less willing to support schools raise little or no local revenues for instruction, paying teachers largely from state funds. It is also claimed that instructional costs for Negro schools are maintained on a low level in some divisions and state funds allocated on the basis of Negro children are used to lighten the burden for white teachers'

[3] Virginia State Board of Education, *School Laws*, p. 56, 1936.

Table 33

PERCENTAGE OF SALARIES OF INSTRUCTIONAL STAFF DERIVED FROM STATE FUNDS, SELECTED COUNTIES, VIRGINIA, 1930-39

County	1930-31	1931-32	1932-33	1933-34	1934-35	1935-36	1936-37	1937-38	1938-39
Group I. Most-Participating Counties									
I-a	70.68	72.67	73.61	68.40	71.62	77.00	76.86	70.40	69.86
I-b	54.03	60.96	60.08	55.33	62.95	58.43	65.70	65.19	73.45
I-c	84.66	82.35	83.26	78.04	73.30	77.87	83.23	83.52	82.13
I-d	51.13	53.40	43.97	37.50	46.72	45.50	49.69	50.62	52.06
I-e	42.11	40.34	41.35	36.71	50.51	47.48	46.60	41.22	42.62
I-f	79.19	86.81	85.86	80.64	77.72	85.83	92.30	89.84	92.68
I-g	44.81	45.78	43.97	42.59	55.02	53.05	51.53	52.18	54.68
I-h	41.64	43.23	43.28	39.41	47.46	46.40	48.97	44.69	47.40
I-i	49.58	52.65	56.70	50.97	54.45	47.58	44.56	43.63	54.08
I-j	52.61	48.66	51.17	43.31	53.13	46.69	50.24	45.87	56.72
I-k	67.04	69.93	74.21	66.65	67.75	64.48	67.08	72.67	78.08
Mean	57.95	59.71	59.77	54.50	60.06	59.12	61.52	59.98	63.98
Group II. Least-Participating Counties									
II-a	46.93	47.06	42.32	43.25	59.93	64.13	56.17	60.49	64.81
II-b	64.93	66.92	68.16	63.03	83.39	90.55	88.83	95.20	84.18
II-c	72.06	74.26	77.18	56.48	68.19	68.43	70.37	68.80	93.66
II-d	69.73	78.77	76.55	74.39	84.89	74.10	83.70	75.01	89.56
II-e	80.86	83.18	76.96	70.67	69.87	72.55	79.59	82.17	83.37
II-f	52.17	54.92	55.18	52.43	62.87	61.86	67.92	64.06	66.11
II-g	83.76	83.90	87.04	83.34	86.08	83.00	89.07	89.85	81.42
II-h	63.63	70.28	67.80	62.23	70.59	70.93	77.59	77.68	70.31
II-i	75.20	82.13	77.28	76.04	79.25	74.84	77.42	70.39	75.04
II-j	65.66	74.77	67.69	61.09	79.83	69.27	73.59	72.99	76.76
II-k	52.17	55.05	61.61	51.55	56.86	58.14	59.25	53.17	60.07
Mean	66.10	70.11	68.89	63.13	72.89	71.62	74.86	73.62	76.84

Source: Virginia State Board of Education, *Annual Report of the Superintendent of Public Instruction.*

salaries. In either case the effect is to decrease the percentage of instructional salaries raised locally. Beginning in 1936, the state aid appropriation law required local divisions to pay at least twenty per cent or, in exceptional cases, ten per cent of instructional costs; this requirement was raised to thirty and twenty per cent for the biennium 1938-40. Percentages showing the extent to which counties depend on state funds for the payment of salaries of the instructional staff should give, therefore, an indication of the willingness, or unwillingness, of the citizens of a county to tax themselves so they might pay better salaries to teachers. Such data for the two groups of counties included in this study are given in Table 33.

In general the most-participating counties went beyond state aid to a much greater extent than did the least-participating counties in providing better salaries for the instructional staff. The mean percentage of instructional costs derived from state funds over the nine-year period for the Group I counties was 59.67 per cent, while it was 70.97 per cent for the least-participating group, a difference of 11.30 per cent. This difference, when tested by an analysis of variance, as shown in Table 34, is found to be highly significant. These two groups of coun-

Table 34

ANALYSIS OF VARIANCE OF PERCENTAGE OF SALARIES OF INSTRUCTIONAL STAFF
DERIVED FROM STATE AID (TABLE 33)

Source of Variation	Sum of Squares	df	Mean Square	F Values		
				Obtained	5% Level	1% Level
Between two groups of counties	6,292.44	1	6,292.44	33.42	3.89	6.76
Among years	2,022.81	8	252.85	1.34	1.98	2.60
Among counties in one group for one year ..	33,890.84	180	188.28			
Interaction	318.67	8	39.83	4.73	2.96	4.91
Total	42,524.76	197				

ties are not random samples from the same population, so it is evident that groups of counties selected as extremes on the criterion of participation in the Virginia state curriculum program differed significantly in the percentage of instructional costs derived from state aid, with the least-participating group depending most extensively on state funds.

LIBRARIES AND TEXTBOOKS

Library facilities and expenditures for library books in the two groups of counties are particularly important items for investigation. The type of curriculum organization recommended in the tentative course of study developed as a part of the program encourages, and, in fact, almost requires the wide use of reference books and supplementary reading material.

Since 1908 Virginia has had state aid for the purchase of school library books. Under the plan in effect during most of the period covered by this study, 1930-1939, the State Department of Education, through its division of school libraries and textbooks, has added ten dollars to each thirty dollars sent it by local school divisions for the purchase of a forty-dollar unit of library books. But beginning July 1, 1938, the law was changed to provide that the state should pay one-half of the cost of each sixty-dollar unit order; also instead of granting aid on all orders as they were received until the state fund was exhausted, as was formerly true, an allocation scheme was initiated and efforts were made to get all counties to use their allotments.

Table 35 shows that the most-participating counties as a group spent on the average far more per 100 pupils for library books each year during the period from 1930 to 1939 than did the least-participating counties. Except for the year 1938-39, the per-pupil expenditure in the former group of counties was about two to three times as great as it was in the least-participating group, and even for the last year of the period, after the Group I counties had made heavy investments in library materials for four years previously they spent over one-and-one-half times as much per pupil. These figures, moreover, are for all schools, white and Negro, elementary and high school, since it was impossible to segregate expenditures on these bases. There is some indication that the difference would be more pronounced if figures on the amount of money spent exclusively for elementary schools had been used, and even more so for white elementary schools. The figures given here represent only expenditures by the local divisions, and hence do not show additional book purchases made available by state matching.

Table 35

EXPENDITURE BY LOCAL DIVISION FOR LIBRARY BOOKS PER 100 PUPILS ENROLLED, ALL SCHOOLS, SELECTED COUNTIES, VIRGINIA, 1930-39

County	1930-31	1931-32	1932-33	1933-34	1934-35	1935-36	1936-37	1937-38	1938-39
Group I. Most-Participating Counties									
I-a	$64.357	$26.476	$11.321	$17.275	$15.792	$27.734	$43.151	$46.468	$26.472
I-b	4.330	5.661	6.911	17.913	10.237	23.318	18.295	18.655	31.919
I-c	12.490	4.478	7.994	19.750	13.226	34.566	31.075	43.773	27.531
I-d	15.160	11.958	7.241	8.961	19.466	22.600	33.076	34.467	28.044
I-e	18.203	22.102	4.317	12.960	34.667	40.473	30.552	48.465	57.127
I-f	8.325	5.228	4.437	12.554	19.284	26.857	29.079	24.988	20.715
I-g	23.003	17.472	11.794	5.271	47.395	10.787	16.946	24.270	21.578
I-h	14.060	7.059	4.665	2.164	19.487	11.391	34.776	33.068	22.590
I-i	14.562	3.441	10.729	23.676	45.581	109.104	91.744	86.473	31.601
I-j	15.022	27.913	10.774	8.455	27.062	27.469	36.413	32.723	31.820
I-k	9.533	13.162	5.103	19.549	37.591	51.529	46.300	33.193	55.979
Mean	$18.095	$13.177	$7.762	$13.503	$26.353	$35.075	$37.401	$38.777	$32.307
Group II. Least-Participating Counties									
II-a	$16.391	$27.680	$22.871	$9.630	$24.300	$27.998	$29.797	$26.691	$27.609
II-b			16.600		4.397	8.200	7.230	29.215	12.034
II-c	4.435	3.608	1.161	4.049	3.662	4.278	11.461	14.245	12.045
II-d	4.125	4.874	3.250	6.772	9.733	6.594	14.214	24.644	22.531
II-e	2.954	10.018	1.341	3.687	8.084	7.747	19.717	10.224	20.273
II-f	14.440	0.386	5.701	12.638	3.002	47.442	38.119	39.557	55.077
II-g	0.427				1.388	33.893	18.895	14.289	38.212
II-h	4.692	3.629	3.651	9.485	15.186	10.638	10.020	9.487	14.652
II-i	23.036	3.945	1.993	4.000	7.808	8.606	11.192	22.991	18.627
II-j	0.701	2.214	4.536		4.714	3.562	5.743	4.314	19.393
II-k	9.081	5.291	4.850	5.718	12.464	20.265	16.080	26.802	20.592
Mean	$7.298	$5.604	$5.995	$5.089	$8.613	$16.293	$16.588	$20.224	$23.731

Source: "Annual School Report" of Division Superintendent of Schools to State Department of Education.

Table 36 shows a highly significant difference between the two groups of counties with respect to library expenditures.

Table 36

ANALYSIS OF VARIANCE OF LIBRARY EXPENDITURES PER 100 PUPILS ENROLLED (TABLE 35)

Source of Variation	Sum of Squares	df	Mean Square	F Values		
				Obtained	5% Level	1% Level
Between two groups of counties	7,805.38	1	7,805.38	46.57	3.89	6.76
Among years	14,801.26	8	1,850.16	11.04	1.98	2.60
Among counties in one group for one year ..	30,165.94	180	167.59			
Interaction	1,909.15	8	238.64	1.42	2.96	4.91
Total	54,681.73	197				

The trends in library expenditures, shown graphically in Figure II, reveal an interesting divergence between the two groups of counties. In 1934-35, the first year the revised course of study was ready for general use in the schools, the difference between the two groups became marked. The rate of acceleration of the curve for the Group I counties is greater than it is for the Group II counties from 1933-34 until 1938-39. The decline in per-pupil library expenditures in Group I counties in the last year was doubtless due to a county allotment plan which placed a limit on the state-aid funds available for any one county. Per-pupil expenditures in Group I counties rose more rapidly than they did for all the counties of the state taken as a whole for this same period, while those for Group II counties failed to maintain the same rate of increase as did the total group. But it should be noted that the mean per-pupil expenditures for Group I counties exceeded both the mean for Group II counties and for all counties even prior to the initiation of the curriculum program in 1931-32.

The annual report of the divisions to the State Department for 1938-39 called for a statement of the number of volumes contained in room and central libraries at the end of the year. The number of books per pupil in average daily membership reported for white elementary and secondary schools is given in Table 37.

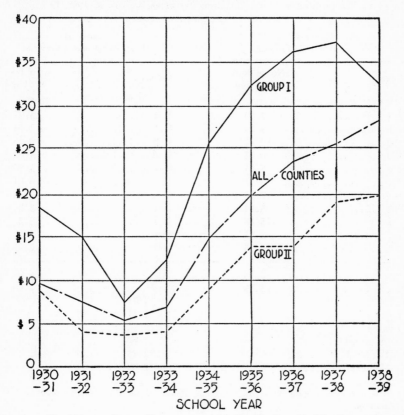

FIGURE II. Library Expenditures per 100 Pupils Enrolled,* Group I and Group II Counties and All Counties in the State, Virginia, 1930–1939

———— Group I Counties
------- Group II Counties
— ·— All Counties

* Group means are weighted means so that all would be comparable, hence they differ slightly from those given in Table 35.

As is to be expected from the data on expenditures, the most-participating counties reported over twice as many library books per pupil as did the least-participating group. The range for the Group I counties was from 5.13 to 15.98 books; for Group II counties it was from 0.65 to 6.61 books. The difference between the means is highly significant.

Table 37

LIBRARY BOOKS PER PUPIL IN AVERAGE DAILY MEMBERSHIP, WHITE ELEMENTARY AND
SECONDARY SCHOOLS, SELECTED COUNTIES, VIRGINIA, 1938–39

GROUP I Most-Participating Counties		GROUP II Least-Participating Counties	
County	No. of Books Per Pupil	County	No. of Books Per Pupil
I-a	9.60	II-a	5.92
I-b	5.20	II-b	2.13
I-c	10.77	II-c	0.65
I-d	6.65	II-d	4.03
I-e	5.13	II-e	3.96
I-f	8.37	II-f	6.61
I-g	7.32	II-g	5.25
I-h	5.92	II-h	3.83
I-i	15.98	II-i	5.34
I-j	5.51	II-j	3.78
I-k	15.75	II-k	2.96
M	8.75		4.04
σ	3.79		1.64
d_{m}		4.71	
σ_d		1.31	
t value			
Obtained		3.60	
1% level		2.85	
5% level		2.09	

Source: Virginia State Board of Education, *Annual Report of the Superintendent of Public Instruction.*

From interviews with division superintendents some general observations about school textbooks can be made: four counties in Group I were using a fee or rental system whereby pupils pay a flat sum of money for the use of textbooks during the year. The board of education buys and owns the books. In one other county, books were furnished free to the children in two out of four magisterial districts but pupils purchased their own textbooks in the remaining districts. In the other six counties in Group I pupils bought their own books. Group II counties all report that pupils bought their own textbooks.

In all four Group I counties using a rental system a variety of textbooks was provided for use in a class, with no single text prescribed.

However, in all but two of the six Group I counties requiring pupils to purchase textbooks, it was reported that most teachers also arranged for the pupils in any one class to buy a variety of titles rather than all purchase the same book. Use of a uniform text was the usual practice in the other two counties, as well as in the case of a few individual classrooms where the teachers preferred uniform texts in the other nine counties. Without exception, Group II division superintendents re-

Table 38

EXPENDITURES FROM BOARD OF EDUCATION FUNDS FOR EDUCATIONAL
SUPPLIES PER 100 PUPILS ENROLLED, ALL SCHOOLS, SELECTED
COUNTIES, VIRGINIA, 1930–31, 1934–35, 1938–39

County	1930–31	1934–35	1938–39
Group I. Most-Participating Counties			
I-a	$ 8.489	$13.022	$19.821
I-b	15.469	17.242	16.894
I-c	5.279	10.945	3.683
I-d	15.575	10.988	16.163
I-e	20.830	18.617	37.242
I-f	4.200	4.618	0.777
I-g	16.850	4.985	15.586
I-h	17.888	7.983	20.169
I-i	19.302	16.492	10.981
I-j	13.415	12.998	15.034
I-k	17.717	19.591	45.923
Mean	$14.092	$12.498	$18.388
Group II. Least-Participating Counties			
II-a	$ 7.515	$12.113	$14.551
II-b	4.380	0.703	3.493
II-c	1.465	2.505	4.312
II-d	4.600	6.341	5.006
II-e	10.802	7.086	7.565
II-f	9.551	8.769	20.847
II-g	10.655	6.159	2.927
II-h	4.658	6.261	3.741
II-i	33.011	6.659	28.171
II-j	0.938	4.644	7.862
II-k	7.789	8.821	13.197
Mean	$ 8.669	$ 6.369	$10.152

Source: "Annual School Report" of Division Superintendent of Schools to State Department of Education.

ported the use of uniform texts as the accepted and common practice in their counties.

EDUCATIONAL SUPPLIES

It seemed desirable to compare the two groups of counties on the purchase of teaching materials and supplies. Figures on expenditures for general supplies, maps, globes and charts, laboratory supplies, and manual training supplies—the four accounting items covering this type of material—per 100 pupils enrolled are given for the years 1930-31, 1934-35, and 1938-39 in Table 38. It is doubtful if the data provide an accurate comparison of the two groups on the availability of teaching materials, however, since practices in both the provision of supplies and to some extent in accounting for such purchases varied from county to county. A fee system for pupil supplies was used in some counties, while in others the pupils purchased some items and the board of education others, the distinction varying from county to county. However, the figures indicate that the Group I counties spent more per 100 pupils from school funds for such supplies as were accounted for under the headings named.

The analysis of variance for these data shows the difference between the two groups of counties to be a significant difference. Table 39 gives this analysis.

Table 39

ANALYSIS OF VARIANCE OF EXPENDITURES FROM BOARD FUNDS FOR EDUCATIONAL SUPPLIES PER 100 PUPILS ENROLLED (TABLE 38)

Source of Variation	Sum of Squares	df	Mean Square	F Values		
				Obtained	5% Level	1% Level
Between two groups of counties	717.15	1	717.15	11.15	4.00	7.08
Among years	260.09	2	130.05	2.02	3.15	4.98
Among counties in one group for one year ..	3,857.20	60	64.29			
Interaction	23.39	2	11.70	5.49	19.47	99.48
Total	4,857.83	65				

TABLE 40

NUMBER OF PUPILS IN AVERAGE DAILY ATTENDANCE, NUMBER OF TEACHERS, AND AVERAGE TEACHER LOAD, WHITE SCHOOLS, SELECTED COUNTIES, VIRGINIA, 1930–31, 1934–35, 1938–39

County	1930–31			1934–35			1938–39		
	Average Daily Attendance	No. of Teachers	Pupils Per Teacher	Average Daily Attendance	No. of Teachers	Pupils Per Teacher	Average Daily Attendance	No. of Teachers	Pupils Per Teacher
Group I. Most-Participating Counties									
I-a	4,207	131	32.11	4,139	111	37.29	3,888	139	27.97
I-b	4,151	193	21.51	4,118	174	23.67	4,506	160	28.16
I-c	575	28	20.54	577	25	23.08	608	29	20.97
I-d	3,426	133	25.77	4,333	151	28.70	5,345	193	27.69
I-e	3,992	144	27.72	4,569	161	28.38	4,928	189	26.07
I-f	737	35	21.06	653	30	21.77	607	23	26.39
I-g	2,672	123	21.72	2,749	115	23.90	2,872	112	25.64
I-h	3,616	134	26.99	3,732	130	28.71	4,006	148	27.07
I-i	1,605	78	20.58	1,562	66	23.67	1,523	63	24.17
I-j	6,307	189	33.37	7,307	221	33.06	8,181	261	31.34
I-k	923	48	19.24	878	45	19.51	831	43	19.33
Mean	2,928.27	112.36	24.60	3,147.00	111.73	26.52	3,390.45	123.64	25.89
Group II. Least-Participating Counties									
II-a	1,147	54	21.24	1,278	46	27.78	1,378	52	26.50
II-b	1,157	53	21.83	1,412	53	26.64	1,609	53	30.36
II-c	4,303	123	34.98	5,064	139	36.43	7,672	175	43.84
II-d	700	30	23.33	724	29	24.97	759	28	27.11
II-e	2,057	77	26.71	2,797	80	34.96	2,677	84	31.87
II-f	862	49	17.59	859	42	20.45	916	41	22.34
II-g	1,603	74	21.66	1,556	65	23.94	1,450	61	23.77
II-h	1,751	75	23.35	1,794	69	26.00	1,631	68	23.99
II-i	3,120	133	23.46	3,416	132	25.88	3,060	126	24.29
II-j	2,388	101	23.64	2,408	100	24.08	2,522	99	25.47
II-k	11,863	318	37.31	11,522	324	35.56	12,047	340	35.43
Mean	2,813.73	98.82	25.01	2,984.55	98.09	27.88	3,280.09	102.45	28.63

Source: Virginia State Board of Education, *Annual Report of the Superintendent of Public Instruction.*

School Size

SIZE OF SCHOOL POPULATION AND TEACHER LOAD

To investigate the possibility that participation in the state curriculum program may be a function of size of school population and number of teachers employed data on these items were analyzed. Table 40 shows the number of white pupils in average daily attendance in both elementary schools and high schools, the number of teachers employed in these schools, and the per-teacher load for the years 1930-31, 1934-35, and 1938-39. The means for the number of pupils in attendance and teachers employed are slightly higher for Group I counties than for Group II counties in all three years. The Group II counties exceeded the Group I counties slightly in mean teacher load. None of these differences, however, are significant when tested by the analysis of variance, the F values for the three items being given in Table 41.

The most important fact revealed by the data in Table 40 is the great variability among the counties in both groups. The Group I counties were a somewhat more uniform group than were the Group II counties, but even here wide differences in number of pupils existed. In Group I, County I–j ranked third while Counties I–c and I–f ranked ninety-fourth and ninety-fifth among the 100 counties of the state in average daily attendance of white pupils in 1938-39. On the other hand in Group II, County II–k had the largest daily attendance of any county in the state, and County II–d ranked ninetieth among all the counties.

Obviously, from the data presented in Tables 40 and 41, it is evident (1) that no significant differences existed between the two groups of counties in size of white school population and the number of teachers employed, and (2) that in view of the wide variation within the groups size of pupil or teacher population does not seem to be an important factor in determining participation in a state curriculum program.

Information on the average daily attendance for the elementary schools alone was available only for the year 1938-39, a revised report form being used that year. Since this study is particularly concerned with elementary teachers and schools, a comparison of the two groups of counties on size of pupil population, number of teachers, and teacher

Table 41

ANALYSIS OF VARIANCE OF NUMBER OF PUPILS IN AVERAGE DAILY ATTENDANCE, NUMBER OF TEACHERS, AND AVERAGE TEACHER LOAD (TABLE 40)

Source of Variation	Sum of Squares	df	Mean Square	F Values		
				Obtained	5% Level	1% Level

I. *Number of Pupils in Average Daily Attendance*

Source of Variation	Sum of Squares	df	Mean Square	Obtained	5% Level	1% Level
Between two groups of counties	275,092.74	1	275,092.74	27.79	252	6,302
Among years	2,391,516.09	2	1,195,758.05	6.39	19.47	99.48
Among counties in one group for one year (Error)	458,611,738.73	60	7,643,528.98			
Interaction	9,214.76	2	4,607.38	1,658.98	19.47	99.48
Total	461,287,562.32	65				

II. *Number of Teachers*

Source of Variation	Sum of Squares	df	Mean Square	Obtained	5% Level	1% Level
Between two groups of counties	4,288.24	1	4,288.24	1.34	252	6,302
Among years	896.39	2	448.20	12.83	19.47	99.48
Among counties in one group for one year (Error)	344,932.55	60	5,748.88			
Interaction	211.30	2	105.65	54.41	19.47	99.48
Total	350,328.48	65				

III. *Average Number of Pupils Per Teacher*

Source of Variation	Sum of Squares	df	Mean Square	Obtained	5% Level	1% Level
Between two groups of counties	37.29	1	37.29	1.33	4.00	7.08
Among years	86.42	2	43.21	1.54	3.15	4.98
Among counties in one group for one year (Error)	1,658.08	60	28.08			
Interaction	15.16	2	7.58	3.70	19.47	99.48
Total	1,823.95	65				

Table 42

NUMBER OF PUPILS IN AVERAGE DAILY ATTENDANCE, NUMBER OF TEACHERS, AND
AVERAGE TEACHER LOAD, WHITE ELEMENTARY SCHOOLS,
SELECTED COUNTIES, VIRGINIA, 1938–39

County	Average Daily Attendance	Number of Teachers	Pupils Per Teacher
Group I. Most-Participating Counties			
I–a	3,069	108	28.42
I–b	3,392	111	30.56
I–c	433	15	28.87
I–d	3,995	136	29.38
I–e	3,411	124	27.51
I–f	411	14	29.36
I–g	2,209	79	27.96
I–h	2,723	89	30.60
I–i	1,005	36	27.92
I–j	5,991	181	33.10
I–k	494	22	22.45
M	2,466.64	83.18	28.74
σ	1,689.25	52.97	2.51
Group II. Least-Participating Counties			
II–a	1,111	39	28.49
II–b	1,312	40	32.80
II–c	7,307	155	47.14
II–d	561	19	29.53
II–e	2,071	50	41.42
II–f	752	32	23.50
II–g	1,105	46	24.02
II–h	1,119	46	24.33
II–i	2,231	88	25.35
II–j	1,976	80	24.70
II–k	10,152	264	38.45
M	2,699.73	78.09	30.88
σ	2,950.52	68.77	7.73
d_m	233.09	5.09	2.14
σ_d	1,075.13	27.45	2.57
t value			
Obtained	0.22	0.19	0.83
1% level	2.85	2.85	2.85
5% level	2.09	2.09	2.09

Source: Virginia State Board of Education, *Annual Report of the Superintendent of Public Instruction.*

load for white elementary schools is pertinent. Table 42 presents this information.

While the Group II counties had a slightly larger average daily attendance in elementary schools, and the Group I counties had on the average about five more teachers per county, neither difference as shown by the *t* value approaches significance. These two conditions produced a slightly smaller per-teacher pupil load in Group I counties, but this difference is of no significance.

Just as in the case of the total school population, wide variability existed among the counties in each group in number of elementary pupils and teachers. In teacher load, the Group I counties were more homogeneous, varying from 22.45 to 33.10 pupils per teacher, while the Group II counties varied from 23.50 to 47.14 pupils.

The evidence presented here would indicate that the number of teachers has no relationship to participation of the elementary corps in a curriculum program.

A factor that may be very important in determining participation is the size of the school faculty in local schools in the county. Table 43 shows the percentage of elementary schools, including both those housed separately and those housed jointly with secondary units, which had a total of but one or two teachers on the elementary staff. These would be the small, often isolated, rural elementary schools. The table reveals a striking contrast between the two groups, and the analysis of variance, given in Table 44, shows that a very significant difference existed between the groups of counties in the total percentage of schools one and two teachers in size, with the most-participating counties having had the smaller percentage of such schools. Furthermore, the mean percentage of these schools in Group I counties declined sharply during the period, while the Group II counties show a much smaller drop. In only two counties in Group II did one-and two-teacher schools comprise less than fifty per cent of the total number of elementary schools in any one year, while six or seven Group I counties fell in this classification in each of the three years.

SUMMARY

During the period under investigation in this study, 1930-1939, some significant differences and several likenesses in important aspects of the

Table 43

PERCENTAGE OF WHITE ELEMENTARY SCHOOLS ONE OR TWO TEACHERS IN SIZE, SELECTED COUNTIES, VIRGINIA, 1930-31, 1934-35, 1937-38

County	1930-31 Per Cent of Schools			1934-35 Per Cent of Schools			1937-38 Per Cent of Schools		
	One Teacher	Two Teachers	Total	One Teacher	Two Teachers	Total	One Teacher	Two Teachers	Total
Group I. Most-Participating Counties									
I-a	35.19	24.07	59.26	75.68	18.92	94.60	52.38	16.67	69.05
I-b	72.28	14.85	87.13	76.39	5.56	81.95	50.00	11.90	61.90
I-c	28.57	28.57	57.14	40.00		40.00	25.00		25.00
I-d	23.53	20.59	44.12	3.85	7.69	11.54	4.55	4.55	9.10
I-e	11.76	5.88	17.64	11.76	5.88	17.64	6.67		6.67
I-f	58.33		58.33	37.50	12.50	50.00	16.67	33.33	50.00
I-g	64.71	7.84	72.55	51.28	15.38	66.66	35.71	14.29	50.00
I-h		14.29	14.29		15.38	15.38		21.43	21.43
I-i	10.00	10.00	20.00	11.11		11.11	11.11		11.11
I-j	6.67	10.00	16.67	6.67	6.67	13.34	7.69	3.85	11.54
I-k		37.50	37.50		28.57	28.57	16.67		16.67
Mean	28.28	15.78	44.06	28.57	10.60	39.17	20.59	9.64	30.23
Group II. Least-Participating Counties									
II-a	59.09	9.09	68.18	18.18	27.27	45.45	25.00	25.00	50.00
II-b	79.31		79.31	76.00		76.00	70.00		70.00
II-c	65.52	24.14	89.66	66.29	25.84	92.13	58.24	31.87	90.11
II-d	71.43	7.14	78.57	63.64	9.09	72.73	60.00	10.00	70.00
II-e		15.38	15.38						
II-f	77.42	3.23	80.65	82.61	4.35	86.96	78.26	4.35	82.61
II-g	74.29	8.57	82.86	55.00	15.00	70.00	28.57	21.43	50.00
II-h	52.00	12.00	64.00	23.53	41.18	64.71	16.67	27.78	44.45
II-i	30.95	35.71	66.66	21.43	38.10	59.53	37.04	37.04	74.08
II-j	51.16	18.60	69.76	61.90	4.76	66.66	62.50	7.50	70.00
II-k	40.66	20.88	61.54	40.63	18.75	59.38	37.11	18.56	55.67
Mean	54.71	14.07	68.78	46.29	16.76	63.05	43.04	16.68	59.72

Source: Virginia State Board of Education, *Annual Report of the Superintendent of Public Instruction.*

Table 44

ANALYSIS OF VARIANCE OF TOTAL PERCENTAGE OF WHITE ELEMENTARY SCHOOLS
ONE AND TWO TEACHERS IN SIZE (TABLE 43)

Source of Variation	Sum of Squares	df	Mean Square	F Values		
				Obtained	5% Level	1% Level
Between two groups of counties	11,183.66	1	11,183.66	18.33	4.00	7.08
Among years	1,443.57	2	721.79	1.18	3.15	4.98
Among counties in one group for one year ..	36,607.63	60	610.13			
Interaction	100.74	2	50.37	12.11	19.47	99.48
Total	49,335.60	65				

educational program existed between the group of counties which participated most extensively and the group which participated relatively slightly in the Virginia state curriculum program.

DIFFERENCES

These chief differences were found among the factors studied:

1. The most-participating counties as a group spent more per pupil enrolled for instruction in white elementary schools than did the least-participating counties. Furthermore, total current expenditures per pupil enrolled for all schools were significantly larger in the most-participating counties.

2. The most-participating counties supplemented state aid in providing funds for salaries of the instructional staff much more extensively than did the least-participating counties.

3. The most-participating counties spent much more per pupil for library books than did the least-participating counties. The number of library books per pupil in white elementary and secondary schools at the end of the period under study was much larger in the most-participating counties.

4. The most-participating counties spent a significantly larger amount on educational supplies in proportion to the number of pupils enrolled than did the least-participating counties.

5. There is some evidence, although not conclusive, that teacher load in white elementary schools was smaller in the most-participating counties in 1938-39 than it was in the least-participating group.

6. A much larger percentage of white elementary schools in the least-participating counties were one- and two-teacher schools than was the case in the most-participating counties.

LIKENESSES

The two groups of counties were found to be alike in the following respects:

1. The two groups of counties did not differ significantly in the effort made to support education as measured by current school expenditures locally raised per $1,000 of locally taxable wealth.

2. In size of the white school population and in number of teachers employed in white schools, the two groups did not differ significantly; hence, the average teacher load in white schools, secondary and elementary, in both groups was practically the same.

CHAPTER VI

Likenesses and Differences in Supervision and Administration

A MOST important set of factors on which the participating and non-participating counties may be compared centers around supervision and administration of the schools. It is quite obvious that important aspects of supervision and administration could have important bearing on participation in a state curriculum program. Certainly this is a fruitful area for investigation.

SUPERVISION

EXTENT OF SUPERVISORY SERVICE

Growing out of a recommendation of the educational survey in 1918,[1] Virginia has followed the policy since that date of granting state aid for elementary supervision in the county school divisions. Under the plan the State Board of Education pays a portion of the salary of supervisors for white elementary schools in county school divisions. Aid is not granted to city divisions nor for high school supervision. Negro supervision is subsidized under another plan and falls outside the scope of this study. Prior to 1922, the State Board of Education paid one-half of the salary of supervisors up to a maximum state contribution of $500. In 1922, the proporton was changed to two-thirds of the salary, with a maximum state contribution of $1,000 per supervisor; then for a time the maximum was increased to $2,000, but in recent years the state has limited its contribution to $1,666.67 per supervisor, or two-thirds of the salary up to a maximum of $2,500.

Employment of elementary supervisors under this plan has been

[1] Virginia Education Commission and Virginia Survey Staff, *Virginia Public Schools*, p. 43.

entirely voluntary with the counties, although the generous provisions for state aid should greatly stimulate counties to employ them. The extent to which the 100 counties of the state have employed elementary supervisors since the inauguration of the plan in 1918 is shown in Table 45. While there is no evidence to indicate a direct relationship, it is, nevertheless, interesting to note that sixteen counties added supervision in 1934-35, the year in which the tentative course of study for elementary schools was available for general use. About three-fourths of the counties now have elementary supervision.

The two groups of counties which are the subject of this study offer a striking contrast with respect to supervision. Table 46 shows that with two exceptions all the most-participating, or Group I, counties have had supervisory service for white elementary schools continuously since 1931-32, the date of inception of the curriculum program. County I–b had employed supervisors from 1919 to 1930, but discontinued the service for five years thereafter and County I–e dropped supervision for one year in 1933-34. On the other hand, but two of the eleven least-participating counties had any elementary supervision from 1931 to 1939. One of these counties, after three years, discon-

Table 45

EXTENT OF ELEMENTARY SUPERVISION FOR WHITE SCHOOLS IN COUNTY SCHOOL DIVISIONS, VIRGINIA, 1918–1939

Year	No. of Counties	No. of Supervisors	Year	No. of Counties	No. of Supervisors
1918–19	13	.. ª	1929–30	37	51
1919–20	28	53	1930–31	48	61
1920–21	28	41	1931–32	47	59
1921–22	21	31	1932–33	53	63
1922–23	21	25	1933–34	52	49
1923–24	23	28	1934–35	68	74
1924–25	16	22	1935–36	75	85
1925–26	18	24	1936–37	78	90
1926–27	17	22	1937–38	79	92
1927–28	21	30	1938–39	75	88
1928–29	31	43			

Source: Virginia State Board of Education: *Annual Report of the Superintendent of Public Instruction* and "Supervisors of Elementary Education."

ª Not available.

Table 46

YEARS SUPERVISORS HAVE BEEN EMPLOYED AND NUMBER EMPLOYED IN THE SELECTED COUNTIES, VIRGINIA, 1918–1939

County	Years Prior to Curriculum Program													Years Since Inception of Curriculum Program							
	1918 –19	1919 –20	1920 –21	1921 –22	1922 –23	1923 –24	1924 –25	1925 –26	1926 –27	1927 –28	1928 –29	1929 –30	1930 –31	1931 –32	1932 –33	1933 –34	1934 –35	1935 –36	1936 –37	1937 –38	1938 –39
Group I. Most-Participating Counties																					
I-a	a	4	3	4	4	3	3	3		3	5	5	5	4	4	3	3	3	3	3	3
I-b		1	2	2		1	1	1	1	3	3	1	1	1	1	1	1	1	1	1	1
I-c													½ᵇ	½	½	½	½	½	½	½	½
I-d		3	1		1	1	1	1	2	2	2	1	1	2	2	1	1	2	2	2	2
I-e					1									1	1	1	1	1	1	1	1
I-fᵇ				1									½ᵇ	½	½	2°	2°	½	½	½	½
I-g	1	4	1	2	2		2		2	2	1	1	1	1	1	2°	1	1	1	1	1
I-h		2	2	1	1				1	1	1	1	1	1	1	1	1	1	1	1	1
I-i	1					1							1	1	1	1	1	1	1	1	1
I-j	1	2	2	1	1				1	1	1	1	1	1	1	1	1	1	2	2	2
I-k													1	1	1	1	1	1	1	1	1
Total	2ᵃ	16	11	9	7	8	5	8	11	15	13	14	14	14	13	11	12	12	15	15	15
Group II. Least-Participating Counties																					
II-a																					
II-b																					
II-c			2	2	1	1	1														
II-d			2	2										1							
II-e																					
II-f																					
II-g										1	1	1	1								
II-h										1	1										
II-i											1	1	1								
II-j			2	1	1	1															
II-k	aᵃ	2	1	1			1						1	1	1			1	1		
Total	2ᵃ	2	5	3	2	1	1	1		1	1	2	2	1	1			1	1		

Source: Virginia State Board of Education, *Annual Report of the Superintendent of Public Instruction* and "Supervisors of Elementary Education."

ᵃ Exact number not available.

ᵇ Counties I-c and I-f have had joint supervision since 1930–31.

° One supervisor spent one day each week supervising and five days teaching.

tinued supervision in 1932 and the other employed supervisors in but two of the eight years. The difference is indicated further by the fact that out of a possible eighty-eight county-years (number of counties times number of years) since 1931 for each group supervisory service has been provided for eighty-three, or 94.3 per cent, of these county-years in the most-participating counties, and for but three, or 3.4 per cent, of the county-years in the least-participating counties.

It is obvious that the provision of supervisory service for white elementary schools since the initiation of the program has been a very important difference between the two groups of counties.

Because of the apparent importance of supervision to participation, Table 46 also shows the extent to which supervision has been provided in the selected counties since the adoption of the state-aid program in 1918. Here again the difference between groups is apparent. One county in Group I has employed supervisors under this plan since the beginning of state aid; another had it in all but two years of the entire period; and a third employed supervisors for all but three of the years. Other counties in Group I had supervision more or less sporadically up to 1930, but all of the counties had begun the service by that year, although County I–b, which had had supervision for eleven years, discontinued it in 1930, only to restore it again in 1935.

In Group II counties, only desultory efforts have been made to provide supervision throughout the twenty-one-year period. Five have not employed any supervisors during that entire time; two had supervisors for but one year each and that was long prior to the present curriculum program; and the other four have had brief periods of supervision, mostly prior to 1931 and hence the curriculum program.

THE SUPERVISORY PERSONNEL

In view of the important affiliation of supervision with participation and the importance which the State Department of Education has placed on supervision in the curriculum program, as stated in Chapter II, a brief statement summarizing some personnel factors about the supervisors employed in the selected counties from 1931-32 to 1938-39 seems pertinent. Such a description may give cues to factors influencing participation.

County I–a. In 1931-32 this county had four supervisors, but one of these positions was discontinued after the following school year. The other three supervisors have served in that capacity continuously since 1927, 1928, and 1929 respectively. One has taken graduate work beyond the Master's degree and has a total of twenty-five years of professional experience, one is a candidate for a Bachelor's degree and has had seventeen years' experience, and the third is taking work for the Bachelor's degree and has had sixteen years of experience. All three have been active in the state curriculum program, among other things serving on state production committees.

County I–b. This county employed a supervisor in 1935 after having been without supervisory service from 1930 to that time. She continued in the position through 1939. She holds a Master's degree and is taking advanced work on the doctorate. She was formerly on the staff of one of the teacher-training institutions in the state and while there served as state consultant in the program for an important elementary subject area. She spent several summers in curriculum workshops in production and reviewing work on the course of study. County I–b also operates a demonstration school for the purposes of experimentation with and demonstration of new curriculum practices.

Counties I–c and I–f. These two counties jointly employed a supervisor in 1930 who continued in the position until 1938, when she joined the staff of the State Department of Education. While supervisor she was acting chairman of a state elementary production committee and in that capacity spent several summers in the central workshop collating, reviewing, and editing the state course of study. She has taken work beyond the Master's degree and has had fifteen years of experience in education. Her position was filled in 1938-39 by one of the teachers in the county who had participated in various phases of the program, particularly summer workshop activities in revising the high school tentative course of study. She is a candidate for the Master's degree and taught nine years in one of these counties before becoming supervisor.

County I–d. Two supervisors were employed in this county in 1931-32, but one position was discontinued thereafter until 1936-37, when the second supervisor was again added. One of the present supervisors has served continuously since 1930; she holds a Master's degree and has a total of seventeen years of experience. The other was appointed in

1936; she is a candidate for the Master's degree and has a total of eight years of professional experience.

County I–e. This county has had the most erratic supervisory service of any of the eleven. Two supervisors were employed in 1931-32 and 1932-33, and then the service was discontinued for one year. A new supervisor was employed in 1934 and she served for four years, when another person took over the position. Meanwhile, in 1936, an additional supervisor was employed. Both of the present supervisors are taking work for a Master's degree; one has had eight years of experience and the other nineteen years. One was a member of a state high school production committee and in that capacity engaged in production work during the summers at the curriculum centers. Also one of the supervisors employed from 1931 to 1933 was a member of the state committee on aims.

County I–g. The same supervisor has served this county continuously since 1930. In addition, the county had a part-time supervisor for two years who worked in one-room schools one day each week and taught a demonstration school of this type the remainder of the week. The full-time supervisor has been very active in the curriculum program, serving as associate chairman of a state production committee and in other capacities. She has a Master's degree and has a total of twenty-four years of experience.

County I–h. The same supervisor has been employed in this county since 1927. She was chairman of one of the important state production committees and spent several summers in curriculum laboratories in production, collation, and review of the state course of study. She is taking advanced graduate work for the doctorate and has twenty-nine years of professional experience.

County I–i. This county, except for one year back in 1923-24, inaugurated supervision in 1930, and the same supervisor has occupied the position since that date. He does not hold a degree. He served on a state production committee and has taken a very active part in curriculum work. He has a total of eighteen years' experience.

County I–j. One of the present supervisors has served this county in that capacity continuously since 1929, except for a one-year leave of absence. A second supervisor was employed in 1936 and has continued in the position since that date. One holds a Master's degree and the other has taken graduate work. Both were members of a state production committee. The former has fourteen years' experience and the latter twenty-four.

County I–k. This county inaugurated supervision in 1928 and the same supervisor has occupied the position since that time. She does not hold a degree and has a total of twenty-seven years' experience. She was a member of a state production committee.

Counties IIa–k. Only two Group II counties have had any supervision since 1931. County II–g discontinued supervision in 1932, after a three-year period. Since this was the year the curriculum program began, there was little opportunity for the supervisor to work with the program. County II–k had supervision in 1932-33; in 1935-36 a member of the extension department of the state university spent the year in the county conducting extension classes and doing a general type of supervision for which state aid was granted.

The above statements show that in nine of the eleven Group I counties at least one supervisor in each instance had served continuously since the inception of the curriculum program in 1931 to the time of the study, except for a one-year leave of absence in one case late in the period and a change in 1938 in the two counties having joint supervision. Thus there has been a continuity of supervision in all but two of the most-participating counties. In contrast to this excellent tenure in Group I counties, investigation shows that out of the sixty-four other counties in the state which had supervision in 1938-39, only thirteen had had the same supervisor throughout the period 1931-39; four others had had the same supervisor for six or seven years of the period. This continuity of supervision by the same person would seem to be an important factor associated with the most-participating counties in contrast even to supervisory service in the remainder of the state. And it must be remembered, of course, that none of the least-participating counties had continuous supervision throughout the program.

Inasmuch as the least-participating, or Group II, counties employed no supervisors in 1938-39, comparisons between the two groups of counties with respect to personnel factors are impossible. It was decided to compare the supervisors in the most-participating, or Group I, counties, therefore, with the supervisory force of the rest of the state to determine if they might have constituted a select group out of the total supervisory corps. Even if no differences are found, the marked contrast in the presence or absence of supervision between the two groups of counties still is of great significance for this study.

TENURE OF SUPERVISORS

Table 47 shows the number of years supervisors employed in 1938-39 had been in their respective positions, including that year, for the Group I counties and the rest of the state. The mean tenure, from ungrouped data, was 7.27 years and 5.15 years respectively. The difference of 2.12 is of doubtful significance, falling between the one per cent and five per cent level of probability of occurrence.

Table 47

YEARS SUPERVISORS IN MOST-PARTICIPATING COUNTIES AND IN
REST OF STATE HAD BEEN IN THEIR RESPECTIVE POSITIONS,
VIRGINIA, 1938–39

	Number of Supervisors		
Years	Group I Most-Participating Counties		Rest of the State
10 and over	6		9
7–9	3		9
4–6	2		27
1–3	4		28
M	7.27[a]		5.15[a]
σ	3.94[a]		3.38[a]
d_m		2.12	
σ_d		1.00	
t value			
Obtained		2.12	
1% level		2.66	
5% level		2.00	

Source: Personnel records in file in State Department of Education.
[a] Calculated from ungrouped data.

TRAINING OF SUPERVISORS

Three of the supervisors in the Group I have taken work beyond the Master's degree, three hold Master's degrees, six have taken graduate work, and three do not hold any degree. Table 48 shows the number of supervisors who held various degrees for the Group I counties and the rest of the state. To compare the Group I counties with the rest of the state in this case the Chi-square technique[2] was used.

Because of the small frequencies expected the data were reclassified according to those with a Bachelor's degree or less and those with a Master's degree and the Yates correction utilized.[3] By this procedure

Table 48

HIGHEST ACADEMIC DEGREE HELD BY SUPERVISORS, VIRGINIA, 1938–39

Degree	Number of Supervisors	
	Group I Most-Participating Counties	Rest of the State
Master's	6	20
Bachelor's	5	37
No degree	3	7

Source: Personnel records on file in State Department of Education.

Chi-square was found to be 1.32, which is clearly not significant since the probability of occurrence of this difference in random samples is from twenty to thirty per cent of all cases.

SALARIES OF SUPERVISORS

The mean salary of supervisors in the Group I, or most-participating counties, and of supervisors in the rest of the state for certain years of the period under study is shown in Table 49. The mean salary was somewhat higher for supervisors in the Group I counties but in only one of the four years studied, 1935-36, is the difference significant, indicating probably that salaries of supervisors in the most-participating counties were raised more quickly after the worst of the depression than in the rest of the state. In general, however, there is no reason to

[2] For discussion of the Chi-square test see:
E. F. Lindquist, *Statistical Analysis in Educational Research*, Chapter II.
Henry E. Garrett, *Statistics in Psychology and Education* (Second Edition), pp. 377-387.
Helen M. Walker, "The Chi-Square Test."
[3] See Paul Rider, *Modern Statistical Methods*, pp. 112-115.

Table 49

MEAN SALARY OF SUPERVISORS IN MOST-PARTICIPATING COUNTIES AND THE REST OF
THE STATE, VIRGINIA, SELECTED YEARS

Year	Mean Salary of Supervisors			*t* Value of Significance		
	Group I. Most-Participating Counties	Rest of the State	Differ-ence	Obtained	5% Level	1% Level
1939–40	$2,072.73	$1,951.37	$121.36	1.49	2.00	2.66
1935–36	2,052.08	1,816.54	235.54	2.72	2.00	2.66
1933–34	1,794.91	1,635.19	159.72	1.13	2.00	2.66
1931–32	2,116.15	1,896.29	219.86	2.10	2.00	2.66

Source: List of supervisors' salaries on file in State Department of Education.

believe that these supervisors represented a highly selected group with respect to salary over the period of years since 1931.

SUPERINTENDENTS OF SCHOOLS

In Virginia the division is the local unit of school administration. A division consists of a county, a combination of two or even in one case three smaller counties, or an independent city. At the head of the school system in each administrative unit is the division superintendent of schools. Obviously this official may have an important relationship to participation of the county in a state curriculum program of the voluntary type carried forward in Virginia. Superintendents in the two groups of counties were studied for important likenesses or differences.

TENURE AND CONTINUITY OF SERVICE

Seven of the eleven counties in Group I, or most-participating group, have had the same superintendent of schools throughout the period since the curriculum program was initiated in 1931. One county, County I–b, changed superintendents at the beginning of the second year of the program, 1932; the other three had the same superintendents during the first six years of the program or until 1937. However, one of these superintendents transferred to another county in the group at that time. Thus there was a continuity of service in all of the counties throughout all or most of the period.

In the eleven Group II, or least-participating counties, ten have had the same superintendent since 1931 or longer; the other made a change in 1937.

With respect to continuity of administration since the initiation of the program, then, there has been no important difference between the two groups of counties, although the least-participating group has had a slightly better record in this respect than the most-participating.

A study of the number of years superintendents in the two groups of counties had held their respective positions at the time of the initiation of the program in 1931-32 reveals, again, no important differences. Table 50 shows this distribution of length of service. The mean years of tenure, calculated from the original data, is 11.80 years for the Group I counties and 10.18 years for the Group II counties. There is nothing in these data as shown by the t value to indicate that number of years administrators have been in their respective positions influ-

Table 50

YEARS DIVISION SUPERINTENDENTS HAD BEEN IN THEIR RESPECTIVE POSITIONS, SELECTED COUNTIES, 1931–32

Years	Number of Superintendents		
	Group I Most-Participating Counties		Group II Least-Participating Counties
21–25	1		
16–20	1		
11–15	3		6
6–10	2		3
1–5	3		2
M	11.80[a]		10.18[a]
σ	7.91[a]		4.22[a]
d_m		1.62	
σ_d		2.90	
t value			
Obtained		0.56	
1% level		2.86	
5% level		2.09	

Source: Virginia State Board of Education, *Annual Report of the Superintendent of Public Instruction* (Directory).

[a] Calculated from ungrouped data.

ences participation of the local unit in such curriculum programs as the Virginia one.

AGE

Distribution of the ages of division superintendents in the two groups of counties as of 1931, shown in Table 51, indicates that superintendents in the most-participating counties tended to be a little older than those in the least-participating group when the curriculum program was initiated. The mean age, from ungrouped data, for the former group was 46.10 years and for the latter group 41.91 years, but this difference is not significant, yielding a t value of but 0.98.

Table 51

AGE OF DIVISION SUPERINTENDENTS, SELECTED COUNTIES, VIRGINIA, 1931

Age in Years	Number of Superintendents		
	Group I Most-Participating Counties		Group II Least-Participating Counties
60 and over	1		1
55–59	1		
50–54	2		
45–49	1		1
40–44	2		3
35–39	2		5
30–34	1		1
M	46.10[a]		41.91[a]
σ	8.93[a]		9.71[a]
d_m		4.19	
σ_d		4.31	
t value			
Obtained		0.98	
1% level		2.86	
5% level		2.09	

Source: Personnel records on file in State Department of Education.
[a] Calculated from ungrouped data.

TRAINING

Table 52 summarizes the amount of college training of all the superintendents who have served in the twenty-two counties since 1931.

Superintendents in the most-participating counties have had somewhat better college training than have those in the least-participating counties. Seven of fourteen superintendents who have served in the former group have had Master's degrees, while only two of the twelve in the latter group have held this degree. However, the difference in level of training is relatively minor. The frequencies are too small to use the usual Chi-square test, but if the table is reduced to a two-by-two table of those holding a Bachelor's degree or less and those with graduate training and this distribution is tested by Yates' modification of the Chi-square test for such small expected frequencies,[4] the two groups are found not to vary significantly in training of superintendents, the Chi-square value being only 0.47, which shows that this difference may occur in fifty per cent of such random samples. The conclusion is that higher level of professional training of superintendents is not a differentiated characteristic with respect to participation.

Table 52

EXTENT OF COLLEGE TRAINING OF DIVISION SUPERINTENDENTS EMPLOYED IN THE SELECTED VIRGINIA COUNTIES DURING 1931–1939

Extent of College Work	Number of Superintendents	
	Group I. Most-Participating Counties	Group II. Least-Participating Counties
Beyond Master's degree	2	
Master's degree	5	2
Some graduate work, but less than Master's ..	5	6
Bachelor's degree	1	2[a]
No degree	1	2

Source: Personnel records on file in State Department of Education.
[a] One of these is an M.D. degree.

While complete information was unavailable and not feasible to secure, there is evidence to indicate that few of the twenty-six superintendents employed since 1931 in these counties have attended higher institutions for professional study in recent years. In fact, personnel

[4] See Rider, *op. cit.*, pp. 112-115.

records reveal the absence of any college work for many years for some of the older superintendents, even in counties which have been most active in the curriculum program. The few superintendents who had studied in a professional institution in recent years were divided rather equally between the two groups of counties. It would seem that recent professional study in higher institutions by the superintendent of schools is not associated with participation in the state curriculum program.

SALARY

The distributions of the salaries of division superintendents in the two sets of counties for 1934-35 and 1939-40 are given in Table 53.

Table 53

DISTRIBUTION OF ANNUAL SALARY OF DIVISION SUPERINTENDENTS, SELECTED COUNTIES, VIRGINIA, 1934–35 AND 1939–40

Salary Group	Number of Superintendents			
	1934–35		1939–40	
	Group I. Most-Participating Counties	Group II. Least-Participating Counties	Group I. Most-Participating Counties	Group II. Least-Participating Counties
$5,000 and above	2		1	
4,500–4,999		1	1	1
4,000–4,499	1		1	
3,500–3,999		1	1	
3,000–3,499	4	1	5	2
2,500–2,999	1	1	1	2
2,000–2,499	2	3		3
Less than $2,000		4		3
M	$3,470.90[a]	$2,401.64[a]	$3,615.00[a]	$2,467.91[a]
σ	1,098.39[a]	1,065.75[a]	680.69	1,011.41
d_m	1,069.26		1,147.09	
σ_d	496.74		399.53	
t value				
Obtained	2.15		2.87	
1% level	2.86		2.86	
5% level	2.09		2.09	

Source: Personnel records on file in State Department of Education.
[a] Calculated from ungrouped data.

One-half of the base salary of division superintendents is paid by the State Department of Education from state funds. This base salary is fixed on the basis of the school census and is set every five years. Most county school boards pay a supplementary salary to the superintendent in addition to their half of the base salary. The figures used here are for the total combined salary of the superintendent. The mean salary for superintendents for both 1934-35 and 1939-40 was much higher in the most-participating counties than it was in the least-participating counties. When the difference in means is tested for significance *t* values of 2.15 for 1934-35 and 2.87 for 1939-40 result. This would indicate that the hypothesis that the two groups of superintendents are random samples from all division superintendents in Virginia with respect to salary should be rejected and the conclusion accepted that superintendents in divisions which participate most extensively do receive significantly higher salaries than superintendents in counties which participate least.

PROFESSIONAL ACTIVITIES

It is enlightening to compare superintendents of the two groups of counties as to membership in the American Association of School Administrators of the National Education Association, or, as it was formerly known, the Department of Superintendence. Membership rolls published in the annual yearbooks of this organization show that eight of the fourteen superintendents who served in the most-participating counties since 1931 had been members sometime during their incumbency, while but two of the twelve serving in the least-participating counties were members at any time during the period 1931-1939. Four of the eight superintendents in the former group who belonged have been members throughout the eight-year period. Membership in the association was held by the superintendent for forty-one of a total of eighty possible county-membership years (number of counties times number of membership years) in the most-participating counties, while membership was held in but eight of a possible eighty-eight county-membership years in the least-participating group.

With respect to serving as an officer in the state professional organization, The Virginia Education Association, no marked differences between superintendents in the two groups of counties were found. Two superintendents, one from each group of counties have been president of the organization for terms of two years each. Six of the superintendents from Group I counties, and one from Group II counties have served as vice-presidents, and hence members of the Board of Directors of the state organization as well as chairmen of their respective district associations.

Three of the division superintendents who have served in these counties during the period from 1931 to 1939 were members of state committees for the curriculum program; two, one of whom was associate chairman of a state secondary production committee and the other a member of another state secondary production committee, were from the most-participating counties and one, a member of the committee on procedures, was superintendent in a Group II county. The two administrators first referred to were very active in summer production work at curriculum centers; the last-mentioned superintendent did not spend the summer of 1932 at the chosen center working with the committee on the procedures bulletin, and the extent of his activities in other respects is not indicated. Undoubtedly, as administrative heads of school divisions, all superintendents had some connection with the program, but the extent of personal participation on state committees is indicated by the above statement.

PERSONAL QUALITIES

It would be highly valuable in this particular study to have some valid and reliable basis for comparing the two groups of superintendents on personal characteristics, attitudes, qualities of leadership, operational viewpoint on basic educational issues and problems, and the like. It is in these respects, the investigator believes, that some very important differences between the two groups of superintendents might be found. Intangible factors centering around the personal qualities and operational philosophy of school administrators and supervisors undoubtedly play an important role in determining the nature and extent of participation of local school units in voluntary state curriculum programs. But the obvious lack of reliable, objective methods of measuring such factors makes it impractical to present evidence on this factor in a study such as this one.

IN-SERVICE EDUCATION AND SUPERVISORY PROGRAM

Policies, programs, and plans for the in-service education of teachers is a most important area for investigation in a study of factors associated with participation in a continuous curriculum program. But unfortunately, reliable objective evidence is difficult to secure, particularly when the survey extends over a period of eight years. Few records describing policies and procedures are available and those that exist give little or no basis for qualitative evaluation; also, in a study of the scope of the present one intensive research in this one aspect was not feasible. In spite of this inadequacy of objective data, however, some pertinent observations may be made.

From interviews with supervisors and division superintendents and a perusal of supervisors' reports to the State Department of Education, general statements characterizing the nature of the in-service education programs of each county are presented. These statements make no attempt to summarize activities carried on by principals in local schools. Also, each county for which information is available reported that the county teachers' association, which is affiliated with the state organization, usually held from two to three meetings annually. These are in charge of the county officers of the association. In most cases these meetings are general in nature, with addresses by outside speakers, reports from delegates to the state convention, and social affairs comprising the bulk of the programs. However, a few associations serve as centers for group study and discussion activities. Since these meetings are common to all counties they are not discussed in each summarization.

GROUP I—MOST-PARTICIPATING COUNTIES

County I–a. The three supervisors in this county meet, with the superintendent also present, at least weekly to plan and coordinate their supervisory activities. One supervisor has responsibility for all grammar grades and the other two have charge of the remaining grades in all larger schools. One- and two-teacher schools are divided among them. In the past eight years many group meetings and conferences of teachers have been held—in fact, there was some feeling that perhaps too many were being held, and the number has been restricted the last year or two. In recent years elementary teachers have organized into upper grade and lower grade groups, which meet at least once each month for study and discussion, the work for the year centering around a subject area, such as art, music, science, and the like. In addition, supervisors, of course, hold innumerable conferences with individual teachers and often hold conferences with local school faculties or with a local group of teachers having a common interest. Problems that arise out of the local situation itself are discussed in these individual and local group conferences.

Inter-school visitation so teachers may observe and study the work of other teachers is encouraged; each teacher is given one day each year with pay for such visitation. Often large groups go as a body to some distant school well-known for its work for observation, although many teachers, particularly new ones, visit within the county.

County I–b. This county began supervision in 1935, after a lapse of five years. Two years prior to that date, a staff member of one of the state teachers colleges had conducted an extension class in the county in which a large percentage of the teachers enrolled. Study was related to the state curriculum program. The following year, 1934, this same instructor spent one day each week in the county visiting schools, after which group conferences with principals were held. Since supervision was restored in 1935 supervisory efforts have been concentrated on schools with four teachers or more. Definite groups of teachers with a fixed schedule of meetings are not organized; rather, informal small groups meet with the supervisor very frequently, with discussion growing out of the needs and interests of the group. In addition, numerous conferences with individual teachers and with local groups of teachers are held. Teachers in the small one- to three-teacher schools have definite meetings about once each month with the supervisor.

This county maintains a demonstration school for observational and experimental purposes. Earlier in the program local school faculties visited it as a group; lately visitation has been on an individual basis. Some visitation is made in schools outside the county, but this is not extensive.

Counties I–c and I–f. County-wide meetings of elementary teachers in each of the two counties comprising this school division are held about six times each year. Discussion usually centers on problems revolving around some area of instruction. On several occasions in 1938-

39 specialists from the State Department and elsewhere visited in the counties and then conducted a conference on special problems related to their respective areas, such as music, art, and the like. Also numerous informal local school meetings under the direction of the supervisor are held. Since the counties are small, the supervisor is able to visit each classroom frequently and to hold numerous personal conferences. A program of inter-school visitation is carried on, with visitation often being made to promising schools in other counties.

County I–d. Some county-wide teachers' meetings are held during the year, at which much attention is given to discussion of curriculum problems growing out of the issues raised by the state program. The two supervisors hold many local group meetings with teachers in various schools and individual conferences are numerous. State Department staff members are drawn upon continuously for aid.

Inter-school visitation is practiced extensively, with provision made for each teacher to do some visiting during the year.

County I–e. The two present supervisors in this county divide the county for supervisory purpose, but coordinate their efforts and cooperate closely. Two county-wide meetings of elementary teachers were held in 1938-39. Also numerous conferences with small groups or the entire elementary staff of local schools are held throughout the year. Individual conferences, of course, follow supervisory visits. The teachers propose problems for discussion and study, both for the county and for local meetings. For several years the work has centered around subject areas. Supervisors teach demonstration classes at intervals during the year and teachers working on the level of the class being taught are invited to observe. Also all teachers are given a holiday on Wednesday before Thanksgiving so they may visit schools in other systems.

County I–g. In recent years, district meetings of elementary teachers have been held once each month. Three groups—primary, intermediate, and grammar—are organized in each of the districts. Committees are appointed to make special studies and the activities of each meeting center around problems proposed by the teachers. The supervisor also holds personal and local school conferences. Teacher visitation to other classrooms is not so common in this county as in others, although some visitation does take place.

County I–h. Turnover is quite a problem in this county so the supervisor in recent years has worked extensively with new teachers. Meetings with these teachers are held early in the year. Throughout the year groups of teachers, either from the same school or from a group of schools, meet with the supervisor for discussion of problems of concern to them. Individual conferences are held extensively. Teacher visitation to observe other teachers is practiced, with teachers visiting schools both within the county and in other schools of promise. Visitation is largely based on individual guidance by the supervisor.

County I–i. This county has emphasized systematic study by teachers in recent years. Four or five regional groups are organized; study is concentrated on pertinent curriculum problems and issues, and teachers are encouraged to read widely in professional literature in conjunction with the study. Study groups meet at least once every two weeks. In addition small groups of teachers meet with the supervisor for discussion and conference as the need arises. In the fall of 1939, for example, the supervisor arranged for groups of elementary teachers to meet with shop instructors to receive instruction in carrying on constructional activities in the classroom. A teacher visitation program is carried on, with groups of teachers going to schools in other counties and, on occasion, to an adjoining state for observation of practice.

County I–j. Reports indicate an intensive in-service education program in this county. All elementary teachers are organized into groups for study and discussion, and each year some study program has been carried on. Early in the program teachers were organized by grade levels and efforts were concentrated in the study program on gaining a thoroughgoing understanding of the viewpoint underlying the course of study and its use in implementing these concepts. In recent years local school faculties are organized as groups and study has been concerned with pertinent curriculum problems, such as child guidance, art, and the like. The teachers themselves plan and conduct the discussion. In addition, teachers in the upper grades and those in the lower grades as groups each have two or three county-wide meetings each year. The supervisors assert that this county has had a continuous study and discussion program since the curriculum program was initiated. Supervisors devote much time to inducting new teachers into the instructional program of the county. Teacher visitation is encouraged, with considerable visitation being made to schools both within and without the county.

County I–k. The small number of elementary teachers in this county permits close personal relationships between the supervisor and teachers, so group meetings are not so frequent. However, the supervisor does hold conferences with elementary teachers of a local school as a group. Earlier in the program study and discussion activities were carried on by the teachers organized in groups. Teachers are required to attend summer school every four or five years and the superintendent often recommends courses to be taken by individual teachers. Inter-school visitation was required of elementary teachers earlier in the program and definite schedules were arranged. In recent years most of this visitation has been eliminated, and few if any teachers now visit other classrooms for observational purposes.

GROUP II—LEAST-PARTICIPATING COUNTIES

General summaries of county in-service education programs in the Group II, or least-participating, counties follow.

County II–a. The superintendent has had a county teachers' institute twice each year, but in the last two years this has been discontinued. Inter-teacher visitation has not been practiced. No other organized efforts at in-service stimulation on a county-wide basis were reported.

County II–b. Two or three county-wide teachers' meetings are held each year in this county. General discussion predominates. There is little inter-school visitation in this county.

County II–c. Groups of teachers have been organized in the larger schools in a number of different years to study curriculum problems and issues raised by the state program. Teachers from surrounding small schools were invited to join these groups. Inter-school visitation is not practiced.

County II–d. No county group meetings of teachers have been held in this county in recent years aside from the three meetings of the county teachers' association, which are inspirational or social in nature. The superintendent stated that he did not propose to teach teachers; it is the job of the colleges to train teachers and not the job of the public school system, he maintained. This county is starting supervision in 1939-40 for the first time. There has been little inter-school visitation of teachers in the past, but it is planned to expand this practice under the guidance of the supervisor in the future.

County II–e. The two or three meetings annually of the county teachers' association comprise all the group meetings of teachers on a county basis held in County II–e. This county is situated near a metropolitan city and some teachers do attend general teachers' meetings and conventions held there. There is no inter-school visitation; the superintendent feels that it is not a satisfactory practice and is apt to cause trouble.

County II–f. Occasional county teachers' meetings are held in this county for group discussion. Local school faculties have had organized study and discussion which centered around the point of view and use of the tentative state course of study. No inter-school visitation is found in this county.

County II–g. Again the only professional meetings of teachers as far as the county is concerned are those of the county teachers' association. Some teachers in this county do take extension courses at a near-by teacher-training institution each year. There has been little or no inter-school visitation in this county in the past.

County II–h. The present superintendent came to this county in 1937, and has since been making an effort to improve the school situation. Supervision is to be added for the first time in 1939-40. County meetings of teachers are called occasionally by the superintendent, unless those of the county association serve the purpose of his program adequately. Also he has meetings with smaller groups of teachers in sections of the county on occasion. Some inter-school visitation was attempted in 1938-39, but in the absence of supervision it was not satisfactory and the effort was abandoned until supervision would be available. Such visitation was largely within the county.

County II–i. The meetings of the county teachers' association are used for professional stimulation. For example, an outside speaker was to discuss art work at a meeting in December, 1939, this to be followed by group discussion. The superintendent plans to have an extension course for teachers on art following this and thus stimulate interest in bettering the art work in the school. Inter-school visitation is not practiced in this county; in the first year or two of the state program some teachers did visit a demonstration school in a near-by county.

County II–j. The general meetings of the county teachers' association, of which there are four to six annually, comprise the total efforts of the administration in this county to carry forward an organized program of stimulation. These meetings are of a general nature. There has been no inter-school visitation in recent years. Early in the program some teachers did visit demonstration schools at two teachers colleges but the situation there was so different from public school conditions in the county that no benefit was derived from the visits, according to the superintendent.

County II–k. High school teachers of the county met monthly in 1938-39 for study and discussion, but elementary teachers were not included in such a program. In 1934-35 and 1935-36, the extension division of the state university conducted extension courses in the county with the instructor each year maintaining residence there. He visited schools and performed a type of supervision, along with the in-service training program. There has been practically no inter-school visitation of teachers in this county.

While these statements do not provide a basis for careful comparisons between the two groups of counties, they nevertheless indicate important differences in the efforts of division superintendents to stimulate and encourage the professional growth and development of teachers. The continuous programs of study, discussion, and conference through both county-wide and small groups found in the Group I counties were in marked contrast to the desultory efforts or even absence of such programs in Group II counties. It might be argued that in-service education naturally centers in the central administrative office in counties which have elementary supervisors, but that similar efforts may be carried forward by principals in the other group of counties. While this aspect of the program was not studied fully, the evidence shows that principals in both groups of counties do make efforts to promote the growth of teachers. Regular principals' meetings with the division superintendent are held in all or practically all counties investigated, and, in turn, local school faculty meetings under the guidance of the principal were reported as being held in all of these counties. In counties with supervisory service the programs of the local principals are often coordinated with those of the supervisors, with the county-wide program of stimulation providing a basis for formulating the local school program of in-service education; but the efforts of principals in these Group I counties appear to be as extensive and comprehensive as those carried forward in Group II schools even though extensive programs are carried forward by the supervisors themselves in the former case. In visitation of teachers during school time in other schools to observe the work of other teachers, a marked difference was found between the two groups of counties. Only one county studied in Group II had encouraged visitation on the part of large numbers of teachers in recent years, while all but two Group I systems have had more or less extensive programs of visitation.

In the matter of professional libraries for teachers major differences between the groups of counties were reported. All but two of the Group I counties reported good professional libraries which are available to teachers generally. The other two were increasing their facilities at the time of the study. In the Group II counties three planned on starting professional libraries in the fall of 1939, one began a professional library in 1938, two had a small library in a central school from which teachers could draw books, and the other five reported no professional library facilities for teachers generally.

There is no question, in the opinion of the investigator, that efforts to promote the professional growth and development of elementary teachers in the most-participating counties far exceeded in extent and merit similar efforts in the least-participating counties. In fact, this seems to be one of the most important differences between the two groups of counties—the dogged, continuous efforts on the part of superintendents, principals, and supervisors to stimulate teachers to improve classroom instruction and to aid them in making such improvements.

SUMMARY

In school supervision and administration and in personnel factors of administrative staffs some important differences existed between the group of most-participating counties and the group of least-participating counties. These differences were as follows.

DIFFERENCES

1. A very great difference existed in the extent of supervisory service for white elementary schools. All of the most-participating counties have employed supervisors since 1930 except for a one-year lapse in one county in 1933-34 and for a five-year interval in one other county

which had no supervisor from 1930 to 1935. But only two least-participating counties employed supervisors at any time since the inception of the curriculum program in 1931—one county had a supervisor in 1931-32, and the other in 1932-33 and again in 1935-36.

2. Superintendents of schools received significantly higher salaries in the most-participating counties.

3. The most-participating counties have carried on much more extensive programs of in-service education for stimulating teacher growth and development than have the least-participating counties, and have provided better professional library facilities for teachers.

LIKENESSES

The important likeness of the two groups of counties in supervision and administration was this:

1. Superintendents of schools in the two groups of counties did not differ as groups in any important respects in tenure, continuity of service in the respective counties, age, and professional training.

SUPERVISORY PERSONNEL

In addition to the study of likenesses and differences in the two groups of counties, supervisors in the most-participating counties were compared in personnel factors to supervisors in the remainder of the state since, with no supervisors employed in the least-participating counties, comparisons between the two sets of counties were impossible. These comparisons showed that:

1. Supervisors had been in their respective positions in the most-participating counties about two years longer than had the rest of the supervisors of the state. The difference, however, is not reliable.

2. In level of professional training, supervisors in the most-participating counties were in no sense a selected group in relation to other supervisors in the state.

3. The average salary of supervisors in the most-participating counties was higher throughout the period from 1931 to 1940 but the difference is statistically reliable only in 1935-36 of the four years tested.

Brief descriptive statements showed a marked continuity of supervisory service in the most-participating counties and a high quality of professional background of the supervisors.

CHAPTER VII

Likenesses and Differences in Teaching Personnel

A COOPERATIVE, voluntary state curriculum program of the Virginia type elevates the teacher to a key position in curriculum development. Chapter I discussed in detail this concept of the role of the teacher in curriculum making. Chapter II described the opportunities for teacher participation in the Virginia plan. It was pointed out that a curriculum study program among teachers was organized, that teachers were enlisted for production work on curriculum materials, that selected teachers tried out preliminary materials in classrooms, and that since the issuance of the course of study efforts have been concentrated on the stimulation of teachers to improve classroom instruction. The whole program has been designed to aid teachers in developing a broadened vision, deeper insights, and keener sensitivity to the needs of children and to the role of education in a democratic society.

In this chapter, a study will be made of the characteristic likenesses and differences of teachers in the two groups of counties with respect to a large number of factors which are pertinent to participation in such a curriculum program. Personnel factors, professional activities, teaching procedures, and educational viewpoint have been analyzed in an attempt to ascertain what differences, if any, existed in the teaching corps and in teaching practices for the two groups of counties. Many school administrators and curriculum directors commonly assume that thoroughgoing curriculum revision is facilitated by, and perhaps only practicable with, a staff of teachers of more than average ability, training, and experience. Failure to undertake a revision program is often excused on the grounds of inferior teaching personnel. It is important that attention be given to likenesses and differences of teachers in counties that participate and those that do not participate extensively in curriculum programs. The two groups of Virginia counties offer opportunities for such investigation.

PERSONNEL FACTORS

Are the teachers in the two sets of counties themselves different in training, experience, salary received, age, and the like? This section seeks to answer this important question.

TEACHERS' SALARIES

Table 54 shows the mean annual salary of teachers in white elementary schools for the nine years from 1930 to 1939, together with the mean of the county means for each group. It will be noted that the mean salary for Group I counties was consistently higher than the Group II mean throughout the entire period. In fact, only one Group I county, County I–b, had a mean county salary lower than the mean salary for the Group II counties as a whole any time during the period, except County I–f, which also falls below the Group II mean one year, 1937-38. On the other hand, only three Group II counties at any time during the nine years paid an average salary equal to the mean for all Group I counties; County II–a exceeded this latter figure during the years 1932-36, County II–e in 1933-34, although this figure while used as published may be in error, and County II–k in 1930-31 and in 1938-39. Thus inspection reveals a great difference between the groups in mean salaries of teachers, and the analysis of variance of these data, given in Table 55, shows that the difference is highly significant with an F value of 96.5—the one per cent level of probability for the number of degrees of freedom applying in this case has an F value of 6.76. Obviously, then, the two groups of counties were significantly different from each other in the mean annual salaries paid teachers of white elementary schools during this period.

These differences, it should be emphasized, existed in 1930-31, prior to the initiation of the curriculum program, and did not develop after counties had been participating in this program. Participation would seem to be associated, therefore, with better paid teachers, and not better paid teachers coming as a result of participation. But participation has not been detrimental to the payment of better salaries as feared by some arch conservatives.

Table 54

MEAN ANNUAL SALARIES OF WHITE ELEMENTARY TEACHERS, SELECTED COUNTIES, VIRGINIA, 1930–1939

County	1930–31	1931–32	1932–33	1933–34	1934–35	1935–36	1936–37	1937–38	1938–39
Group I. Most-Participating Counties									
I-a	$696	$722	$621	$633	$667	$730	$758	$735	$749
I-b	607	550	447	512	573	590	598	598	641
I-c	685	686	623	596	651	652	642	720	747
I-d	809	822	823	819	817	810	816	825	853
I-e	944	951	848	802	799	791	861	1,004	1,023
I-f	695	684	628	596	660	615	623	622	684
I-g	843	811	792	668	724	729	823	801	915
I-h	943	930	878	831	886	878	885	908	933
I-i	888	823	767	746	780	787	793	848	848
I-j	761	763	639	729	661	723	718	754	747
I-k	868	800	711	656	692	710	725	755	794
Mean	$794	$777	$707	$690	$719	$729	$749	$779	$812
Group II. Least-Participating Counties									
II-a	$700	$728	$750	$721	$760	$747	$747	$763	$768
II-b	596	542	500	412	447	459	460	463	544
II-c	611	594	536	579	540	588	573	594	651
II-d	523	472	423	399	440	494	507	521	550
II-e	735	685	674	812	687	690	690	690	731
II-f	585	596	575	510	558	557	559	593	676
II-g	602	650	556	509	545	543	594	615	704
II-h	662	592	587	552	593	624	594	624	691
II-i	608	587	608	512	563	607	624	653	667
II-j	580	523	532	504	519	568	587	601	664
II-k	858	763	682	700	678	666	672	774	815
Mean	$642	$612	$584	$565	$575	$595	$601	$626	$678

Source: Virginia State Board of Education, *Annual Report of the Superintendent of Public Instruction.*

Table 55

ANALYSIS OF VARIANCE OF MEAN ANNUAL SALARY OF WHITE ELEMENTARY TEACHERS
(TABLE 54)

Source of Variation	Sum of Squares	df	Mean Square	F Values		
				Obtained	5% Level	1% Level
Between two groups of counties	997,834.02	1	997,834.02	96.52	3.89	6.76
Among years	260,527.89	8	32,565.99	3.15	1.98	2.60
Among counties in one group for one year ..	1,860,863.85	180	10,338.13			
Interaction	8,504.83	8	1,063.10	9.73	2.96	4.91
Total	3,127,730.59	197				

TRAINING OF TEACHERS

Annual reports made by division superintendents to the State Department of Education show the grade of certificate held by each teacher employed. Certificates in Virginia have been issued on the basis of three levels of professional training: the collegiate professional and collegiate certificates require a baccalaureate degree; the normal professional and special certificates require a minimum of two years of college training; and the elementary, provisional elementary, trade, and local permit certificates may be secured with less than two years of college training. Since 1932 the minimum requirement for certificates for new teachers has been two years of college training, except that trade certificates and local permits which are very limited in number have been issued on the basis of less college training.

Beginning in 1942 no certificates will be issued to new teachers unless they hold a baccalaureate degree. Since teachers in most cases secure a higher grade of certificate as soon as they are eligible—its issuance being automatic in case the training is completed in most of the state teacher-training institutions—the level of college preparation of teachers may be determined by tabulating the type of certificates held. Based on such tabulations Table 56 shows the percentage of white elementary teachers with four years or more, at least two years but not four years, and less than two years of college training for the two groups

Table 56

PERCENTAGE DISTRIBUTION OF WHITE ELEMENTARY TEACHERS ACCORDING TO LEVEL OF COLLEGE TRAINING, SELECTED COUNTIES, VIRGINIA, 1930–31, 1934–35, 1938–39

County	1930-31			1934-35			1938-39		
	4 Years or More	2 and Up to 4 Years	Less than 2 Years	4 Years or More	2 and Up to 4 Years	Less than 2 Years	4 Years or More	2 and Up to 4 Years	Less than 2 Years
Group I. Most-Participating Counties									
I-a	7.61	26.09	66.30	25.58	52.33	22.09	30.39	61.76	7.85
I-b	3.87	23.23	72.90	17.91	55.22	26.87	25.69	66.97	7.34
I-c		44.44	55.56	18.75	68.75	12.50	43.75	43.75	12.50
I-d	5.88	54.90	39.22	20.54	75.89	3.57	27.01	72.26	.73
I-e	9.62	64.42	25.96	15.39	76.92	7.69	34.68	62.90	2.42
I-f	11.54	53.85	34.61	31.82	54.54	13.64	33.33	40.00	26.67
I-g	3.37	43.82	52.81	23.26	45.35	31.39	29.11	51.90	18.99
I-h	3.19	82.98	13.83	4.82	92.77	2.41	17.98	80.90	1.12
I-i	4.26	70.21	25.53	21.43	57.14	21.43	27.78	52.78	19.44
I-j	11.84	40.79	47.37	19.41	66.47	14.12	30.17	67.60	2.23
I-k	6.90	86.20	6.90	7.41	92.59		15.38	84.62	
Mean	6.19	53.72	40.09	18.76	67.09	14.15	28.66	62.31	9.03
Group II. Least-Participating Counties									
II-a	2.27	52.27	45.46	22.86	62.86	14.28	35.00	62.50	2.50
II-b		20.93	79.07		82.50	17.50	5.00	87.50	7.50
II-c	10.53	20.17	69.30	10.08	58.91	31.01	19.60	70.94	9.46
II-d	4.76	28.57	66.67	15.00	60.00	25.00	21.05	47.37	31.58
II-e	7.41	51.85	40.74	3.70	68.52	27.78	22.00	66.00	12.00
II-f	10.26	35.90	53.84	33.33	36.36	30.31	25.00	43.75	31.25
II-g	19.30	80.70		12.25	59.18	28.57	26.09	60.87	13.04
II-h	1.72	46.55	51.73	5.77	65.38	28.85	4.55	88.63	6.82
II-i	6.93	49.50	43.57	16.30	72.83	10.87	16.28	68.60	15.12
II-j	3.80	26.58	69.62	10.13	48.10	41.77	13.75	63.75	22.50
II-k	5.31	33.88	60.81	13.90	84.94	1.16	20.83	78.79	.38
Mean	6.57	40.63	52.80	13.03	63.60	23.37	19.01	67.16	13.83

Source: "Report of Instructional Personnel Under Contract" made annually by division superintendent to State Department of Education.

of counties for the first, fifth, and ninth years of the period under consideration.

The percentage of teachers with at least four years of college training has increased during the period in both groups of counties, but the Group I counties, after starting from the same level in 1930-31, have far outdistanced the Group II counties in this respect in the years

Table 57

ANALYSIS OF VARIANCE OF PERCENTAGE OF TEACHERS HAVING VARIOUS AMOUNTS OF COLLEGE TRAINING (TABLE 56)

Source of Variation	Sum of Squares	df	Mean Square	F Values Obtained	5% Level	1% Level
I. Four Years or More of Training						
Between two groups of counties	412.05	1	412.05	7.59	4.00	7.08
Among years	3,361.16	2	1,680.58	30.96	3.15	4.98
Among counties in one group for one year	3,256.70	60	54.28			
Interaction	281.05	2	140.53	2.59	3.15	4.98
Total	7,310.96	65				
II. Two and Up to Four Years of Training						
Between two groups of counties	252.76	1	252.76	1.07	252	6,302
Among years	4,684.72	2	2,342.36	8.70	3.15	4.98
Among counties in one group for one year	16,153.05	60	269.22			
Interaction	886.11	2	443.06	1.65	3.15	4.98
Total	21,976.64	65				
III. Less than Two Years of Training						
Between two groups of counties	1,310.26	1	1,310.26	5.89	4.00	7.08
Among years	15,005.51	2	7,502.76	33.74	3.15	4.98
Among counties in one group for one year	13,343.09	60	222.38			
Interaction	172.64	2	86.32	2.58	19.47	99.48
Total	29,831.50	65				

since then. Counties II–b and II–h particularly have a low percentage of degree teachers in elementary schools.

Taking each level of training as a separate factor, analyses of variance were made of the three sets of data. These are given in Table 57. From these analyses it is seen that the Group I counties differed significantly from the Group II counties in the percentage of teachers with four years or more of college training. No important difference is found in the percentage of teachers with two years of college work. And it follows from these two comparisons that an important difference, although not entirely statistically reliable, existed in the percentage of teachers having less than two years of training—the Group II counties having the higher percentage in this case.

In view of the great importance attached to this matter of well-trained teachers in relation to curriculum development, it was decided to probe further into this factor in an attempt to isolate differences in relation to years in the program. A Chi-square test of comparison was used for this purpose. Table 58 gives the distribution of the total number of white elementary teachers in the two groups of counties according to levels of training for the three years under investigation. The lower part of the table gives the Chi-square values obtained from these data. Three classifications were used in an effort to locate important differences. First, the two groups of counties were compared with all three categories of training retained as listed in the table. The results show that in all three years studied the two groups of counties differed significantly with respect to training of teachers. When the data were reclassified on the basis of teachers having four or more years of training and those having less than four years, significant differences are noted for 1934-35 and 1938-39, but not for 1930-31. A third test was made with teachers regrouped into those having two years or more and those having less than two years of college work. In this case significant differences are found in 1930-31 and 1938-39, but not in 1934-35.

From the evidence presented in Tables 57 and 58 it may be concluded that the two groups of counties differed significantly in the level of training of teachers even prior to and throughout the period of the curriculum program. In 1930-31, just prior to the program, the difference was found in the numbers of teachers with more and with less

Table 58

DISTRIBUTION OF WHITE ELEMENTARY TEACHERS ACCORDING TO LEVEL OF COLLEGE
TRAINING, SELECTED COUNTIES, VIRGINIA, 1930–31, 1934–35, 1938–39

Level of Training	1930–31		1934–35		1938–39	
	Group I Counties	Group II Counties	Group I Counties	Group II Counties	Group I Counties	Group II Counties
4 years or more	60	57	165	105	258	162
2 up to 4 years	442	330	595	580	601	606
Less than 2 years ..	405	468	135	157	53	81
Total	907	855	895	842	912	849

Chi-square Values

A. Three classifications of training			
Obtained	19.38	13.90	26.42
1% level	9.21	9.21	9.21
5% level	5.99	5.99	5.99
B. Four years or more and less than four years			
Obtained	0.00	12.16	21.13
1% level	6.64	6.64	6.64
5% level	3.84	3.84	3.84
C. Two years or more and less than two years			
Obtained	17.62	3.47	8.81
1% level	6.64	6.64	6.64
5% level	3.84	3.84	3.84

Source: "Report of Instructional Personnel Under Contract" made annually by division superintendent to State Department of Education.

than two years of college work; but in both 1934-35 and 1938-39 the chief differences existed in the number of teachers with four or more years of college training. A staff of better trained teachers is associated with participation in cooperative, long-time curriculum programs.

EXPERIENCE OF TEACHERS

Experience of teachers in most-participating and least-participating counties offers a fruitful area for a study of associated factors. Some

Table 59

TEACHING EXPERIENCE IN THE COUNTY OF WHITE ELEMENTARY TEACHERS, SELECTED COUNTIES, VIRGINIA, 1930–31, 1934–35, 1938–39

County	Average Years' Experience			Per Cent Serving First Year			Per Cent Five Years or Less		
	1930–31	1934–35	1938–39	1930–31	1934–35	1938–39	1930–31	1934–35	1938–39
Group I. Most-Participating Counties									
I-a	8.31	8.34	7.93	3.30	9.76	9.90	38.46	35.37	45.54
I-b	4.88	6.17	8.35	22.30	14.62	9.43	61.49	54.62	37.74
I-c	8.39	8.00	4.93	0.00	0.00	20.00	50.00	40.00	66.67
I-d	3.50	5.48	5.52	18.63	10.71	17.16	77.45	50.89	49.25
I-e	5.03	6.40	7.98	16.35	11.11	8.87	55.77	50.43	43.55
I-f	6.12	5.29	8.93	19.23	19.05	0.00	69.23	52.38	42.86
I-g	4.67	6.23	7.84	7.87	13.95	5.06	66.29	38.37	36.71
I-h	5.24	7.57	7.17	15.05	3.70	16.09	56.99	35.80	48.28
I-i	7.13	10.64	13.69	23.40	2.38	0.00	57.45	30.95	22.86
I-j	5.74	7.46	8.01	15.79	6.51	10.73	53.29	43.20	37.29
I-k	3.97	6.70	7.58	20.69	7.41	11.54	72.41	40.74	38.46
Mean	5.73	7.12	7.99	14.78	9.02	9.89	59.89	42.98	42.66
Group II. Least-Participating Counties									
II-a	2.52	5.89	5.67	15.91	8.57	28.21	86.36	34.29	51.28
II-b	3.07	5.65	6.33	18.60	10.00	17.95	76.74	50.00	41.03
II-c	3.44	4.97	5.06	24.78	13.39	18.37	78.76	55.12	56.46
II-d	5.10	4.24	6.53	19.05	19.05	15.79	71.43	66.67	47.37
II-e	3.11	8.30	9.27	18.87	4.00	12.24	73.58	34.00	34.69
II-f	3.51	5.64	6.66	20.51	18.18	9.38	79.49	42.42	43.75
II-g	5.26	7.29	9.54	12.28	5.88	10.87	50.88	33.33	30.43
II-h	5.81	9.79	10.28	12.28	5.77	13.04	50.88	25.00	23.91
II-i	4.91	6.52	8.75	13.86	7.69	5.95	61.39	47.25	33.33
II-j	6.24	8.70	11.18	12.66	6.33	1.25	49.37	30.38	25.00
II-k	5.33	6.15	7.52	11.48	10.69	10.61	62.70	49.62	45.45
Mean	4.39	6.65	7.89	16.39	9.96	13.06	67.42	42.55	39.34

Source: "Report of Instructional Personnel under Contract" made annually by division superintendent to State Department of Education.

administrators excuse the lack of a forward-looking school program on the grounds of inexperienced teachers or a high turnover rate or both. Do school systems which participate extensively over a period of time in curriculum revision programs have a staff of more experienced or more stable teachers than systems which make little effort to join in such movements? The evidence from Virginia is presented in the following section.

Several factors relative to teachers' experience were studied. Table 59 summarizes these data and the analyses of variance are given in Table 60. First, the two groups of counties were compared with respect to the average number of years of experience in the county of the white elementary teachers who composed the staff in the years for which data were collected. The table shows that white elementary teachers in the Group I or most-participating counties had taught in their respective counties on the whole slightly longer than had similar teachers in Group II counties in the selected years. When analyzed, however, these differences are shown to be insignificant and are no greater than may be expected from random samples of counties. There has been a significant increase in length of service during the period covered by the study, but this increase has occurred in both groups of counties.

The next factor investigated was the percentage of white elementary teachers who were serving their first year in the county during the year under consideration. In other words, these percentages, given in Table 59, show the proportion of teachers on the staff who were new teachers in the county for the years 1930-31, 1934-35, and 1938-39. The data give an indication of the problem of inducting new teachers into service; if the percentage is small, it is possible that a continuous program of improving instruction may be carried forward more easily. Energies of administrators and supervisors would not be dissipated in initiating new teachers into the work of the schools. These percentages also give a crude measure of turnover. An exact study of turnover was impractical because of the necessity of detailed investigation of all new teachers to discover if they replaced former teachers or were an addition to the staff. Table 59 shows that in Group I counties on the whole a slightly lower percentage of teachers were serving their first year in their respective counties for each of the three years. However, the difference has no significance when tested by the analysis of variance.

Table 60

ANALYSIS OF VARIANCE OF TEACHING EXPERIENCE IN THE COUNTY OF WHITE
ELEMENTARY TEACHERS. (TABLE 59)

Source of Variation	Sum of Squares	df	Mean Square	F Values		
				Ob-tained	5% Level	1% Level
I. Average Years of Experience						
Between two groups of counties	6.66	1	6.66	2.16	4.00	7.08
Among years	93.62	2	46.81	15.15	3.15	4.98
Among counties in one group for one year ..	185.60	60	3.09			
Interaction	4.40	2	2.20	1.40	19.47	99.48
Total	290.28	65				
II. Percentage of Teachers Serving First Year						
Between two groups of counties	59.95	1	59.95	1.57	4.00	7.08
Among years	425.51	2	212.76	5.58	3.15	4.98
Among counties in one group for one year ..	2,286.30	60	38.11			
Interaction	14.41	2	7.21	5.29	19.47	99.48
Total	2,786.17	65				
III. Percentage of Teachers with Five Years or Less Experience						
Between two groups of counties	26.18	1	26.18	4.72	252	6,302
Among years	6,988.34	2	3,494.17	28.28	3.15	4.98
Among counties in one group for one year ..	7,413.78	60	123.56			
Interaction	346.66	2	173.33	1.40	3.15	4.98
Total	14,774.96	65				

To push this point of length of experience in the county further, a
comparison was made of the percentage of white elementary teachers
who had been teaching in their respective counties five years or less,
including that year. This point seems important, especially in Virginia
where the curriculum program has been a continuous effort since 1931,
for if a county had a much larger proportion of its teachers continue

in service for an extended period of years it is possible that participation in the program would be facilitated. Table 59 reveals, again, that no important difference existed between the two groups of counties with respect to the percentage of teachers who had taught in the county five years or less.

One other aspect of teaching experience seems pertinent to this study.

Table 61

AVERAGE NUMBER OF YEARS OF EXPERIENCE OUTSIDE OF
COUNTY OF WHITE ELEMENTARY TEACHERS, SELECTED
COUNTIES, VIRGINIA, 1930–31, 1934–35, 1938–39

County	1930–31	1934–35	1938–39
Group I. Most-Participating Counties			
I-a	1.57	2.48	2.74
I-b	1.51	1.30	1.46
I-c	.50	.27	2.20
I-d	1.86	2.01	3.43
I-e	5.10	3.81	4.51
I-f	1.30	2.33	2.93
I-g	2.68	2.75	2.12
I-h	.63	.55	.80
I-i	1.66	1.46	1.20
I-j	2.64	2.37	2.35
I-k	1.86	1.56	1.34
Mean	1.94	1.90	2.28
Group II. Least-Participating Counties			
II-a	2.32	1.54	1.46
II-b	.44	.58	.41
II-c	1.24	1.17	1.44
II-d	.23	.47	1.42
II-e	1.63	2.34	2.24
II-f	1.02	2.42	1.15
II-g	2.51	2.38	1.98
II-h	2.19	2.23	1.65
II-i	1.74	1.50	1.91
II-j	1.71	1.54	1.93
II-k	1.18	.57	.64
Mean	1.47	1.52	1.48

Source: "Report of Instructional Personnel Under Contract" made annually by division superintendent to State Department of Education.

The three previous comparisons relate to experience in the respective counties themselves. But it is possible that the counties in one group may have tended to employ teachers who had had more years of experience elsewhere before employment in these counties. Table 61, which gives the average number of years of experience of white elementary teachers prior to employment in the county, shows that teachers in Group I counties had slightly more years of previous experience than did teachers in Group II counties. The analysis of variance, Table 62, indicates that the F value falls between the one and five per cent levels of significance, and hence that the difference has doubtful significance.

The conclusion is reached from these data that white elementary teachers in the most-participating counties, while exceeding teachers in the least-participating counties somewhat in length of experience in the county, as well as in experience prior to employment in the county, did not differ markedly from the latter group. Also it was found that the least-participating counties had a slightly higher percentage of teachers without previous experience in the county and of teachers who had served five years or less in the system, but the difference was not great enough to approach statistical reliability.

Table 62

ANALYSIS OF VARIANCE OF YEARS OF EXPERIENCE OUTSIDE OF COUNTY (TABLE 61)

Source of Variation	Sum of Squares	df	Mean Square	F Values		
				Obtained	5% Level	1% Level
Between two groups of counties	4.96	1	4.96	5.70	4.00	7.08
Among years	0.42	2	0.21	4.14	19.47	99.48
Among counties in one group for one year ..	52.15	60	0.87			
Interaction	0.57	2	0.29	3.00	19.47	99.48
Total	58.10	65				

CHARACTERISTICS OF NEW TEACHERS

It seemed important in this study to investigate certain characteristics of teachers employed for the first time by the school system during the period of the curriculum program in an effort to determine if the counties which participated extensively tended to select different types of teachers with respect to training and previous experience than did the least-participating counties. Is the employment of better trained or more experienced teachers when vacancies occur associated with participation in a curriculum program? Tabulations were made of the number of years of experience prior to employment in the county and the level of training of all white elementary teachers employed for the first time in 1930-31, 1934-35, and 1938-39. These data for the two groups of counties are given in Tables 63 and 64, together with the Chi-square values.

With respect to years of prior service no statistically reliable difference occurred until 1938-39, although the Chi-square value for 1934-35 was much larger than that for 1930-31, and approaches significance. As revealed by data for these three selected years, then, Group I or most-participating counties have during the period of the program gradually selected white elementary teachers with greater numbers of years of

Table 63

YEARS OF PREVIOUS EXPERIENCE OF NEWLY EMPLOYED WHITE ELEMENTARY TEACHERS SELECTED COUNTIES, VIRGINIA, 1930–31, 1934–35, 1938–39

Years of Experience	1930–31		1934–35		1938–39	
	Group I Counties	Group II Counties	Group I Counties	Group II Counties	Group I Counties	Group II Counties
Five and over	18	14	9	4	23	4
Four	5	4	3	3	3	4
Three	9	7	4	1	5	5
Two	12	5	4	2	6	7
One	10	14	12	3	5	3
None	82	87	53	69	55	78
Total	136	131	85	82	97	101
Chi-square values						
Obtained	4.54		11.86		18.02	
1% level	15.09		15.09		15.09	
5% level	11.07		11.07		11.07	

Source: "Report of Instructional Personnel Under Contract" made annually by division superintendent to State Department of Education.

previous experience than that possessed by new teachers employed in the least-participating counties.

The Chi-square values for level of training, however, reveal exactly opposite trends. The two groups differed greatly in this respect in 1930-31, but the difference had largely disappeared by 1934-35. The important difference in recent years between the two groups of counties

Table 64

LEVEL OF COLLEGE TRAINING OF NEWLY EMPLOYED WHITE ELEMENTARY TEACHERS, SELECTED COUNTIES, VIRGINIA, 1930–31, 1934–35, 1938–39

Level of Training	1930–31		1934–35		1938–39	
	Group I Counties	Group II Counties	Group I Counties	Group II Counties	Group I Counties	Group II Counties
Four years or more .	22	23	42	31	48	41
Two and up to four years	93	48	42	51	48	60
Less than two years	21	60	1		1	
Total	136	131	85	82	97	101
Chi-square value						
Obtained	33.11		3.51		2.77	
1% level	9.21		9.21		9.21	
5% level	5.99		5.99		5.99	

Source: "Report of Instructional Personnel Under Contract" made annually by division superintendent to State Department of Education.

in the percentage of teachers with four years or more of college training, shown earlier in Table 56, evidently came about in the main through a better trained staff of teachers to start with, coupled with continued study of teachers in the system.

The conclusion is that the most-participating counties have, during the period since the inception of the curriculum program, tended to employ new teachers with more experience than those employed in least-participating but with no more college training than the latter group.

AGE

Age of teachers may be a factor associated with participation in a progressive curriculum program. It is possible that young teachers, whose training is recent, may be more willing to participate in a progressive curriculum program than much older teachers who may have fallen into a traditional pattern of teaching. On the other hand, it is possible that older teachers, with a good background of experience, realize deficiencies in their work and feel the need of professional stimulation and are anxious to experiment and try new methods. Principals and supervisors often assume, however, that it is difficult to get older teachers to make major changes in their methods or to look with favor on disruptive innovations and experimentation with new practices. Certainly the association of age with participation is worth investigation.

Ages of teachers were secured from the teacher questionnaires described in Chapter I. The respondent teacher was asked to indicate

Table 65

MEAN AGE OF WHITE ELEMENTARY TEACHERS, SELECTED COUNTIES, VIRGINIA, 1939

Group I Most-Participating Counties		Group II Least-Participating Counties	
County	Mean Age	County	Mean Age
I–a	33.4	II–a	31.7
I–b	33.5	II–b	.. [a]
I–c	30.0	II–c	32.1
I–d	31.7	II–d	31.7
I–e	36.4	II–e	33.5
I–f	30.0	II–f	30.3
I–g	33.8	II–g	33.0
I–h	29.8	II–h	41.0
I–i	40.3	II–i	38.3
I–j	32.3	II–j	37.0
I–k	31.5	II–k	31.6
M	33.0		34.0
σ	3.0		3.4
d_m		1.0	
σ_d		1.5	
t value			
Obtained		0.71	
1% level		2.86	
5% level		2.09	

Source: Questionnaire form used in this study.
[a] Since only two replies were received, this county is not used in the calculations.

his age group by checking the proper blank. Table 65 shows the mean age of white elementary teachers in each county in 1939 as calculated from the frequency distribution of the replies, together with the mean of the county means for each group and the *t* value of the difference of these group means. County II–b is not included in the county tabulations of data secured by the questionnaire since only two forms were returned by teachers in that county. The data show that the two groups were quite similar with respect to age of teachers in 1939, and there is no reason to believe, in view of the facts concerning experience of teachers in the two groups which were given previously in this chapter, that any important difference existed in earlier years of the program. The original data show that only 21.1 per cent of all teachers in Group I counties and 20.6 per cent in the Group II counties were forty years of age or over in 1939. Thus both groups of counties had a relatively young corps of teachers. Certainly the least-participating group cannot claim that participation was difficult either because of too many young teachers or too large a proportion of old teachers, in view of their similarity to the Group I counties.

HOME TEACHERS

The employment of teachers who have been living in the local community, or professional inbreeding as it is often called, is usually assumed to be an undesirable practice in school administration. Mort and Cornell maintained, for example, that " the percentage of teachers which before teaching had lived in the local community . . . has been found to yield a negative correlation with the school program."[1] Perhaps professional inbreeding is also associated with failure of school systems to participate extensively in a curriculum revision program. Teachers included in this study were asked on the questionnaire form to check "yes" or "no" to the question, "Was your home in this county when you first started to teach in it?" Table 66 summarizes these replies. It shows that the Group II counties, on the whole, have selected a larger percentage of their white elementary teachers from residents of the local county, although the difference is not great and

[1] Paul R. Mort and Francis G. Cornell, "A Digest of School Survey Data from Field Studies of Selected Pennsylvania Communities," p. 9.

Table 66

PERCENTAGE OF WHITE ELEMENTARY TEACHERS TEACHING IN HOME COUNTY, SELECTED
COUNTIES, VIRGINIA, 1939

Group I. Most-Participating Counties				Group II. Least-Participating Counties			
County	No. of Home County Teachers	No. Re-plying	Per Cent Home County	County	No. of Home County Teachers	No. Re-plying	Per Cent Home County
I–a	48	76	63.2	II–a	5	24	20.8
I–b	47	86	54.7	II–b	2	2	.. [a]
I–c	5	14	35.7	II–c	63	103	61.2
I–d	31	88	35.2	II–d	14	18	77.8
I–e	26	84	31.0	II–e	15	40	37.5
I–f	8	12	66.7	II–f	7	15	46.7
I–g	33	45	73.3	II–g	21	25	84.0
I–h	34	58	58.6	II–h	10	15	66.7
I–i	26	31	83.9	II–i	27	31	87.1
I–j	138	176	78.4	II–j	32	49	65.3
I–k	6	16	37.5	II–k	43	52	82.7
Total ..	402	686		Total ..	239	374	
M			56.2				63.0
σ			18.0				20.9
d_m					6.8		
σ_d					8.9		
t value							
Obtained					0.76		
1% level					2.86		
5% level					2.09		

Source: Questionnaire form used in this study.
[a] Insufficient returns.

lacks much of being statistically reliable. Wide variation existed among the counties in each group. It seems obvious that neither a large proportion of home teachers nor of outside teachers is associated in any important respect with participation.

PROFESSIONAL ACTIVITIES

In this section white elementary teachers will be compared with respect to certain professional activities, such as attending summer school, taking extension work, reading professional books and magazines, attending conventions, and enrolling in professional organizations. These would seem to be important factors that might conceivably be affiliated in one way or another with participation in a cooperative state curriculum program. The comparisons are based on replies to the questionnaire distributed to teachers, and apply only to teachers serving in the schools in the fall of 1939, and then only insofar as the teachers replying are truly representative of all teachers in the county in that particular factor. It would have been enlightening to have studied such professional activities of teachers just prior to the outset of the curriculum program—that is, in 1930-31—and again near the middle of the period, say 1934-35, so that trends during the course of the program could have been studied and comparisons made. But this was not done and was impossible to do in this study. All that can be said at this stage of the endeavor is that certain differences or likenesses existed after eight years of the program.

CONTINUED STUDY AT INSTITUTIONS OF HIGHER LEARNING

Certainly a most important factor for investigation is the extent to which teachers continue after employment to study at higher institutions. Have teachers employed in school systems which have participated in a broad, cooperative curriculum program like the Virginia one in which teachers are encouraged not only to study but to aid in production of materials and the like attended summer school or taken extension courses more than have teachers in least-participating counties? Has participation in a curriculum program encouraged or required more professional study at higher institutions of learning? The answer to these questions, on the basis of the facts found in this study of Virginia conditions, according to Tables 67, 68, and 69, is a rather emphatic "No."

Table 67 gives the percentage of white elementary teachers in each county answering the questionnaire who have attended college since June, 1930, or if they were not teaching at that time, since the person began teaching—in other words, study after employment or after 1930, if employed prior to that date. Teachers were divided into three classes according to length of experience prior to the then present school year, 1939-40, and the percentages given in Table 67 show the number in each category of experience who attended higher institutions

Table 67

PERCENTAGE OF WHITE ELEMENTARY TEACHERS IN EACH CATEGORY OF EXPERIENCE
WHO HAVE ATTENDED SUMMER SCHOOL[a] SINCE BEGINNING TEACHING OR
SINCE JUNE, 1930, SELECTED COUNTIES, VIRGINIA, 1939

County	Per Cent Attending Summer School[a]		
	0-3 Years' Experience	4-7 Years' Experience	8 or More Years' Experience
Group I. Most-Participating Counties			
I-a	50.0	77.8	97.9
I-b	21.7	77.3	82.9
I-c	22.2	100.0	100.0
I-d	15.8	75.0	77.8
I-e	7.1	50.0	84.7
I-f	0.0	100.0	80.0
I-g	11.1	58.3	75.0
I-h	15.4	83.3	79.3
I-i	66.7	40.0	78.3
I-j	26.9	67.6	78.2
I-k	14.3	100.0	100.0
M	22.8	75.4	84.9
σ	18.5	19.4	9.2
Group II. Least-Participating Counties			
II-a	45.5	100.0	91.7
II-b	..[b]	..[b]	..[b]
II-c	51.5	88.0	84.8
II-d	75.0	80.0	77.8
II-e	15.4	100.0	83.3
II-f	75.0	100.0	100.0
II-g	33.3	75.0	83.3
II-h	..[c]	..[c]	93.3
II-i	0.0	50.0	81.8
II-j	40.0	60.0	74.4
II-k	23.8	40.0	77.3
M	39.9	77.0	84.8
σ	23.9	21.4	7.6
d_m	17.1	1.6	0.1
σ_d	10.0	9.6	3.9
t value			
Obtained	1.71	0.16	.03
1% level	2.86	2.86	2.86
5% level	2.09	2.09	2.09

Source: Questionnaire form used in this study.

[a] A very small number of teachers included in these figures attended college during the academic term rather than the summer session.

[b] Insufficient returns.

[c] No cases in this classification.

under these conditions. Practically all attendance was at summer sessions, although a few teachers had taken off an academic year for study.

No important differences between teachers in the two groups of counties with respect to continued study are revealed by the table. Almost identically the same percentage of teachers with eight or more years of experience—that is, those who were teaching when the curriculum program was initiated in 1931-32—have attended college since 1930. In all counties at least three-fourths of all such teachers have continued their professional study. Teachers with four to seven years of experience—teachers who first began teaching in the early years of the program, 1932 to 1935—also attended summer school in about equal proportions in the two groups of counties. In fact, the percentage is a little higher in the least-participating counties. And in the case of newer teachers, those employed since the fall of 1936, the Group II counties make a somewhat better record, although the difference is not statistically reliable.

In view of the importance of this factor and because of the small number of cases falling in the categories for some counties, it was decided to take the totals for the most-participating counties as a group and the totals for the least-participating counties as a group, and calculate the significance of the difference in percentages of those attending summer school in each category of experience. In other words, this procedure gives a weighted mean percentage for each group of counties. For teachers with eight or more years of experience, 82.79 per cent attended school in Group I counties and 82.61 per cent in Group II counties. When tested by the accepted technique for difference between percentages[2] an x/σ value of 0.06 is obtained, which clearly is not reliable. For teachers with four to seven years of experience the percentages are 69.70 and 73.33 respectively and the difference again is not reliable, having a x/σ value of 0.51. For teachers with no prior experience to three years of experience, the percentages are 22.99 for Group I and 39.81 for Group II. This difference gives a x/σ value of 3.05, which is reliable, so that taken as a single group more teachers in Group II or least-participating counties with three years or

---

[2] For a discussion of this test see: Helen M. Walker, "Reliability of the Difference Between Two Per Cents."

less of prior experience have attended summer school than have such teachers in the most-participating counties.

Although the percentage of teachers who have attended summer school is approximately the same in the two groups of counties, except for the newer teachers, it may be that teachers in one group have attended more frequently than those in the other group. Perhaps the curriculum program has stimulated more frequent attendance among teachers in systems which have participated extensively. Table 68 gives the dis-

Table 68

DISTRIBUTION OF WHITE ELEMENTARY TEACHERS WHO HAVE ATTENDED SUMMER SCHOOL[a] SINCE BEGINNING TEACHING OR SINCE JUNE, 1930, ACCORDING TO NUMBER OF SESSIONS ATTENDED AND YEARS OF TEACHING EXPERIENCE, SELECTED COUNTIES, VIRGINIA, 1939

Number of Summer Sessions Attended[a]	8 or More Years' Experience		4–7 Years' Experience		0–3 Years' Experience	
	Group I Counties	Group II Counties	Group I Counties	Group II Counties	Group I Counties	Group II Counties
Five or more	35	23	7	3		
Four	34	26	7			
Three	73	45	17	6	4	5
Two	70	43	14	6	8	3
One	109	45	53	26	27	19
Total	321	182	98	41	39	27
Chi-square value						
Obtained	5.03		3.48		0.00[b]	
1% level	13.28		13.28		6.64	
5% level	9.49		9.49		3.84	

Source: Questionnaire form used in this study.

[a] A few teachers included here attended college during the academic year; one academic year is classified as three summer sessions.

[b] Because of small number of expected frequencies, these data were reclassified into "one summer session" and "two or more summer sessions" for the Chi-square test.

tribution of the number of teachers in each category of experience who have attended school, according to the number of sessions attended. These data were compared for any differences by means of the Chi-square procedure and in no case was anything approaching a reliable difference found between the two groups of teachers in the amount of summer school attendance.

In addition to summer school attendance, teachers may continue their professional study for credit through college extension work. Apparently a considerable amount of college work is carried in extension courses in Virginia. This may be done through correspondence, and also by attending evening and Saturday classes at near-by institutions. But in Virginia several institutions, especially the University of Virginia, organize classes in cities throughout the state for college study. Often these classes are organized upon the invitation and with the cooperation of local school officials. Such classes provide excellent opportunity for in-service training and study as well as permitting teachers to earn college credit. The work may well be more vital and stimulating than regular summer school attendance. Table 69 shows the number and percentage

Table 69

NUMBER AND PERCENTAGE OF WHITE ELEMENTARY TEACHERS WHO HAVE TAKEN
COLLEGE EXTENSION COURSES SINCE BEGINNING TEACHING OR SINCE
JUNE, 1930, SELECTED COUNTIES, VIRGINIA, 1939

Group of Counties	8 or More Years' Experience		4–7 Years' Experience		0–3 Years' Experience	
	Number	Per Cent	Number	Per Cent	Number	Per Cent
Group I counties ...	188	50.5	42	31.8	23	12.3
Group II counties ..	78	37.7	12	20.0	10	9.2
d_p		12.8		11.8		..[a]
σ		4.8		7.0		
$\sigma_{p1\text{-}p2}$						
x/σ value						
Obtained		2.67		1.69		
1% level		2.58		2.58		
5% level		1.96		1.96		

Source: Questionnaire form used in this study.
[a] Insufficient cases to make test of significance.

of teachers who had taken college extension courses since they began teaching or if that was prior to 1930 since June, 1930. The differences in percentages in the first two classifications of experience were tested for significance; and in the case of teachers with eight years or more of experience a reliable difference was found between the two groups, that is to say, teachers in the most-participating counties who have been teaching since the inception of the curriculum program have taken a significantly greater amount of extension work than have teachers in the least-participating counties. In the other two categories of experience a larger percentage of teachers in the most-participating counties took extension work, but significance of the differences could not be established.

The facts concerning continued professional study at higher institutions by teachers in white elementary schools may now be summarized as follows: In spite of much urging by leaders of the curriculum program in Virginia and the stimulation to such study that presumably might come from participation in the program, the evidence indicates that teachers in the most-participating counties had no better record in summer school attendance, either as to the percentage who attended or the amount of attendance by those who did continue study, than had teachers in the least-participating counties. In fact, the data reveal that the latter group of teachers have done slightly better than the former group. It must be remembered, however, that summer school attendance is extensive in both groups of counties and that four out of every five teachers who have taught four years or more have attended summer school since they began teaching or since 1930 if they began teaching prior to that year. Teachers in the most-participating counties who have taught throughout the period of the program, however, have taken more college work by extension than have the similar group of teachers in the least-participating counties. A more detailed investigation might show that county school systems which were taking an extensive part in the curriculum program provided more opportunities for study for college credit during the school year through locally held extension classes. The question remains as to the extent these figures can be relied on in drawing conclusions for all white elementary teachers in these counties. Over seventy per cent of the teachers returned questionnaire forms in the most-participating counties but only about forty per cent returned them in the least-participating group. Did the teachers who had good records of continued study at summer school tend to fill out the forms in larger proportions than other teachers? A more thoroughgoing study would need to be made to answer this question than is possible in the present one.

PROFESSIONAL READING

Three questions on the inquiry form sought information about the professional reading of teachers. The purpose was to determine if the two groups of teachers differed importantly in the extent to which they carried on voluntary professional study. The question to which an answer is sought here is this: Is extensive participation in the curriculum program associated with increased reading of professional books and magazines? One of the questions on the form asked teachers to give the number of different "educational magazines," not including the state education association journal or similar magazines received as a part of dues in a professional organization, which they had received by personal subscription sometime during the period from September, 1938, to December, 1939. The second question asked them to give the number of "books dealing specifically with education" which they had read during the same period but not including any read or studied in conjunction with college courses taken during summer session or in extension. This presumably represented the voluntary, free professional reading of teachers. Table 70 reports the replies to these questions. No statistically reliable difference was found between the means of the two groups of counties for either item. It will be noted that a larger mean percentage of white elementary teachers subscribed to professional magazines in the least-participating counties, while a larger percentage of teachers in the most-participating counties read professional books. Several counties make a rather poor showing on these items, Counties I–k and II–d in particular.

To determine if the teachers in either group of counties who do report such items tended to subscribe to more magazines or read more books per person, a Chi-square test was made for the total group. The values obtained were 3.01 for number of magazines and 3.58 for number of books, which clearly indicate that no important differences, in the number of subscriptions or books read, existed between the two groups of teachers who subscribed to professional magazines and who read professional books. One point more in this connection: Since teachers might not subscribe to professional magazines as extensively if they had access to them in a professional library they were asked on the form also to list the number of such magazines read regularly but to which they did not subscribe personally. An analysis of the summary

Table 70

PERCENTAGE OF WHITE ELEMENTARY TEACHERS WHO SUBSCRIBED TO
ONE OR MORE PROFESSIONAL MAGAZINES[a] AND WHO READ ONE
OR MORE PROFESSIONAL BOOKS[b] FROM SEPTEMBER, 1938,
TO DECEMBER, 1939, SELECTED COUNTIES, VIRGINIA

County	Per Cent Subscribing to Magazines	Per Cent Reading Books
Group I. Most-Participating Counties		
I-a	82.9	80.0
I-b	74.4	57.7
I-c	64.3	64.3
I-d	59.1	73.6
I-e	63.5	78.8
I-f	41.7	75.0
I-g	80.0	56.8
I-h	73.8	69.5
I-i	83.9	96.4
I-j	72.2	79.4
I-k	47.1	50.0
M	67.5	71.0
σ	13.3	12.6
Group II. Least-Participating Counties		
II-a	75.0	83.3
II-b	..[c]	..[c]
II-c	68.3	52.9
II-d	55.6	50.0
II-e	67.5	65.0
II-f	100.0	71.4
II-g	84.0	40.0
II-h	80.0	60.0
II-i	76.7	72.4
II-j	81.6	59.2
II-k	71.7	54.7
M	76.0	60.9
σ	11.2	11.9
d_m	8.5	10.1
σ_d	5.7	5.6
t value		
Obtained	1.5	1.8
1% level	2.86	2.86
5% level	2.09	2.09

Source: Questionnaire form used in this study.

[a] Does not include journals received by virtue of membership in organizations.

[b] Does not include books read or studied in conjunction with college courses.

[c] Insufficient returns.

of replies to this question shows that these figures so nearly duplicate the data for personal subscription to magazines that it was decided not to include them here. The important thing is that no differences existed in this respect which might have been a factor in explaining the data presented above.

While the data in Table 70 show that no statistically reliable differences existed between the two groups of counties in professional reading when the county is taken as the unit, it is possible that a few counties have influenced greatly the comparisons because of the fact that only twenty-two cases constitute the total number for comparative purposes. Any widely divergent county produces a high standard error under such conditions. Therefore, a comparison of the total groups of teachers, considering the teacher as the unit, was made of the percentage who subscribed to magazines and of the percentage who had read professional books. Four hundred and seventy-eight teachers, or 69.18 per cent, out of a total of 691 Group I teachers reported subscribing to magazines compared to 274, or 73.66 per cent, out of a total of 372 Group II teachers. The difference of these percentages divided by its standard error gives a value of 1.53, which shows that the difference is not reliable since it might occur in about twelve per cent of such random samples. With regard to professional books, 498, or 73.24 per cent, of 680 teachers in Group I counties reported having done such reading, compared to 218, or 58.76 per cent, of the 371 Group II teachers. This difference of 14.48 per cent divided by its standard error gives a value of 4.81, which indicates that the difference is highly reliable.

From the evidence presented in this section it appears that on the whole a larger proportion of teachers in the most-participating counties read professional books than did teachers in the least-participating counties. However, several counties apparently have not stimulated teachers in free reading of such books, with the result that when counties are taken as units the difference between the two groups of counties, while large, is not statistically reliable because of the large error variance that results from the influence of these extremes. The percentage of teachers who reported professional reading of books seems to correlate closely with the emphasis placed on reading, study, and group discussion by the county administrative and supervisory officers. The summaries of the programs of professional stimulation given in Chapter VI are worth a re-study in this connection. Those statements showed that Counties I–a, I–e, I–i, I–j emphasized study in their supervisory programs to a much greater extent than the other counties, and in Table 70 these four counties rank as the top four counties in percentage of teachers who have done professional reading. The record of County I–i should be particularly noted. This county has had a systematic study program during the last few years, and 96.4 per cent of the teachers reported having done professional reading. On the other hand, Counties I–b and I–k, according to Chapter VI, have not stressed organized study in recent years, turning attention more to informal group and individual conferences, and these two counties are low in percentage of teachers who have done free professional reading. In Group II counties, where little if any organized county study programs are carried on, only three counties exceed even the mean of the Group I counties. These bits of evidence would indicate that about fifty to sixty per cent of the white elementary teachers will as a matter of practice read at least one professional book in the course of a year, but that well-planned programs of stimulation are necessary to get many of the remaining part of the staff to read.

The evidence with respect to the percentage of teachers who subscribe to professional magazines is a bit confusing. The Group II counties make a slightly better showing in this respect. A guess may be hazarded that teachers in the most-participating counties, having supervision and the aid that comes from being a participant in the program, do not feel the need for or get help from the usual professional magazines on teaching methods and devices which seem to constitute an important item in the professional equipment of many elementary teachers.

The third aspect of professional reading which was investigated was the extent to which teachers had access to professional literature in libraries or other sources. Of all white elementary teachers in Group I counties who reported, 93.7 per cent stated that they had access to professional books and magazines, while 60.4 per cent of the Group II teachers reported having sources from which they could get such materials. In only one Group I county did any appreciable number of teachers report the lack of such facilities and even then it was but one out of every four teachers. On the other hand, in five of the ten Group II counties for which returns are available a large proportion (in four cases over one-half) of the teachers reported lack of any professional library facilities.

With respect to the location of professional literature only four out of ten Group II teachers reported that the school system, either the county itself or the local school, provided professional literature, while eight out of ten Group I teachers reported such provisions. Surprisingly, too, three times as large a percentage of teachers in Group I counties reported having access to professional books and magazines in public libraries. Thus facilities for carrying on professional reading were much more available to teachers in most-participating counties than to teachers in the least-participating group, as was pointed out in Chapter VI.

PROFESSIONAL ORGANIZATIONS

Information on membership in state and national professional organizations and attendance at educational conventions was secured by means of the inquiry form. The returns show that white elementary teachers in the Group I, or most-participating, counties tended to participate in professional organizations to a somewhat greater extent than teachers in least-participating counties. Practically all teachers in Virginia belong to the state education association, so no important differences are found there. However, 33.8 per cent of the Group I teachers reported holding membership in the National Education Association sometime during the period from September, 1938, to December, 1939, contrasted to 15.2 per cent of the Group II teachers. This is a signficant difference. Only fourteen Group I teachers and five Group II teachers listed membership in any other professional organizations.

One hundred and ninety-four, or 28.0 per cent, of the Group I teachers attended one or both of the annual meetings of the state education association held in 1938 and 1939, while seventy-nine, or 21.0 per cent, of the Group II teachers attended one or both of these meetings. This difference in percentages is significant. Four Group I and no Group II teachers reported attending meetings of the National Education Association during the period.

TEACHING PROCEDURES

Since the Virginia curriculum program has primarily stressed the improvement of classroom instruction it would be enlightening not only to those in charge of the program in the state, but to curriculum workers generally to ascertain if any significant differences actually are found between teaching procedures used by teachers in counties which have participated extensively in the program and those used by teachers in counties which have participated least. Are differences in procedures associated with participation? It was not the purpose of the present broad investigation to go into this aspect of the educational program intensively—that could well be the subject for a thoroughgoing study in itself—but it was felt that some indication of whether important differences existed might be gained by including a number of questions on important aspects of teaching in the inquiry form. These questions sought information about matters that have received much emphasis in the Virginia program. Tables 71, 72, and 73 following summarize these findings.

An explanation of the treatment of the data should be made at the outset. For this phase of the study teachers were classified into categories of those teaching in the lower grades, or grades kindergarten to four inclusive, in the upper grades, or grades five to seven inclusive (most Virginia schools have seven elementary grades), and in one-teacher schools, or grades one to seven inclusive. Since a much larger percentage of total returns in Group II counties was from the rural or one-teacher schools than was true in Group I counties it was considered advisable to eliminate these teachers in most of the comparisons. The peculiar conditions prevailing in such schools might cause these teachers to respond differently to many of the questions relating to teaching procedures, and thus invalidate the comparisons between the two groups of counties. Taking the two categories of lower grades and upper grades as totals gives a very similar teaching group for the two sets of counties. In the Group I counties 56.2 per cent of the teachers replying were in the lower grade group and 43.8 per cent in the upper grade group when these two were used as the total; in Group II counties the percentages were 57.3 per cent and 42.7 per cent respectively.

In developing broad units of work in keeping with the recommendations of the Virginia tentative course of study, a flexible daily program of work is desirable, if not necessary. In suggestions for use of the course of study, it is stated that "The daily program should provide for flexibility in time allotment. . . . The program should provide for

Table 71

PERCENTAGE OF WHITE ELEMENTARY TEACHERS NOT INCLUDING THOSE IN ONE-TEACHER
SCHOOLS, REPORTING FLEXIBLE DAILY CLASS SCHEDULE, CLASS EXCURSIONS
AND TRIPS, AND CLASS STUDY OF COMMUNITY LIFE, SELECTED
COUNTIES, VIRGINIA, 1939

County	Per Cent of Teachers Who Report		
	Flexible Time Schedule for Class Work	Class Excursions and Trips	Class Study of Community Life
Group I. Most-Participating Counties			
I–a	64.1	55.1	53.2
I–b	82.5	44.4	67.1
I–c	71.4	46.2	69.2
I–d	69.3	34.1	51.3
I–e	63.1	23.5	55.7
I–f	63.6	8.3	45.5
I–g	71.4	20.9	52.5
I–h	61.7	27.9	64.9
I–i	75.9	41.9	35.7
I–j	65.9	48.0	63.8
I–k	17.6	47.1	64.7
M	64.2	36.1	56.7
σ	15.9	13.7	9.9
Group II. Least-Participating Counties			
II–a	20.0	28.6	35.0
II–b	. . [a]	. . [a]	. . [a]
II–c	26.9	26.1	50.9
II–d	25.0	0.0	0.0
II–e	31.6	20.0	47.4
II–f	20.0	40.0	40.0
II–g	43.5	21.7	22.7
II–h	36.4	40.0	35.7
II–i	25.0	42.9	28.0
II–j	41.0	15.0	41.2
II–k	34.1	40.9	55.0
M	30.4	27.5	35.6
σ	7.9	13.2	15.1
d_m	33.8	8.6	21.1
σ_d	5.9	6.3	5.9
t value			
Obtained	5.7	1.4	3.6
1% level	2.86	2.86	2.86
5% level	2.09	2.09	2.09

Source: Questionnaire form used in this study.
[a] Insufficient returns.

long, uninterrupted work periods."[3] Two questions were, therefore, included on the inquiry form dealing with daily program: One asked the teacher to indicate by checking "Yes" or "No" if he had a definite time schedule for each day of the week which he followed regularly in holding recitations; and another asked the teacher to give the number of recitation or activity periods, in lieu of recitations, which were twenty minutes or less, over twenty minutes and up to one hour, and one hour or over in length. The percentage of lower and upper grade teachers combined, that is, all teachers except those in one-teacher schools, who stated that they did not have a definite daily time schedule which they followed regularly—in other words, those that had a flexible schedule—is shown in Table 71. And it reveals a decided difference between the practices of teachers in the two groups of counties. From six to eight teachers out of every ten in the Group I counties, except County I–k, reported flexible schedules, but only two to four teachers in every ten had flexible daily programs in the least-participating counties. The difference between the mean percentages for the groups is highly significant. Taking the teachers in each group of counties as a whole so that an extreme situation in individual counties would not affect so strongly the comparison, it is found that 67.1 per cent of the teachers in Group I counties and 31.1 per cent in Group II counties had flexible schedules. The difference of 36.0 per cent is over ten times its standard error, hence also highly significant.

The total number of class recitation or activity periods in lieu of recitations classified according to length is as follows:

	Group I Counties	Group II Counties
One hour and over...........	545	56
Over twenty minutes and up to one hour in length.........	1,449	605
Twenty minutes or less.......	1,170	729

The Chi-square value obtained in comparing the two groups is 182.2, which shows a highly reliable difference between the groups. This would seem to be due to the large number of periods one hour and over in length in the Group I counties.

[3] Virginia State Board of Education, *Tentative Course of Study for Virginia Elementary Schools, Grades I-VII,* p. 33.

Apparently, then, teachers in the most-participating group of counties did provide for flexibility in scheduling the work of the class and in doing so provided much greater opportunity for pupils to work for long periods on the activities under way.

The Virginia curriculum program, in seeking improvement of classroom instruction, has particularly emphasized the importance of relating school experiences of pupils to community life or, better, developing the broad units of work out of the familiar aspects of community living. The tentative course of study suggests "Community Life" as the center of interest for the entire year's work in the second grade, and throughout the elementary grades practically every area of study suggests pupil activities which are community centered. Two questions touching on the extent to which teachers utilized the community for study were included in the questionnaire form to determine if any differences existed betweeen the practices of teachers in the two groups of counties. One asked them to give the number of excursions or trips away from the school building on which they had taken pupils during school hours since the opening of school that fall (1939), and the other asked teachers if any of their classes had studied more or less intensively during the same period any community problems or aspects of community life growing out of their own communities. Table 71 shows both the percentage of teachers who reported such excursions and those who had developed units on community life.

In the case of excursions, wide variation in practice is found with one-half the teachers in some counties but only one-fifth or less of the teachers in other counties in Group I reporting class trips. None of the Group II counties had as good a record in this respect as had five Group I counties. The difference between the mean percentages is 8.6, which is not statistically reliable. When the teachers are considered as total groups, the percentages remain about the same as the mean for county percentages, being 38.8 and 26.9, but this difference is significant, with a ratio of 3.6 betweeen the difference of 11.9 and the standard error.

Group I teachers reported much more study of community life than Group II teachers; the difference between the group means is highly reliable with a t value of 3.6 and the difference between the percentages for the groups taken as a whole is also significant, the ratio being 4.7.

The evidence warrants the conclusion that teachers in the most-

Table 72

PERCENTAGE OF WHITE ELEMENTARY TEACHERS NOT INCLUDING THOSE IN
ONE-TEACHER SCHOOLS REPORTING DEVELOPMENT OF LARGE UNITS OF WORK,
AND INTRODUCTION OF MAJOR CHANGES IN TEACHING, SELECTED COUNTIES,
VIRGINIA, 1939

County	Per Cent of Teachers Who Report	
	Large Units of Work	Major Changes in Teaching
Group I. Most-Participating Counties		
I–a	82.8	81.8
I–b	78.7	92.2
I–c	85.7	68.4
I–d	85.2	81.3
I–e	74.3	90.8
I–f	91.7	77.8
I–g	82.5	85.0
I–h	87.1	55.6
I–i	51.1	77.8
I–j	78.3	80.1
I–k	64.3	72.7
M	78.3	78.5
σ	11.1	9.8
Group II. Least-Participating Counties		
II–a	62.5	45.5
II–b	....ᵃ	....ᵃ
II–c	64.1	73.8
II–d	62.5	81.8
II–e	69.4	70.6
II–f	60.0	80.0
II–g	43.5	40.9
II–h	87.5	53.8
II–i	40.0	77.8
II–j	40.5	86.1
II–k	63.4	70.3
M	59.3	68.1
σ	13.9	15.0
d_m	19.0	10.4
σ_d	5.8	5.8
t value		
Obtained	3.3	1.8
1% level	2.86	2.86
5% level	2.09	2.09

Source: Questionnaire form used in this study.
ᵃ Insufficient returns.

participating counties by and large did give much more attention to community life in the school instructional program than did teachers in least-participating counties. In some of these former counties few teachers seemed to utilize the class trip as a teaching procedure, but in all counties emphasis, although in a varying degree, was placed on a correlation of classroom work with community life.

Broad units of work to whose development materials from all subject fields contribute comprise the basis of curriculum organization recommended in the Virginia tentative course of study. To ascertain whether teachers in the two sets of counties actually differed in the extent to which they used the broad unit organization, teachers were asked to state if they had developed any large units of work in their classes so far that school year in which pupils organized their study, work, and class activities for some period of time around a major problem or area, such as transportation, recreation, communication, production and similar problems listed in the course of study. Table 72 shows the percentage of teachers, excluding those in one-teacher schools, who reported that they had developed such units. In nine Group I counties at least seven out of every ten teachers utilized broad teaching units as a teaching procedure. And even in the Group II counties from four to six out of every ten teachers in most counties had developed such units. The groups were more uniform within themselves than usual, so that the difference between means, 19.0 per cent, is highly significant. Almost the same percentages were secured when the two total groups of teachers were considered; 78.2 per cent of all Group I and 58.7 per cent of the Group II teachers reported the development of units. The difference between these percentages is also reliable.

Teachers in the most-participating counties, it may be concluded, did give much more attention to the broad unit plan of curriculum organization than did teachers in the least-participating counties.

Teachers were asked baldly whether they had made any major changes during the previous five years in their teaching procedures or in the way in which they organized the subject matter taught. Approximately eighty per cent of Group I teachers and seventy per cent of Group II teachers, as is shown in Table 72, reported making major changes. If these changes really are major, the curriculum program in Virginia has indeed had a tremendous influence. The difference

Table 73

PERCENTAGE OF TEACHERS, CLASSIFIED BY GRADE LEVEL, FOLLOWING VARIOUS TEACHING PRACTICES, SELECTED COUNTIES, VIRGINIA, 1939

Practice	Lower Grade Teachers			Upper Grade Teachers		
	Group I Counties	Group II Counties	d_p / σ_{p1-p2}	Group I Counties	Group II Counties	d_p / σ_{p1-p2}
1. Letting pupils read library books and the like only after they have completed daily assignments	19.5[a]	25.0	1.47[b]	24.3	35.2	2.29[b]
2. Making much more use of things in the community in developing class work	80.3	59.3	5.16	77.0	63.3	2.91
3. Drastically reducing the amount of time usually spent on drill and practice work	42.9	21.5	4.83	35.5	24.2	2.27
4. Insisting that pupils attain at least approximately the standards set for the grade before being promoted or passed	58.7	76.2	3.95	56.4	76.6	3.92
5. Having pupils regularly share in planning the activities in which they engage in carrying forward their work	91.1	72.1	5.78	83.5	66.4	3.90
6. Insisting that at least most of the pupils master the required work before going to a new topic or subject	61.1	64.5	0.68	67.9	75.8	1.62
7. Planning a variety of activities in which pupils may engage as they carry forward a unit of work	91.3	70.4	6.34	87.2	53.9	7.46
8. Scheduling long periods in the day during which pupils may work on the development of a unit of work	52.9	25.0	5.54	67.9	21.9	8.70
9. Organizing most of the school work into a program of study which centers around the major aspects of social living	70.8	39.0	6.21	63.9	34.4	5.58
10. Using the textbooks as the basis for teaching the subjects	50.0	75.6	5.62	55.4	85.9	6.02

Source: Questionnaire form used in this study.

[a] Interpret the table as follows: Of 380 teachers in Group I counties who teach in the kindergarten to fourth grade inclusive, 74 or 19.5 per cent checked this item as one teaching practice.

[b] The one per cent level of probability is 2.58 and the five per cent level is 1.96.

between the two mean percentages is not reliable. However, if again the total group of teachers is considered, the percentage of teachers who reported making major changes is 80.5 per cent for Group I counties and 68.5 per cent for Group II counties. The difference in this case is significant, so that as a group a significantly larger proportion of teachers in the most-participating counties have made major changes in their teaching procedures or in organization of subject matter.

The most common changes reported by teachers may be summarized as changes which provided much greater flexibility in the classroom work. A more flexible pattern of instruction, use of a wider variety of pupil activities, group work, and the granting of more freedom to children were commonly listed under this type of change. Many teachers gave as their major change the use of large units of work as the basis of organizing instruction, and another large group of changes listed may be characterized as the giving of much greater attention to both individual and group interests and needs.

The last item on the questionnaire which sought to secure an insight into teaching procedures was a check list of ten practices, reproduced in Table 73. Teachers were requested to check those which they practiced in their teaching. The list contained statements of both practices recommended and encouraged throughout the curriculum program and of some which would be in conflict with the spirit and interest of the program. Since teachers had quite a choice of selection, the results should give a good insight into those things which teachers emphasize in their classroom instruction. Table 73 gives the percentages of teachers in each group of counties teaching in the kindergarten through fourth grades and in the fifth to seventh grades inclusive who checked the various practices.

It is interesting that the percentage checking the first item, which is a practice certainly not in keeping with present-day thinking, is about the same as the percentage reporting that they had not introduced any major changes in teaching procedures. While a higher percentage of Group II teachers checked this practice, the difference is not so great as to be entirely reliable. A much larger proportion of Group I teachers made greater use of community resources in their class work than did Group II teachers. This confirms findings presented in Table 71. Item number three on the list is enlightening; over forty per cent of the lower grade teachers in the most-participating counties indicated that they were giving much less time to drill teaching. This is in keeping with the principles of the Virginia program. But at least three out of every four Group II teachers stated that they still devoted as much time as formerly to drill work. Replies to the fourth practice show that Group I teachers were relaxing rigid, arbitrary grade standards to a much greater extent than Group II teachers. The very large percentages of teachers even in the Group II counties who checked items number five and seven, pupil sharing in planning the class work and use of a variety of activities, shows that two of the chief tenets of the Virginia program were being quite widely practiced by all teachers. In both cases the differences between the percentages, however, are highly significant. Replies to item number nine on the list, organization of the instructional program around the major aspects of social living, show that a much larger proportion of teachers in the Group I counties sought to follow the plan of organization set up in the state tentative course of study, while the replies to the last item show that the textbook dominated teaching to a much greater extent in the least-participating counties. In general, then, the results reported in Table 73 confirm what has been presented earlier in this section with respect to teaching practices. And they reveal again that teachers in the group of most-participating counties have made great strides forward in adopting progressive practices.

This section of the study has summarized the reported classroom practices and procedures of white elementary teachers, not including rural teachers, in the two groups of counties. Important differences were found, with a significantly larger percentage of teachers in the most-participating counties reporting the use of procedures which are emphasized by the Virginia curriculum program. More general use by teachers of what are generally considered to be desirable teaching procedures is associated with participation of the school system in the curriculum program. And these differences existed even though teachers in the least-participating counties undoubtedly have been influenced, perhaps greatly, by the program. The comparison here is not between teachers cooperating in the program and teachers entirely ignorant of it, but between teachers in school systems in the same state which have participated extensively and those which have participated slightly in the program over an eight-year period.

TEACHER VIEWPOINT

Part III of the inquiry form distributed to teachers, as stated in Chapter I, was the Mort-Cornell-Hinton opinionnaire called "What Should Our Schools Do?," except that the last five statements of Part III, Numbers 101 to 105 inclusive, were added to the opinionnaire for the purposes of this study. The first 100 statements constituting the Mort-Cornell-Hinton scale were scored and treated as a unit, the last five added statements being used in another connection. As will be seen from an examination of the opinionnaire, which is reproduced in the Appendix, it is composed of a series of statements about educational practice with which the respondent is asked to express his agreement or disagreement. Thus the form is designed to secure some measure of viewpoint on educational issues and was used in the present study to gain an insight into the educational point of view held by teachers in the two groups of counties. Teachers' replies were marked right or wrong in accordance with the key provided with the scale. The authors state that the accepted answers in the key are based on the "way in which a jury of professors and advanced students of education judged the manner in which a person willing to accept the implications of newer education practices would respond to the items." A score of 100 would indicate that the person had marked each statement in accordance with the views of an overwhelming majority of forward-looking educational leaders who participated in marking the scale for use in preparation of the key.

The scores made by white elementary teachers on the scale are given in Table 74 and the mean score for each county is shown in Table 75. The mean score for Group I teachers taken as a whole is 76.10 and for Group II teachers 73.19. The difference of 2.91 points is highly significant. Taking the counties as units, the mean of the mean county scores is 76.78 for Group I counties and 72.88 for Group II counties. Again, the difference is statistically reliable. Table 75 shows that not a single Group II county has a mean score as high as the group mean for the Group I counties and, on the other hand, that not a single Group I county falls below the group mean of the least-participating counties. Moreover, seven Group I counties exceeded the highest Group II county in mean score. Incidentally, the high score made by County

Table 74

DISTRIBUTION OF SCORES OF "WHAT SHOULD OUR SCHOOLS DO?" MADE BY WHITE
ELEMENTARY TEACHERS, SELECTED COUNTIES, VIRGINIA

Score	Group I Counties	Group II Counties	Score	Group I Counties	Group II Counties
98–100		1	65–67	31	36
95– 97	3		62–64	21	25
92– 94	2	2	59–61	15	10
89– 91	16	2	56–58	10	6
86– 88	41	9	53–55	3	6
83– 85	84	34	50–52		4
80– 82	97	43	47–49	2	
77– 79	111	47	44–46		1
74– 76	110	57	41–43		1
71– 73	78	43		—	—
68– 70	66	44	Total	690	371

M	76.10[a]		73.19[a]
σ	7.68[a]		8.32[a]
d_m		2.91	
σ_d		0.51	
t value			
Obtained		5.70	
1% level		2.58	
5% level		1.96	

Source: First 100 questions of Part III of questionnaire form used in this study.
[a] Calculated from ungrouped data.

I–i is interesting since this is the same county in which 96.4 per cent of the teachers, according to Table 70, had engaged in free reading of professional books during the preceding year.

It is evident, then, that insofar as educational viewpoint is measured by the scale "What Should Our Schools Do?" white elementary teachers in the most-participating counties had a more progressive, forward-looking philosophy than teachers in the least-participating counties.

The scores made by two other sets of teachers on the opinionnaire are available, so the two groups of Virginia teachers may be compared to teachers in other situations. The manual of directions for the scale gives the percentile scores made by 1,546 teachers in Pennsylvania and by teachers in a large mid-western city. Examination of the original data shows that 774 teachers were included in the latter group. Comparative

Table 75

MEAN SCORE OF WHITE ELEMENTARY TEACHERS ON "WHAT SHOULD OUR SCHOOLS DO?" SELECTED COUNTIES, VIRGINIA

Group I Most-Participating Counties		Group II Least-Participating Counties	
County	Mean Score	County	Mean Score
I–a	78.47	II–a	75.13
I–b	77.31	II–b	....ᵃ
I–c	82.14	II–c	72.91
I–d	75.77	II–d	71.61
I–e	76.31	II–e	73.41
I–f	75.00	II–f	74.50
I–g	76.80	II–g	71.08
I–h	73.60	II–h	69.80
I–i	80.42	II–i	71.86
I–j	74.42	II–j	73.92
I–k	74.35	II–k	74.60
M	76.78		72.88
σ	2.54		1.66
dₘ		3.90	
σd		0.99	
t value			
Obtained		3.94	
1% level		2.86	
5% level		2.09	

Source: First 100 questions of Part III of questionnaire form used in this study.
ᵃ Insufficient returns.

percentile and mean scores are given in Table 76. The Pennsylvania and mid-western city groups included both elementary and high school teachers. The table shows that both Virginia groups made better scores than the mid-western city teachers. However, Pennsylvania teachers made about the same quartile scores as the most-participating group in Virginia and somewhat above those made by the least-participating group. The data are inconclusive insofar as they give any clue as to how Virginia teachers' viewpoint compares to the views of teachers in other sections.

Some insight into likenesses and differences in the expressed viewpoint of the two groups of Virginia teachers might be gotten by study-

Table 76

QUARTILE AND MEAN SCORE ON "WHAT SHOULD OUR SCHOOLS DO?"
OF FOUR GROUPS OF TEACHERS

	Virginia		Pennsylvania Teachers	Teachers in Large City
	Group I Counties	Group II Counties		
Third quartile	82	79	82	78
Median	77	74	76	71
First quartile	71	68	70	64
Mean	76.10	73.19		70.12

Source: "Manual of Directions for What Should Our Schools Do?" and Table 74 above.

ing the replies to certain key statements on the questionnaire form. Table 77 gives the percentage of white elementary teachers in the two groups of counties who expressed agreement with selected statements. The ratio of the difference between the two percentages to its standard error is also given. It should be noted that the figures show the percentage of teachers agreeing with the statement, regardless of what the keyed answer might be. The table is self-explanatory, and discussion of each item is unnecessary here. A study of the replies to statements number 9, 22, and 104, however, is particularly revealing; in the case of teachers in most-participating counties a marked consistency of viewpoint is found, with the results showing that about twenty to twenty-five per cent of this group were unsympathetic with any efforts which would abolish traditional subjects or drastically change traditional procedures. It will be recalled in this connection that almost this same percentage of Group I teachers, as shown in Table 72, reported that they did not use the unit procedure of teaching at all and had not made any major changes in their teaching procedures or in methods of organizing subject matter in the past five years. This would seem to indicate that about one teacher in every four in the most-participating counties is unsympathetic with the viewpoint and procedures emphasized in the Virginia curriculum program. Here is a challenge to supervisors, superintendents, and State Department of Education staff members in even the school systems which have been most active in the program.

Oddly enough, about the same proportion of teachers in the least-

Teaching Personnel

Table 77

PERCENTAGE OF WHITE ELEMENTARY TEACHERS WHO AGREE WITH CERTAIN STATE-
MENTS FROM "WHAT SHOULD OUR SCHOOLS DO?" AND ADDED ITEMS, SELECTED
COUNTIES, VIRGINIA

Statement	Per Cent Who Agree		$\dfrac{d_p{}^a}{\sigma_{p1-p2}}$
	Group I Counties	Group II Counties	
5. Social studies should not be limited to the traditional subjects, such as geography, history and civics, but should emphasize contemporary problems like slum clearance, conservation of natural resources, crime prevention, safety, etc.	98.3	93.5	.. ᵇ
8. Children should repeat work when tests reveal that they have not attained mastery of minimum essentials in the work	76.5	83.6	2.69
9. The entire curriculum of both elementary and high school should be organized round life problems, such as making a home, raising children, running a business, being a consumer, being a citizen, and using leisure	76.8	74.7	0.78
10. The schools should consolidate and pass on the cultural gains achieved in the past; changes in society should be initiated by other agencies ..	40.0	44.7	1.50
13. There is enough to do in schools now without adding more subjects or activities for children to take	37.1	37.5	0.12
14. Progress cannot be expected in school practices unless there is experimentation	93.5	88.1	2.98
22. Reading, writing, and arithmetic should be taught much less through the medium of spelling books, readers, formal drill, and texts and more in connection with activities, such as planning a home and running a miniature store ...	75.5	74.9	0.21
26. A teacher should not be judged in terms of the amount of subject matter his pupils have learned	91.0	85.2	2.91
29. The community life itself should be the source of many of the problems given consideration by children in regular school work	99.1	98.7	.. ᵇ
30. Textbook learning should give way to increased learning through experience	84.9	84.9	0.01
35. In current school practice children are required to learn too many things which are of no value to them	51.3	58.5	2.25
40. In the traditional subject-matter divisions, such as reading, writing, arithmetic, Latin, and literature, there is sufficient preparation for the			

Table 77 (*Continued*)

| Statement | Per Cent Who Agree | | $d_p{}^a$ |
	Group I Counties	Group II Counties	σ_{p1-p2}
everyday problems of living, such as making a home, using leisure, and good citizenship	13.9	15.1	0.52
42. Most new ideas in education are all right in theory but not in practice	35.7	48.5	4.07
53. Pupils should be free to move about the classroom and to talk in groups about class work ..	92.3	77.9	6.74
54. The increase in the number of subjects in the curriculum has resulted in sacrifice of thoroughness	45.5	52.0	2.04
61. Young children would benefit by having more social experiences and less formal instruction in reading and arithmetic	80.6	73.8	2.53
78. New types of activities—excursions, art and dramatic projects, and the like—should not involve reduction of time given to the three R's	41.3	43.4	0.66
82. Grades and marks are indispensable for stimulating pupils to do their best	29.0	36.9	2.65
83. Experimentation is desirable in schools only if it does not interfere with the regular school program	24.4	32.4	2.80
98. If the school program is changed to suit the interests of individual children, the results will be aimless waste of time	11.3	20.2	3.95
99. Mathematics instruction is justified as a required course because it is a means of training the mind	41.3	53.4	3.76
101. Curriculum revision has been made so rapidly in the past five years that it has upset teachers and harmed education	34.4	40.2	1.87
102. All children in the same class should be doing about the same things	21.2	36.9	5.53
103. Considerable use of library reference materials tends to interfere with complete mastery of the regular textbook, resulting in a loss of desirable development of the pupil	6.5	13.8	3.91
104. For the elementary school, I favor a curriculum which in large part represents an organization in terms of separate subjects	20.7	42.6	7.52
105. Educational experts rather than classroom teachers should make the curriculum	9.4	11.9	1.24

Source: Part III of questionnaire form used in this study.

ᵃ To be a statistically reliable difference this ratio should be 2.58, that being the one per cent level of probability. The five per cent level of probability is 1.96.

ᵇ The percentages are too large to test the significance of difference by the procedure used here.

participating counties as in the Group I counties agreed to the desirability of utilizing broad units of work organized around meaningful experiences of children, but in statement number 104 they showed a much greater reluctance to depart from the traditional subject matter basis of organization.

Some of the important differences between the two composite groups of teachers with respect to viewpoint are found in these items: insistence on the mastery of subject matter (items 8, 26, and 103); the need for experimentation and change (items 14, 42, and 83); teaching procedures with respect to pupil freedom (items 53, 102, and 61); efficacy of formal discipline (item 99); use of failure as a motivating procedure (items 8 and 82); and subject matter orientation of the curriculum (items 35, 54, 98, and 104).

Replies to the last five statements given in Table 77, which were appended to the original Mort-Cornell-Hinton scale, are particularly revealing. The answers to statement 101 show that only one teacher in three in the most-participating counties has been particularly disturbed by the curriculum revision program in spite of its tempo and broad sweep in Virginia. It is generally recognized that the leaders of the state program have incessantly encouraged and worked for basic curriculum revision. Those school systems which have joined wholeheartedly in the program have moved forward rapidly, relatively speaking, in reorganizing instruction, in making a break with tradition, and in embarking on a new program of instruction. Chapter VI showed the constant efforts being made in these counties to stimulate, to encourage, and to help teachers modify their practice, yet two-thirds of the teachers feel that progress has not been too fast nor too disruptive. This is a tribute to the professional spirit and understanding of the teachers in the eleven most-participating counties and to the high quality of leadership provided by county school superintendents and supervisors and, primarily by the State Department of Education.

On the other hand, forty per cent of the teachers replying from the least-participating counties were disturbed by curriculum revision. In view of the lack of any important participation in these counties, this would seem to represent a fear of the program by teachers who have done little or have been unable to do little in it. These are probably the teachers who fear that if the program is pushed they will be engulfed in it, but who feel unable to make the necessary adjustments entailed in more active participation.

A sharp difference in views regarding pupil freedom and teaching procedures is evident in replies to statements 102 and 103. Replies to statement 104 show, as previously stated, that about one-fifth of the teachers in the most-participating counties believed the subject basis of organizing the curriculum to be the most satisfactory procedure. Two out of every five teachers in the least-participating counties likewise favor the separate subject basis of organization. It is apparent even from this expressed willingness to make a change that much professional study and discussion is necessary in these Group II counties before widespread progress can be made. It is significant that practically all the teachers in both sets of counties accept the present-day view of progressive educators as to who should make the curriculum.

In summary, it appears that in expressed points of view on many basic educational problems and issues teachers in both the most-participating and the least-participating counties were much alike in their thinking. However, on several important educational principles a much smaller percentage of teachers in the least-participating counties were willing to accept the more progressive point of view than were teachers in the most-participating counties. This cleavage in opinion occurred particularly with respect to the place of subjects and subject matter in the curriculum and in teaching procedures to be used in carrying on learning activities in the school.

SUMMARY

DIFFERENCES

The following differences were found to exist with respect to the white elementary teaching personnel and to certain teaching practices and procedures and the expressed point of view of these teachers in the two groups of counties.

1. Teachers in the most-participating group of counties received higher salaries on the average than teachers in the least-participating group of counties throughout the entire period under study—1930-1939.

2. By and large white elementary teachers were better trained in the most-participating counties. This difference seemed to be due to a smaller proportion of teachers with less than two years of training in

1930-31 and to a larger proportion of teachers with four years or more of training in 1934-35 and 1938-39.

3. When segregated as a class, teachers with three years or less of previous teaching experience in 1939 had attended summer school during the period of their experience in much larger numbers, proportionately, than had similar teachers in the most-participating counties.

4. A larger percentage of teachers in the most-participating counties than in the least-participating counties had taken college extension courses. The difference is statistically reliable in the case of teachers with eight and more years of experience.

5. As a total group, teachers in the most-participating counties had read more professional books, but had subscribed to fewer professional magazines during the year previous to December, 1939, than had teachers in the least-participating counties. The difference is reliable in the first case but not in the second. However, wide variations were found among counties in each group, so that differences in group means are not reliable in either instance.

6. A much greater percentage of teachers in the most-participating counties reported access to professional literature in school and public libraries and other sources than did teachers in the least-participating counties.

7. In teaching procedures, a higher percentage of white elementary teachers in the most-participating counties reported using a flexible daily program for class work, taking class excursions, developing units on community life, using broad units of work in their teaching, and making major changes during the past five years in their teaching procedures than did teachers in the least-participating counties. If these percentages are taken for the groups of teachers as a whole all are significant, but differences in group means when the county is used as the unit are not reliable in all cases.

8. A check list of teaching practices revealed further important differences between procedures practiced by the two groups of teachers.

9. When educational point of view is measured by means of the Mort-Cornell-Hinton scale "What Should Our Schools Do?" teachers in the most-participating counties made a reliably higher average score than did the teachers in the least-participating counties. Also, very important differences of opinion were revealed in answer to key questions.

LIKENESSES

The likenesses in personnel and teaching factors were found to be as follows:

1. The two groups of counties were much alike in the tenure of teachers, whether measured by the average length of service in the county of teachers serving in any one of the years 1930-31, 1934-35, and 1938-39, by the percentage of teachers serving their first year in their respective positions in the same years, or by the percentage who had been in their then present position five years or less in the three selected years.

2. The average age of white elementary teachers in 1939 was 33.0 years in the most-participating counties and 34.0 years in the least-participating counties—an unimportant difference.

3. A somewhat higher percentage of the 1939 teaching staff in the least-participating counties were teaching in their home county than in the most-participating counties, but the difference was not reliable.

4. As a total group, teachers in each set of counties had attended summer school to about the same extent during the period of their teaching experience since 1930. This is true both of the proportion of teachers attending and the number of sessions attended during the period. However, as stated above, teachers in the least-participating counties with three years or less of previous experience attended summer school in much larger proportion than did similar teachers in the most-participating counties.

CHAPTER VIII

Conclusions and Implications

UTILIZING the method of analyzing the characteristic likenesses and differences of a group of counties which have participated most extensively and of a group which have been least active in the Virginia state curriculum program some forty or more factors have been investigated to determine those which are associated with participation in a comprehensive, cooperative type of state curriculum program.

The findings will not be repeated here; their import can only be correctly understood by a careful study of the supporting data in Chapters IV, V, VI, and VII, and summaries at the close of each chapter have already brought together the more important results of the study. The conclusions concerning each factor investigated are important to curriculum workers, administrators, state school officials, and educational leaders generally. Much emphasis has been given in recent years and is being given to curriculum development through voluntary, cooperative state programs, and it is important for all concerned in the organization and direction of such movements to know whether a factor, be it geographic, sociologic, economic, educational, or professional in nature, facilitates and is congenial to cooperation of local school systems in such state-wide ventures or whether it is not a differentiated characteristic with respect to extent of participation of school systems in the program. In other words, the conclusions are significant regardless of whether the two groups of counties were alike or unlike in the characteristic, so long as the factor is relevant to efforts to improve instruction in the classroom.

What are the implications of the findings? In light of them, what of state curriculum development programs in the future? How should they be organized to be most effective? What difficulties need be overcome? What conditions may be utilized to best advantage in furthering

232

significant participation? Two factors emerge from all the evidence of the study as being basic to extensive participation by local school systems in a state cooperative curriculum program of the type organized and developed in Virginia—leadership and, relatively speaking, high economic ability to finance schools. Perhaps the two are in a measure inextricable, but extensive participation may be found in local school units of low economic ability if good leadership is present. On the other hand, high economic ability does not insure the presence of good leadership in administrative and supervisory staff. Leadership would seem to be the crux of the matter. But insofar as a high per-capita level of wealth enables the local school governing body to employ administrative and supervisory officers with vision, ability, imagination, and the other traits so essential to leadership and to provide funds whereby these officers may employ teachers of ability and provide facilities and equipment that aid in the carrying forward of a progressive school program, it is a basic factor in participation.

The difference in the economic ability of the two groups of counties studied with respect to participation was marked, regardless of the measure used to determine this ability. The group mean of the amount of locally taxable wealth per pupil enrolled for the most-participating counties was at least fifty per cent greater than that for the least-participating counties for each of the nine years of 1930 to 1939. And from two to almost three times as many people proportionately paid a state income tax in the most-participating counties as in the least-participating counties in respective years of this same period. In total wealth per capita, value of farm land, and other factors, the much greater economic resources of the most-participating counties are conclusively shown in the study.

The influence of this superior economic ability on other associated factors is seen in several very important instances: Although the average size of the county school system as measured by the number of white elementary pupils in average daily attendance is somewhat larger in the case of the least-participating group of counties, the average annual salary of superintendents of schools is much higher in the most-participating group of counties. Even if it be recognized that both of these averages are greatly affected by one or two extreme cases and that the inclusion of Negro children would change the comparison with respect to the size of the school system, nevertheless inspection of the data shows that superintendents in the least-participating counties are not paid salaries comparable to those paid in the most-participating counties. The question in this connection, then, becomes: Have the most-participating counties secured a higher type of educational leadership through the paying of better salaries? The writer believes this to be the case. And ability and leadership in the superintendent are factors of utmost importance in participation. In fact, a dynamic superintendent of schools can, if he so desires, probably overcome almost any handicap to participation by his school system in a state cooperative curriculum program of the stimulative type organized in Virginia.

The influence of a dynamic superintendent of schools on participation is forcefully brought out in the case of several counties in each group. They cannot be singled out by name because of possible embarrassment, but on the basis of other key factors associated with participation three counties which have taken a very active part in the curriculum program would be expected to rank low in the extent of actual participation. But familiarity with the situation indicates that the leadership of the superintendents of schools has counterbalanced the effect of these factors and has resulted in active participation. On the other hand, a study of the data for individual counties would lead one to believe that on the basis of these same important factors at least two counties in the least-participating group should be very active participants and perhaps should fall in the class of most-participating counties. Again the superintendent of schools seems to be the answer as to why they are not actively participating counties.

The influence on participation of both the factor of high economic ability and that of the leadership of the superintendent is again evident in the employment of elementary school supervisors. All of the most-participating counties employed supervisors for white elementary schools during the entire period under analysis—1930-1939—with two minor exceptions, while none of the least-participating counties had supervision except for one year in one county and two years in another county early in the period. Under the very generous state-aid plan for supervision the local county pays only one-third of the salary of a supervisor for white elementary schools. Thus most counties pay but $500 to $800 for such supervision from their own funds—certainly an insignificant sum in a county school budget. Yet none of the least-participating counties have consistently provided such service. That low financial ability is more an excuse than a reason is indicated by the fact that two of the counties, both with serious school financial problems, were adding supervision in 1939-40.

Supervision appears to be a crucial factor in participation. A dynamic supervisor who is sympathetic to the point of view, principles, and method underlying the state curriculum program and who has the active support, cooperation, and sympathetic guidance of the superintendent is the catalytic agent in securing the active, enthusiastic participation of a school system in a state cooperative program. In fact, supervision with these two necessary correlates seems to be basic to participation. And that again is where leadership comes in—not only in the supervisor himself but in the superintendent who, envisaging the possibilities inherent in supervision of the right sort for the improvement of instruction, makes provision in his school program for supervision and releases the creative abilities of a supervisor with vision and imagination. With one or two possible exceptions supervision has not been provided in the least-participating counties apparently because superintendents of schools do not appreciate the possibilities inherent in supervision of the type found in the most-participating counties, or, in their complacency, do not wish to seek improvement in classroom instruction through such an agency as supervision. Leadership—again and again it has so forcefully been brought to the investigator's attention how important this factor is to participation.

High economic ability is evident, again, in teachers' salaries. It was shown in Chapter VII that the salaries of white elementary teachers were significantly higher throughout the period from 1930 to 1939 in the most-participating counties than they were in the least-participating counties. However, it is questionable whether the most-participating counties paid higher salaries so they could employ better teachers than would otherwise have been employed or were employed in the least-participating counties, or if the teachers employed in the former counties were simply paid better salaries because of the greater financial resources of these counties. In other words, it is impossible to determine if participation would have been hindered if the salary level had not been as high, relatively speaking, as it was.

A fourth set of factors associated with participation which may be a concomitant of high economic ability was the much more generous provision of educational materials, such as library books and supplies, which was found in the most-participating counties. And in a curriculum program which subscribes to the point of view underlying the Virginia one, ample provision of such materials is important to the success of the program. Generous state aid in the purchase of library books reduces greatly the influence of variation in economic ability, so that an appreciation of the need for such books seems to be more a factor in their provision than taxable wealth. But the important fact remains that counties which participate extensively provide library facilities to a much greater extent than do least-participating counties. Merely furnishing library books will not bring about participation—the State Department of Education could not insure participation by sending out quantities of books—but school administrators who are sympathetic to the point of view of curriculum development underlying the Virginia program seem to appreciate the necessity of providing children with a wide variety of worth-while books and materials. Or on the other hand, it may be that placing much greater emphasis on such things is indicative of an operational philosophy of education that also would generate interest and active cooperation in a broad curriculum program. Again vision and leadership are requisites, for a choice of values is involved.

Isolation, both physical and cultural, seems to be significantly associated with the lack of participation in a number of counties. This isolation, which originates in physical factors, becomes, it seems, a psychological and cultural condition; the people of such communities become ingrained with a feeling of segregation, of backwardness, perhaps of helplessness, and certainly of unconcern with what other communities in more favored sections may do. Isolation may become a mental hazard to progress. This seemed to be the case in several of the least-participating counties. The superintendent of schools expressed a feeling of helplessness, of inability to overcome admittedly serious handicaps; teachers in written statements on the inquiry form excused their failure to use some recommended practice on the basis of their personal inability to cope with the local situation. Henderson[1] has

[1] H. Ruth Henderson, *A Curriculum Study in a Mountain District.*

shown in remarkable detail the impact of this isolation on the social and cultural life of a community and its implications for education.

And usually little is done to overcome the effects of this isolation on the life of the people. Commonly people in the rest of the state simply discuss the situation as an accepted condition and turn their attention to other matters. Officials of state agencies of government are inclined to center their efforts on more promising situations—there was some indirect evidence, for example, that this was true among the staff of the State Department of Education. So many demands are made on staff members that it is natural that the least promising sections of the state would be given less attention than groups much more willing to join wholeheartedly in carrying forward a program.

But this factor of isolation—in some states amounting to no more than sheer distance from the cultural and educational centers of the state—is something that must be faced by state curriculum directors and educational officials. Any program for advancement should be planned so as to overcome as much as possible this condition.

The evidence of the study indicates, then, that the state cooperative curriculum program as it has been planned and developed in Virginia has not succeeded in enlisting the active cooperation and aggressive participation of the county school units which are highly rural, more or less isolated, relatively poor, and lacking in dynamic leadership. Here, it seems, lies the crux of the matter in the planning of such programs in the future, both in Virginia and in other states: Are such programs to be planned and organized, perhaps deliberately, so as to stimulate, facilitate, and aid by and large only the more promising local situations— those where leadership, progressiveness, and ability already exist—in carrying forward an intelligently conceived program for the improvement of instruction, or are they to be planned so that all sections of the state and all types of local school situations are encouraged and definitely aided in improving their respective instructional program?

Throughout the period covered by this study the Virginia state program apparently has proceeded, whether by design or not, on the former basis. It will be remembered from the evidence presented that in practically every respect in which a real difference was found between the two groups the most-participating counties excelled in that factor in the year prior to the inauguration of the state program as well as in later years.

They were already employing supervisors, they paid higher administrative and teacher salaries, they spent more per pupil for instruction, they spent more per pupil for library books, they had fewer one- and two-teacher white elementary rural schools proportionately, they employed somewhat better trained teachers, and they had somewhat better tenure. The counties which did not have supervision, which were highly rural, which had low economic ability, which had inferior educational leadership, and which had less well trained teachers have been relatively little affected by the program. Should blame be attached to these less privileged counties for their failure to participate more actively? Their limiting conditions are facts which the responsible authorities must recognize and must overcome if they desire more effective participation. The challenge is to develop a plan of action which will work for and actually secure improvement in the curriculum under all types of local conditions. That is the challenge that faces state department officials in Virginia and state curriculum directors generally. This study has sought to reveal the handicaps that must be overcome and the types of local situations which have been relatively unaffected by the current type of program. Such programs as are exemplified by the Virginia program apparently have a selective appeal; they have not been formulated so as to stimulate all types of local schools to aggressive action in carrying forward a program of instructional improvement. If the interest and cooperation of all schools is to be secured some revision in plans and procedures is necessary so as to overcome conditions which militate against effective participation in the present type of program.

Bringing together the findings of this study in one brief concluding statement the investigator would make these recommendations for the consideration of curriculum workers, directors of instruction, state school officials, city school officials, and educators generally with respect to the planning and organization of cooperative programs for the improvement of instruction:

1. In any effort to improve instruction through curriculum development programs it is essential that attention be given to the alleviation of the effects of low economic ability of a local district on the financial support of the educational program.

2. Provisions should be made for supervisory service in all local

school systems, but it must be provided as a result of felt need for such service by the professional staff of the system.

3. It is particularly important that forward-looking, creative, and dynamic leadership be secured in administrative and supervisory positions in local school systems. This may be fostered through (*a*) generous state aid for the payment of salaries of such officials, (*b*) insistence on high professional standards of attainment as a basis for eligibility for such offices, and (*c*) the development of a program of professional stimulation of in-service growth of these officials.

4. A continuous and vigorous program of stimulation and professional development for the entire staff should be carried forward in each local school system through the support and cooperation of the state department of education. Regional curriculum centers readily accessible to all local school systems may be a valuable means of furthering cooperative programs of professional development. Such centers might provide consultative service and guidance, work facilities for local groups or individual teachers, and an adequate professional library of all types of useful materials.

5. Combining one- and two-teacher schools into larger local units of attendance would by and large provide a more favorable situation for professional development and curriculum improvement.

Bibliography

Alexander, William M. *State Leadership in Improving Instruction.* New York: Bureau of Publications, Teachers College, Columbia University, 1941.

Board of Public Education, School District of Philadelphia. *The Course of Study in English—Grades One to Eight.* Board of Education, 1917.

Bonser, Frederick. *The Elementary School Curriculum.* New York: The Macmillan Company, 1920.

Bruner, Herbert. "Curriculum Making in American Public Schools." *South Dakota Education Association Journal,* Vol. 5, pp. 263-266, January, 1930.

Caldwell, Otis and Courtis, Stuart A. *Then and Now in Education 1845:1923.* Yonkers-on-Hudson: World Book Company, 1924.

Caswell, Hollis L. "Current Studies in Curriculum Making." In *Proceedings of the Eleventh Annual Educational Conference.* Bulletin of the Bureau of School Service, University of Kentucky, Vol. 7, No. 2, December, 1934.

Caswell, Hollis L. "State Curriculum Programs." *The School Executive,* Vol. 56, pp. 205-207, February, 1937.

Caswell, Hollis L. and Campbell, Doak S. *Curriculum Development.* New York: American Book Company, 1935.

Cocking, Walter D. *Administrative Procedures in Curriculum Making for Public Schools.* Contributions to Education, No. 329. New York: Bureau of Publications, Teachers College, Columbia University, 1928.

County Superintendent's Section of Illinois State Teachers Association, Standing Committee on State Course of Study. *Course of Study for the Common Schools of Illinois.* Springfield: State Department of Education, 1925.

Cubberley, Ellwood. "Courses of Study." In *Cyclopedia of Education* (Paul Monroe, edr.). Vol. 2. New York: The Macmillan Company, 1911.

Cubberley, Ellwood. *Readings in the History of Education.* Boston: Houghton Mifflin Company, 1920.

Cubberley, Ellwood P. *The History of Education.* Boston: Houghton Mifflin Company, 1920.

Denver, Colorado, Public Schools. *Course of Study in Geography and Nature Study.* Board of Education, 1918.

Denver, Colorado, Public Schools. *Course of Study Monographs.* Board of Education, 1923 and subsequent years.

Department of Supervisors and Directors of Instruction and the Society for Curriculum Study, Joint Committee on Curriculum. *The Changing Curriculum* (Henry Harap, chr.). New York: D. Appleton-Century Company, 1937.

Division of Field Studies, Institute of Educational Research, Teachers College, Columbia University. *Report of the Survey of the Schools of Chicago, Illinois.* Vol. 3. New York: Bureau of Publications, Teachers College, Columbia University, 1932.

Report of the Survey of the Schools of St. Louis, Missouri. Complete Report. Vol. 5. St. Louis, Missouri: Board of Education, 1939.

Ebey, George W. *A Study of Adaptability in the City of St. Louis, Missouri.* New York: Bureau of Publications, Teachers College, Columbia University, 1940.

Garrett, Henry E. *Statistics in Psychology and Education.* Second Edition. New York: Longmans, Green and Co., 1937.

Good, Carter, Barr, A. S., and Scates, Douglas. *The Methodology of Educational Research.* New York: D. Appleton-Century Company, 1936.

Hall, Sidney B. "Teacher Training in Virginia in Relation to the New Curriculum." *Virginia Journal of Education,* Vol. 27, pp. 221-224, February, 1934.

Henderson, H. Ruth. *A Curriculum Study in a Mountain District.* Contributions to Education, No. 732. New York: Bureau of Publications, Teachers College, Columbia University, 1937.

Hopkins, L. Thomas. *Curriculum Principles and Practices.* New York: B. H. Sanborn and Co., 1930.

Idaho State Superintendent of Public Instruction. *Courses of Study and Teachers Manual for the Public Schools of Idaho.* Boise: State Board of Education, 1908 and subsequent years.

Inglis, Alexander. *The Rise of the High School in Massachusetts.* Contributions to Education, No. 45. New York: Bureau of Publications, Teachers College, Columbia University, 1911.

John Dewey Society. *Democracy and the Curriculum.* Third Yearbook (Harold Rugg, edr.). New York: D. Appleton-Century Company, 1939.

Langvick, Nina M. *Current Practices in the Construction of State Courses of Study.* U. S. Office of Education, Bulletin 1931, No. 4. Washington, 1931.

Lindquist, E. F. *Statistical Analysis in Educational Research.* Boston: Houghton Mifflin Company, 1940.

Mississippi State Department of Education. *Study Program.* Bulletin No. 1, Mississippi Program for the Improvement of Instruction. Jackson, Mississippi, 1934.

Mort, Paul R. and Cornell, Francis G. "A Digest of School Survey Data from Field Studies of Selected Pennsylvania Communities." Mimeographed. Distributed by authors. 1939.

Mort, Paul R. and Cornell, Francis G. *Adaptability of Public School Systems.* New York: Bureau of Publications, Teachers College, Columbia University, 1938.

Mort, Paul R., Cornell, F. G., and Hinton, Norman. *What Should Our Schools Do?* A Poll of Public Opinion on the School Program. New York: Bureau of Publications, Teachers College, Columbia University, 1938.

National Education Association, Department of Superintendence. *The Elementary School Curriculum.* Second Yearbook. Washington, 1924.

National Education Association, Department of Superintendence. *The Superintendent Surveys Supervision.* Eighth Yearbook. Washington, 1930.

National Education Association, Department of Superintendence, Committee on Superintendent's Problems. "Report—Part I, Administrative Cooperation in the Making of Courses of Study in Elementary Schools." In *Addresses and Proceedings,* Vol. 57, pp. 675-716, 1919.

National Education Association, Research Division. *Keeping Pace with the Advancing Curriculum.* Research Bulletin, Vol. 3, No. 4-5, September-November, 1925.

National Education Association, Research Division. *The Efforts of the States to Support Education.* Research Bulletin, Vol. 14, No. 3, May, 1936.

National Society for the Study of Education. *The Foundations and Technique of Curriculum-Construction.* Twenty-Sixth Yearbook, Parts 1 and 2 (Harold Rugg, chr.). Bloomington, Illinois: Public School Publishing Company, 1927.

————. *Report of the Society's Committee on Arithmetic.* Twenty-Ninth Yearbook, Part 1 (F. B. Knight, chr.). Bloomington, Illinois: Public School Publishing Company, 1930.

Philbrick, John D. *City School Systems in the United States.* U. S. Bureau of Education, Circular of Information, 1885, No. 1. Washington, 1885.

Reinoehl, Charles M. *Analytic Survey of State Courses of Study for Rural Elementary Schools.* U. S. Bureau of Education, Bulletin 1922, No. 42. Washington, 1923.

Reisner, Edward H. *The Evolution of the Common School.* New York: The Macmillan Company, 1930.

Rider, Paul R. *Modern Statistical Methods.* New York: John Wiley and Sons, 1939.

Rugg, Harold. *American Life and the School Curriculum.* Boston: Ginn and Company, 1936.

Russell, John H. "Diversity of Real Estate Assessment Levels Among Political Subdivisions." *The Commonwealth,* Vol. 6, pp. 7-11, November, 1939.

St. Louis, Missouri, Public Schools. *Outline of the Course of Study,* 1902. Board of Education, 1902.

San Francisco, California, Public Schools. *Course of Study in the Public Schools of San Francisco,* 1897-1898. Board of Education, 1897.

————. *Courses of Study for the Public Schools,* 1900. Board of Education, 1900.

Shearer, Allen E. "Procedures in Curriculum Revision Programs of Selected States." Unpublished Ph.D. Dissertation, George Peabody College, Nashville, 1937.

Snedecor, George W. *Statistical Methods.* Revised. Ames, Iowa: Collegiate Press, Inc., 1938.

State of Colorado. *State Course of Study for the Public Schools of Colorado,* 1890-1893. Denver: State Superintendent of Public Instruction, 1890.

State of Indiana. *Forty-Second Report of Superintendent of Public Instruction,* 1895 and 1896. Indianapolis: State Superintendent of Public Instruction, 1896.

————. *Thirty-Second Report of Superintendent of Public Instruction,* 1883 and 1884. Indianapolis: State Superintendent of Public Instruction, 1884.

————. *Uniform Course of Study for Elementary Schools of Indiana,* 1916-1917. Indianapolis: State Superintendent of Public Instruction, 1917.

State of Kansas. *Course of Study for the Common Schools of Kansas.* Topeka: State Superintendent of Public Instruction, 1907.

———. *Course of Study for the Public Schools of the State of Kansas.* Topeka: State Superintendent of Public Instruction, 1896.

State of Massachusetts. *Forty-Eighth Annual Report of the Board of Education,* 1883-84. Boston: State Board of Education, 1885.

———. *Sixty-Third Annual Report of the Board of Education,* 1898-99. Boston: State Board of Education, 1900.

State of Pennsylvania. *Report of the Superintendent of Common Schools,* 1874. Harrisburg: State Superintendent of Public Instruction, 1874.

State of South Dakota. *Fifteenth Biennial Report of Superintendent of Public Instruction,* 1918-1920. Pierre: State Superintendent of Public Instruction, 1920.

———. *Preliminary Reports on Approaches to and Theories Regarding Curriculum Construction, General Aims, and Guiding Principles of Education.* Pierre: State Superintendent of Public Instruction, 1930.

State of Virginia. *Course of Study for the Primary and Grammar Grades of the Public Schools of Virginia.* First Edition. Richmond: State Board of Education, 1907.

———. *State Course of Study for Elementary Schools.* Richmond: State Board of Education, 1915.

———. *State Course of Study for Rural and Elementary Schools of Virginia.* Richmond: State Board of Education, 1923.

Stout, John E. *The Development of High School Curricula in the North Central States from 1860 to 1918.* Chicago: University of Chicago Press, 1921.

Thorndike, Edward L. *Your City.* New York: Harcourt, Brace Company, 1939.

Trillingham, Clinton C. *The Organization and Administration of Curriculum Programs.* Los Angeles: University of Southern California Press, 1934.

U. S. Bureau of the Census. *Fifteenth Census of the United States: 1930. Agriculture,* Vol. 2, part 2. *Population,* Vol. 1; Vol. 3, part 2; Vol. 6. Washington: Government Printing Office.

———. *United States Census of Agriculture: 1935.* Vol. 1; Vol. 2. Washington: Government Printing Office.

U. S. Department of Commerce, Bureau of Foreign and Domestic Commerce. *Consumer Market Data Handbook, 1939 Edition.* Washington: Government Printing Office, 1939.

Virginia Education Commission and Virginia Survey Staff. *Virginia Public Schools.* Yonkers-on-Hudson: World Book Company, 1920.

Virginia State Board of Education. *Annual Report of the Superintendent of Public Instruction.* School Years 1930-31 to 1938-39. Richmond: Division of Purchase and Printing.

———. *Brief Description of Virginia Program for Improving Instruction.* Richmond: Division of Purchase and Printing, 1939.

———. *Illustrative Materials from Tentative Course of Study for Virginia Elementary Schools.* Richmond: Division of Purchase and Printing, 1933.

———. *Organization for Virginia State Curriculum Program.* Richmond: Division of Purchase and Printing, 1932.

Virginia State Board of Education. *Procedures for Virginia State Curriculum Program.* Richmond: Division of Purchase and Printing, 1932.

————. *School Laws.* Richmond: Division of Purchase and Printing, 1936.

————. "Supervisors of Elementary Education." Yearly Mimeographed Directory. Richmond: State Department of Education.

————. *Study Course for Virginia State Curriculum Program.* Richmond: Division of Purchase and Printing, 1932.

————. *Tentative Course of Study for the Core Curriculum of Virginia Secondary Schools—Grade VIII.* Richmond: Division of Purchase and Printing, 1934.

————. *Tentative Course of Study for Virginia Elementary Schools—Grades I-VII.* Richmond: Division of Purchase and Printing, 1934.

Virginia State Department of Agriculture and Immigration. *Virginia.* Richmond: Division of Purchase and Printing. (No date.)

Virginia State Department of Taxation. *Report of the Department of Taxation.* Fiscal Years Ending June 30, 1931 to June 30, 1939. Richmond: Division of Purchase and Printing.

Virginia State Planning Board. *Land Use and Agriculture.* Vol. 4-A, Sections 1 and 2. Richmond: The Board, 1937.

Walker, Helen M. "Analysis of Variance." "Formulas for the Standard Error of a Mean." "The Chi-Square Test." "Reliability of a Difference Between Means." "Reliability of the Difference Between Two Per Cents." "Standard Error Formulas." Mimeographed Materials Distributed by the Author.

Walker, Helen M. and Durost, Walter N. *Statistical Tables—Their Structure and Use.* New York: Bureau of Publications, Teachers College, Columbia University, 1936.

Appendix

Richmond, Virginia
December 1, 1939

STUDY OF INSTRUCTIONAL PROCEDURES

(*Form for White Elementary Teachers*)

Directions:

This form is sent as a part of an important study on some aspects of teaching in 22 Virginia counties. The study is being made with the approval and cooperation of your Division Superintendent and the State Department of Education.

The form appears rather formidable but we believe that Virginia teachers are willing to make this kind of contribution to the success and validity of the study. Your cooperation will be greatly appreciated and your name will never appear.

Please fill in or check the items in Part I and II. Instructions for Part III are given there.

A stamped envelope is enclosed for your reply and we are depending on a 100 per cent return.

All information will be confidential and replies will appear only in tabulated summaries. Do *NOT* sign your name.

Name of County..................... Grade or Position.....................

PART I—GENERAL

1. How many years have you taught in this county prior to the present year?.......; in Virginia?.............

2. Was your home in this county when you first started to teach in it? (*Check one*)
   ......Yes   ......No

3. Indicate your age by checking the appropriate blank:

   ......Under 20 years   ......30-39 years   ......50-59 years
   ......20-29 years   ......40-49 years   ......60 years and over

4. Beginning with June, 1930, or whenever you began teaching after that time list all of your attendance at college. Give the year, state whether summer session or academic year, the institution, and number of semester hours taken in courses on some phase of curriculum making or use and construction of courses of study.

Year	Summer or Academic Year	Institution	Sem. Hrs. in Curr. Courses
....	....	....	....
....	....	....	....

....　　..............　　..................　　............

....　　..............　　..................　　............

....　　..............　　..................　　............

5. Do the same for any work taken in extension or in any other manner.

Year	Sponsoring Institution	Total Sem. Hours Credit	Sem. Hrs. in Curr. Courses
....	....	....	....
....	....	....	....
....	....	....	....

6. Have you done any work at a college or curriculum center since June, 1930 in producing curriculum materials, such as units, course of study materials, and the like,
either in conjunction with a college course or a curriculum production committee?
......Yes　　......No. If so, give dates, place, and nature of work.

....

....

7. List the names of all State and National education organizations to which you have
belonged at any time during the period since September, 1938.

....

....

8. How many different educational magazines have you received by personal subscription since September, 1938, not counting any received as a part of membership in
above organizations?............................
How many more do you read quite regularly, but to which you do not personally
subscribe?........................

9. How many books dealing specifically with education have you read since September,
1938, not counting any studied in conjunction with courses taken as a part of work
listed in questions 4 and 5?........................;
On how many, if any, of these did you take an examination for renewing your
certificate?........................

10. Do you have access to any library or other source of professional educational books
and magazines?　　......Yes　　......No. If so, where?

....

11. What educational conventions or meetings other than local or divisional have you
attended since September, 1938?..

12. On how many, if any, excursions or trips away from the school building during
school hours have you taken pupils since the opening of school this Fall?.........

13. Do you have a definite time schedule for each day of the week which you follow
regularly in holding recitations?　　......Yes　　......No. If not, what
is your practice?..

....

14. How many recitation periods or activity periods in lieu of recitations do you have
during a typical day which are:

　　　　......Twenty minutes or less in length
　　　　......Over twenty minutes and up to one hour in length
　　　　......One hour and over in length

15. Have any of your classes studied more or less intensively since the opening of school this Fall any community problems or aspects of community life growing out of your own community?

......Yes ......No. If so, please state them.....................

....

....

16. Have you developed any large units of work in your classes so far this year in which pupils organized their study, work, and class activities for some period of time around a major problem or area, such as transportation, recreation, communication, production, and the like? ....Yes ......No. If so, please list them and indicate grade. ....

....

....

17. Have you introduced any major changes in your teaching procedures or nature of organizing the subject-matter taught during the past five years? ...Yes ......No. If so, please describe briefly.

....

....

....

18. What is the chief source you use in determining the subject-matter or units to be studied by your classes during the year?

....

19. Which, if any, of the following things are you now practicing in your teaching? (*Check those practiced*)

......Letting pupils read library books and the like only after they have completed
...... daily assignments.

......Making much more use of things in the community in developing class work.

......Drastically reducing the amount of time usually spent on drill and practice
...... work.

......Insisting that pupils attain at least approximately the standards set for the
...... grade before being promoted or passed.

......Having pupils regularly share in planning the activities in which they en-
...... gage in carrying forward their work.

......Insisting that at least most of the pupils master the required work before
...... going to a new topic or subject.

......Planning a variety of activities in which pupils may engage as they carry
...... forward a unit of work.

......Scheduling long periods in the day during which pupils may work on the
...... development of a unit of work.

......Organizing most of the school work into a program of study which centers
...... around the major aspects of social living.

......Using the textbooks as the basis for teaching the subjects.

PART II—RELATIONSHIP TO STATE CURRICULUM PROGRAM

Since 1931, the State Department of Education has been conducting a State Curriculum Program. Teachers have been given an opportunity to participate voluntarily in various phases of this program. Please answer the following questions relative to your participation. The questions relate to participation regardless of where you were teaching in the State at the time. If you have not taught in Virginia continuously since 1931, answer questions which do cover your period of teaching.

A. The Study Program

The first phase of the Program was on organized study of curriculum problems by teachers. It was recommended that each county organize study groups in 1931-32 or the Fall of 1932.

1. Have you engaged in any curriculum study program organized as an aspect of the State Curriculum Program since 1931? ......Yes ......No.
2. If your answer is "Yes," please answer the following:
    a. Was this study carried on by you independently or as a member of a study group? ......Independently ......Study group.
    b. Was the "Study Course" Bulletin prepared by the State Department in 1932 followed in the study program? ......Yes ......No.
    c. If you were a member of a group, how many meetings were held?.............
    d. Did you attend any regional meetings called by the State Department or a Curriculum Center relative to the *study program*? ......Yes ......No.
    e. Have you had any additional opportunity to study and discuss curriculum problems in an organized way since the original study? ......Yes ......No. If so, explain. ....
    ....

B. Production of Curriculum Materials

The second phase of the State Curriculum Program was the production of curriculum materials. These materials might be: Descriptions or lists of activities, units of work, content, methods, and the like; plan sheets for units; inventories of children's interests or needs; or any material useful in formulating a course of study. It was recommended that teachers engage in such production during 1932-34.

1. Did you engage in preparing any curriculum materials in conjunction with the State Curriculum Program? .....Yes ......No.
2. If your answer is "Yes," please answer the following:
    a. Did you work independently or with a group or committee? ......Independently ......Group.
    b. List the local, division, or state production committees on which you served or with which you worked...
    ....
    c. Did you do any production work during the summers at a curriculum center? ......Yes ......No. If so, describe..............................
    ....
    d. Did you attend any regional or state conferences held in conjunction with production work? ......Yes ......No. If so, how many?...............
3. Apart from the State program, have you produced any materials since 1931 for possible use in your division or school in developing a course of study or curriculum materials? ......Yes ......No. If so explain.........................
....
....

C. Try-out Period

An experimental edition of the course of study was prepared in the Summer of 1933. A limited number of teachers tried out this edition in classrooms during 1933-34. Other teachers could obtain a brief Bulletin of Illustrative Materials for study and use in developing some broad units of the type recommended.

1. Were you one of the teachers who tried out the experimental course of study? (The large mimeographed edition issued in 1933) ......Yes ......No.
2. If you were not a "try-out" teacher did you have a copy of the Illustrative Bulletin? ......Yes ......No. Did you undertake the development of any broad units of work during the year? ......Yes ......No.

D. Use of the Tentative Course of Study

The "Tentative Course of Study for Virginia Elementary Schools," formulated as a part of the Program, was issued in the Fall of 1934. Use of this Course is entirely voluntary so far as the State Department is concerned.

1. Have you used this Course of Study in your work? ......Yes ......No.
2. If your answer is "Yes":
   a. Give the year when you started to make use of it?..................
   b. Check the statement (or add your own) which best describes your present use of this Course of Study:
      ......Follow it quite closely in organizing classroom instruction; class work has been reorganized in accordance with its recommendations and plans.
      ......Use it for suggestions in developing some broad units, but do not follow it systematically and regularly.
      ......Use it to get suggestions and ideas for activities, references, and the like in teaching the regular subjects.
      ....
3. If you do not follow the Course of Study closely or do not use it at all, please state reasons. ....
....

E. Miscellaneous

1. Have you taken any courses at college or elsewhere since 1934 which considered extensively the plan and use of the State Tentative Elementary Course of Study? .....Yes ......No.
2. Have you observed any demonstration school teachers or teachers in regular schools teaching the revised curriculum? ......Yes ......No. If so, how many times?...........................
3. If you taught first grade in 1936-37, did you make the study of retardation carried out by the State Department that year? ......Yes ......No.
4. If you taught 5th, 6th, or 7th grade in 1937-38, did you make the study of "drop-outs" carried out by the State Department that year? ......Yes ......No.
5. Do you feel that the State Curriculum Program as a whole has been of value to you? (*Check one*).
   ......Of much value ......More harmful than helpful
   ......Of some value ......Know nothing about it.
   ......Of little or no value

6. If it has been of value, what do you consider these chief values to be?...........

. . . .

. . . .

7. Do you believe that you have made progress in improving the quality of your class-room instruction in recent years? ......Yes ......No. If so, what factors have aided you in making improvement?

. . . .

. . . .

PART III—WHAT SHOULD OUR SCHOOLS DO?*

The following statements represent various points of view regarding educational matters. Please indicate your opinion on these statements by underlining your immediate reaction to each. You are not asked to show whether or not the statements are right or wrong but to indicate whether or not you agree with them.

Please remember that there is no single right answer to most of these problems. We are simply asking you to show whether or not your opinions agree with the statements listed. Please give your own personal views, regardless of what someone else may believe.

Directions for Marking

If you agree with the statement, underline the word *Agree* at the left of the statement.
If you disagree with the statement, underline the word *Disagree*.

Please mark all statements one way or the other. If you would not completely agree or disagree with the item, mark it the way which would be nearest to your opinion or judgment on the issue.

Agree Disagree   1. Schools should not expect all children to reach the same standard of achievement.

Agree Disagree   2. Changes in public school programs are not justified if they require the expenditure of more money.

Agree Disagree   3. Kindergarten programs are mostly play and therefore are not essential.

Agree Disagree   4. Schools should be concerned more with the educative effects of non-school agencies—the home, the church, the movies, etc.

Agree Disagree   5. Social studies should not be limited to the traditional subjects such as geography, history and civics, but should emphasize contemporary problems like slum clearance, conservation of natural resources, crime prevention, safety, etc.

Agree Disagree   6. The learning of facts is of no importance unless the ability to apply facts is also acquired.

Agree Disagree   7. Many practices in education exist simply because of tradition.

Agree Disagree   8. Children should repeat work when tests reveal that they have not attained mastery of minimum essentials in the work.

Agree Disagree   9. The entire curriculum of both elementary and high school should be organized around life problems, such as making a home, raising children, running a business, being a consumer, being a citizen, and using leisure.

Agree Disagree   10. The schools should consolidate and pass on the cultural gains achieved in the past: changes in society should be initiated by other agencies.

* Items 1 to 100 are from Mort-Cornell-Hinton, *What Should Our Schools Do?*

Agree Disagree 11. Pupils and teachers should be free to seek and discuss all available facts on controversial issues.

Agree Disagree 12. There should be more men teachers in public schools.

Agree Disagree 13. There is enough to do in schools now without adding more subjects or activities for children to take.

Agree Disagree 14. Progress cannot be expected in school practices unless there is experimentation.

Agree Disagree 15. The danger of Communism is so great that children should not be given any information regarding Russia.

Agree Disagree 16. Children with extreme mental handicaps should not be put in separate classes but should be scattered widely among classes of normal children.

Agree Disagree 17. If adults of this generation had been better educated, they would be in a better position to cope with modern problems of living.

Agree Disagree 18. Children have as much need for practicing restraint as they have for practicing freedom.

Agree Disagree 19. There is as much need for research to develop new methods in education as there is to develop new products in industry.

Agree Disagree 20. Education should not be a fixed thing. It should be forever in a state of change.

Agree Disagree 21. A great many of our adults neeed more education and our schools seem to be one proper place for obtaining it.

Agree Disagree 22. Reading, writing and arithmetic should be taught much less through the medium of spelling books, readers, formal drill and texts and more in connection with activities such as planning a home, and running a miniature store.

Agree Disagree 23. Superintendents or principals should devote over half their time to helping teachers improve instruction.

Agree Disagree 24. In connection with the educational program all school children should have frequent opportunities to visit farms, factories, government offices, and points of public interest in or about the community.

Agree Disagree 25. Education can go only so far in building character. It is impossible to change human nature.

Agree Disagree 26. A teacher should not be judged in terms of the amount of subject matter his pupils have learned.

Agree Disagree 27. Schools are handicapped in making needed changes by not having enough money.

Agree Disagree 28. It is a primary function of American schools to inculcate the idea that America and her government are in every respect the best in the world.

Agree Disagree 29. The community life itself should be the source of many of the problems given consideration by children in regular school work.

Agree Disagree 30. Textbook learning should give way to increased learning through experience.

Agree Disagree 31. Schools in the United States have traditionally over-emphasized the point of view of big business.

Agree Disagree 32. Athletic contests between schools should be replaced by programs of intramural games in which nearly all the children of the school can participate.

Agree Disagree 33. Children should be taught both what to think and how to think.

Agree Disagree 34. Changes in school organization or administration should never be made unless they improve opportunities for the development of boys and girls.

Agree Disagree 35. In current school practice children are required to learn too many things which are of no value to them.

Agree Disagree 36. If properly qualified local teachers are available for vacancies in teaching positions, they should be given preference over out-of-town teachers.

Agree Disagree 37. School buildings are comparatively unimportant. It is what is taught that counts.

Agree Disagree 38. Efficiency in schools is not always to be attained by reducing costs.

Agree Disagree 39. School teachers should be permitted all the freedom of normal social life allowed members of other professional groups in the community.

Agree Disagree 40. In the traditional subject-matter divisions, such as reading, writing, arithmetic, Latin, and literature, there is sufficient preparation for the everyday problems of living, such as making a home, using leisure, and good citizenship.

Agree Disagree 41. Under no circumstances is physical punishment or scolding a satisfactory corrective for pupil misbehavior.

Agree Disagree 42. Most new ideas in education are all right in theory but not in practice.

Agree Disagree 43. Schools should seek to improve society.

Agree Disagree 44. Children should not know about blunders of the United States government in its relation with foreign countries.

Agree Disagree 45. It is more important to give tests to children in order to find out what to teach than it is to find out how well it has been learned.

Agree Disagree 46. In modern schools there should be provisions whereby each child will experience success more frequently than failure.

Agree Disagree 47. The extension of high school and college education to all youth tends to produce a generation not willing to knuckle down to work.

Agree Disagree 48. The kindergarten offers small children many worthwhile experiences which are seldom provided in the home.

Agree Disagree 49. Classes in leisure training for adults should not be held at public expense.

Agree Disagree 50. School teachers are too inclined to become set in their ideas.

Agree Disagree 51. Competition among children for marks is not fair to pupils who are naturally slow.

Agree Disagree 52. The school system should see that proper medical service is provided all children needing it.

Agree Disagree 53. Pupils should be free to move about the classroom and to talk in groups about class work.

Agree Disagree 54. The increase in the number of subjects in the curriculum has resulted in sacrifice of thoroughness.

Agree Disagree 55. Speakers with radical views should not be permitted to speak in high school assembly programs.

Agree Disagree 56. Teachers should present to their pupils the point of view most nearly in accord with the prevailing opinion of a majority of inhabitants of the community.

Agree Disagree 57. All the arithmetic needed in adult life could be learned in half the time now devoted to this subject in school.

Agree Disagree 58. Children should have an opportunity to participate to some extent in planning the work of their classes.

Agree Disagree 59. Changes in education should be made only on the condition that the basic fundamentals of the solid subjects are to be retained.

Agree Disagree 60. The more the schools know about their pupils, the more the pupils are likely to benefit from their schools.

Agree Disagree 61. Young children would benefit by having more social experiences and less formal instruction in reading and arithmetic.

Agree Disagree 62. If new ideas are to be developed in educational practice, they will have to be tried out by classroom teachers themselves.

Agree Disagree 63. Since people are constantly up against "tests" in the life struggle, education should not be made easy.

Agree Disagree 64 Modern teaching cannot take place in rooms with desks screwed to the floor.

Agree Disagree 65. It is contrary to standards of American ideals to teach evolution in schools.

Agree Disagree 66. Each child is different from every other child and each should be treated individually in the schools.

Agree Disagree 67. The chief purpose of education should be training children for vocations.

Agree Disagree 68. Elaborate landscaping and ornamental trimming on school buildings are extravagant non-essentials.

Agree Disagree 69. Each child failed in a grade or in a subject is evidence of failure on the part of the school to adapt its program to the individual differences of children.

Agree Disagree 70. The amount of money that could be profitably spent for education could be greatly increased if educational practices were changed.

Agree Disagree 71. A winning football team is more beneficial to a community than a good curriculum.

Agree Disagree 72. There is no reason for paying high school teachers more than elementary school teachers, provided the same standard of service is maintained.

Agree Disagree 73. Book knowledge goes in deeper than things learned through play.

Agree Disagree 74. The proper place for sex instruction is in the home, not in the school.

Agree Disagree 75. Things are constantly changing in the economic and social world; hence the schools must also modify their programs to keep up with changes of living in a modern world.

Agree Disagree 76. The federal government should help pay the costs of public education.

Agree Disagree 77. The course of study in any grade should never be considered fixed or permanent.

Agree Disagree 78. New types of activities—excursions, art and dramatic projects, and the like—should not involve reduction of time given to the three R's.

Agree Disagree 79. Boys should not be encouraged to follow studies of homemaking, as this subject is more in line with the interests and needs of girls.

Agree Disagree 80. Success in learning is greatest when learning results from the natural incentives and interests of children.

Agree Disagree 81. There is an early need for children to associate wtih youngsters of the same age.

Agree Disagree 82. Grades and marks are indispensable for stimulating pupils to do their best.

Agree Disagree 83. Experimentation is desirable in schools only if it does not interfere with the regular school program.

Agree Disagree 84. Students should have the opportunity of going, at public expense, as far in our educational system as they are capable of benefiting therefrom.

Agree Disagree 85. If schools are to educate children they must educate parents too.

Agree Disagree 86. Children are often too early an age to conform to adult ways of looking at things.

Agree Disagree 87. All children are entitled to the advantages of a high school education.

Agree Disagree 88. Instruction and classroom activity of all sorts should be adapted to the individual interests, aptitudes and capacities of each child.

Agree Disagree 89. Teachers should have the same social and economic status as other professional groups (lawyers, doctors, dentists).

Agree Disagree 90. Public education should be universally free to both children and adults.

Agree Disagree 91. Many of the social and economic ills of America may be solved by providing more and better public education.

Agree Disagree 92. The college entrance objectives of high schools have been given far too much weight in shaping high school courses of study.

Agree Disagree 93. Only a few students who will probably go to college should study Latin.

Agree Disagree 94. The reading of children in all grades should consist of more reading for research, appreciation, and recreation, and less reading for recitation from textbooks.

Agree Disagree 95. Extra-curricular activities as such should be abandoned in the high school. If these activities have educational value they should become a part of the regular school program.

Agree Disagree 96. Contemporary social problems should not be discussed except as they arise in connection with regular lessons.

Agree Disagree 97. It should be possible to recruit public school teachers from the most capable people in the country.

Agree Disagree 98. If the school program is changed to suit the interests of individual children, the results will be aimless waste of time.

Agree Disagree 99. Mathematics instruction is justified as a required course because it is a means of training the mind.

Agree Disagree 100. Children should be taught to be willing to give their lives for their country in case war or catastrophe requires this of them.

Agree Disagree 101. Curriculum revision has been made so rapidly in the past five years that it has upset teachers and harmed education.

Agree Disagree 102. All children in the same class should be doing about the same things.

Agree Disagree 103. Considerable use of library reference materials tends to interfere with complete mastery of the regular textbook resulting in a loss of desirable development of the pupil.

Agree Disagree 104. For the elementary school, I favor a curriculum which in large part represents an organization in terms of separate subjects.

Agree Disagree 105. Educational experts rather than classroom teachers should make the curriculum.